Adult Protection a [illegible] Law in Scotland

Shaina
Best wishes
Sandra
Feb. '25

Adult Protection and the Law in Scotland

Third edition

Nicola Smith
Solicitor, Cairn Legal

and

Nairn R Young
Principal Solicitor, North Lanarkshire Council

Bloomsbury Professional
EDINBURGH • LONDON • DUBLIN • NEW YORK • NEW DELHI • SYDNEY

BLOOMSBURY PROFESSIONAL
Bloomsbury Publishing Plc
50 Bedford Square, London, WC1B 3DP, UK
1385 Broadway, New York, NY 10018, USA
29 Earlsfort Terrace, Dublin 2, Ireland

British Library Cataloguing-in-Publication Data

A catalogue record for this book is available from the British Library.

ISBN:	PB	978 1 52652 340 2
	ePDF	978 1 52652 342 6
	ePub	978 1 52652 341 9

Typeset by Evolution Design and Digital Ltd (Kent)
Printed and bound by CPI Group (UK) Ltd, Croydon, CR0 4YY

To find out more about our authors and books visit www.bloomsburyprofessional.com. Here you will find extracts, author information, details of forthcoming events and the option to sign up for our newsletters

This book is dedicated with love by Nicola to Neil, Carys and Connor; and by Nairn to his mother and father, and to Adriana and Anna.

FOREWORD

Recent years have seen a busy period in relation to the practice, policy and guidance to the Adult Support and Protection (Scotland) Act 2007. Since the Act was actively implemented in October 2008, practice has massively evolved. We now have more than 15 years of experience in utilising the Act to facilitate the support and protection of those adults who require this.

It makes this new third edition of 'Adult Protection and the Law in Scotland' even more relevant and welcome. Previous versions of this authoritative and helpful resource have graced the shelves of numerous professionals across all the sectors. It has long been a stalwart of anyone attempting to navigate the complex framework of adult support and protection law and practice, whilst ensuring that knowledge remains current within the changing landscape.

The most recently revised ASP Code of Practice was published by the Scottish Government in July 2022 and the associated consultation exercises and revision of the document itself, was produced against the very recent backdrop of the Covid-19 pandemic. Whilst not all of the impacts will have been fully understood at the time of the revision exercise, and it may be some years yet before all the ways the pandemic impacted on these adults has been documented, it is clear that the concerns for vulnerable adults at that time and a better understanding of the potential impacts of trauma on an adult's ability to engage with supports on offer, are threaded throughout the revised Code. As a result, it feels like the general tone of the Code of Practice encourages practitioners to consider impacts of trauma in their risk assessments and in the way they apply the ASP criteria. As a result of more trauma informed practice, the categories of adults at risk of harm have widened to potentially include those affected by modern slavery, homelessness, hoarding, eating disorders and problematic use of alcohol and drugs.

This edition takes cognisance of this potential wider categorisation of adults at risk of harm, as well as legislative developments arising from the Mental Health (Scotland) Act 2015 and the Self-directed support (Scotland) Act 2013. It also encompasses the revised ASP Code of Practice which supports the Act, bringing this guidance up to date with relevant changes. There is also a section providing practical information on a range of issues relating to court measures of protection.

In addition, as well as the general updates throughout this revised edition, of particular interest will be the substantive changes to the chapters on Adult Protection Committees (Chapter 3), harm – which now includes very helpful information in relation to the issue of 'coercive control' (Chapter 6), financial harm (Chapter 7) and the transition from childhood to adulthood (Chapter 11).

I am certain you will find that this new edition of 'Adult Protection and the Law in Scotland' will provide you with a practical navigation aid to assist you in negotiating the complex landscape of Adult Support and Protection.

Brenda Walker
National Adult Support and Protection Coordinator
Iriss
August 2024

PREFACE

There is never a perfect time to publish a book on adult protection in Scotland. The law and policy are constantly evolving, as we try to develop practice and find better ways to promote and protect individual rights. Increased understanding of the often complicated and nuanced reasons adults experience harm, means a single intervention is unlikely to help and we need to think more broadly about the support and services available. Ideas that seemed innovative when introduced no longer represent best practice. For example, general principles that were widely welcomed when introduced are now criticised as not giving appropriate weight to the will and preferences of those subject to the legislation.

At the time of writing, as with previous editions, changes to the law are being considered. We expect new legislation following the *Review of Mental Health Law in Scotland*, and a consultation on changes to the Adults with Incapacity (Scotland) Act 2000 is in progress. Where appropriate we have referred to these proposals. However, we know that some of these might not happen, some might be substantially amended and provisions we have not even considered may be enacted. For this reason, we have primarily tried to focus on the law as it stands at September 2024.

One thing that remains constant is that, when it comes to relationships and lifestyles, things are rarely simple. It is unrealistic to expect any law to eliminate the very real dilemmas encountered by those attempting to protect adults at risk. Interfering in an individual's life is a serious matter, and will require those involved to balance risk with the sometimes conflicting views of the adult and carers. The law needs to try and provide the best framework within which all these decisions can take place.

We hope that the book is accessible and of practical help to lawyers, doctors, social workers, mental health officers, independent advocates and other professionals: as well as private and voluntary organisations and, of course, individual service users and their families and carers. It can be read from start to finish, but equally we have tried to make sure that each chapter can be read on its own.

The early chapters provide a broad overview of the legislation, key organisations, adult protection committees, the definition of 'harm' and the general principles. Later chapters consider investigating harm, how to deal with emergencies and applying for court orders. Chapter 11 looks at specific considerations where younger adults are involved and the transition from child to adult protection. Human rights underpin domestic law, and human rights law has important things to say both about the respect to be shown to human autonomy and about the duties of public authorities to protect people at risk. Chapter 14 looks at this in more detail.

We are very grateful to Paula O'Connell of Bloomsbury Professional for her encouragement to keep going with this edition when life kept getting in the way. We would like to thank Brenda Walker for her generous foreword and Michelle Afford for her patience and keeping us on track with our extensive edits.

We would like to acknowledge the very many people who provided insight, comments and guidance on various drafts, as well as other support, including: Karen Reid, Abby Somers, Fiona Brown, Yvonne Bennett, Paula John, Sandra Smith, Iain Nisbet and Sophie Dobson. We also renew our thanks to all those who have contributed to the previous editions, especially Hilary Patrick, who co-wrote the first and edited the second. Any errors in the text are entirely the responsibility of the authors.

We would like to say a very big and personal thank you to friends and family who supported us through the writing of this book. Especially to Neil and Adriana, without whom it would simply have been impossible for us to complete it.

The law is as stated at 1 September 2024.

Nairn Young
Nicola Smith
September 2024

CONTENTS

Foreword *vii*
Preface *ix*
Table of Cases *xix*
Table of Statutes *xxiii*
Table of Statutory Instruments *xxix*
Table of Conventions *xxxi*

Chapter 1 – The development of adult protection law in Scotland **1**
Introduction to adult protection 2
Scope of legislation 3
Balancing risk and protection 3
The wider context 4
Conclusion 4

Chapter 2 – The legal framework **6**
Adult Support and Protection (Scotland) Act 2007 6
  Adults covered by Act 7
  The concept of 'capacity' and the Act 8
  'Unwilling or unable' 8
  Scope of Act 9
  Potential use of Act 10
  Information needs of adults, relatives and carers 11
Mental Health (Care and Treatment) (Scotland) Act 2003 12
  People covered by Act 12
  Scope of Act 13
  Relevance to adult protection 14
  Information needs of adults, relatives and carers 15
Adults with Incapacity (Scotland) Act 2000 15
  Adults covered by Act 16
  Scope of Act 16
  Relevance for adult protection 19
  Information needs of adults, relatives and carers 19
Codes of Practice 19
Other relevant legislation 20
  Vulnerable Witnesses (Scotland) Act 2004 20
  Social Work (Scotland) Act 1968 20
  Chronically Sick and Disabled Persons Act 1970 21

Social Care (Self-directed Support) (Scotland) Act 2013 21
Protection of Vulnerable Groups (Scotland) Act 2007 23
Housing (Scotland) Act 1987 24
Conclusion 24

Chapter 3 – Adult protection committees **25**
Role and functions of adult protection committees 26
Membership 27
Procedures 30
Governance and accountability 31
Learning reviews and large scale investigations 33
Conclusion 35

Chapter 4 – Key organisations and individuals **36**
Local authorities 36
Council officers 37
Health care providers 37
Social Care and Social Work Improvement Scotland ('The Care Inspectorate') 38
Inspections 39
Complaints 40
Enforcement 41
Healthcare Improvement Scotland (HIS) 41
Inspections 42
Enforcement 42
Public guardian 43
Investigations 43
Overlap with other bodies 44
Mental Welfare Commission 45
Investigations 45
Inquiries 46
Visits 47
Overlap with other bodies 47
Care providers 48
Professional regulators 49
Individuals supporting an adult 49
Attorneys, guardians and people authorised under intervention orders 50
Named person 51
Independent advocacy 52
Criminal justice system 52
The police 53

Crown Office Procurator Fiscal Service 53
Conclusion 55

Chapter 5 – Principles in adult protection law 56
Background to principles 56
Principles in Adults with Incapacity (Scotland) Act 2000 57
Mental Health (Care and Treatment) (Scotland) Act 2003 principles 61
Adult Support and Protection (Scotland) Act 2007 62
Social Care (Self-directed Support) (Scotland) Act 2013 64
Human rights concepts 65
Legal impact of principles 66
Adults with Incapacity (Scotland) Act indemnity 66
Promoting the principles 67
Conclusion 67

Chapter 6 – Harm and abuse 68
Legal definitions of harm and abuse 68
Mental Health (Care and Treatment) (Scotland) Act 2003 69
Adults with Incapacity (Scotland) Act 2000 71
Adult Support and Protection (Scotland) Act 2007 71
Common categories of harm and abuse 73
Physical abuse 73
Psychological abuse 73
Sexual abuse 74
Neglect by a third party 75
Self harm, neglect or abuse 75
Alcohol and drug abuse 77
Domestic abuse and 'coercive control' 77
Forced marriage 80
Human trafficking 80
Financial abuse 80
Recognising harm or abuse 81
Disclosure by adult 81
Disclosure by a third party 81
Concerns raised following behaviour changes 81
Medical care and treatment 81
Conclusion 82

Chapter 7 – Financial harm and abuse 83
Legal definitions of financial harm and abuse 83
Common categories of financial harm and abuse 85
Misuse of formal authority 85

Harm by individual with no formal role	86
Harm by companies or strangers	86
Remedies	88
Appointment or removal of financial attorney	88
Appointment or removal of financial guardian or intervener	91
Appointment or removal of appointee	93
Appointment or removal of withdrawer	94
Criminal offences	95
Banning order	96
Residents' finances in care homes	97
Misuse of direct payments	98
Recovery of funds	100
Conclusion	102
Chapter 8 – Local authorities' duty to investigate harm	**103**
Powers and duties under Adult Support and Protection (Scotland) Act 2007	104
Duty to investigate	104
Visits	105
Warrant for entry	106
Medical examinations	108
Assessment orders	109
Access to records	113
Outcome of inquiries	114
Adults with Incapacity (Scotland) Act 2000: investigatory duties	114
Duty to investigate	115
Powers and duties under Mental Health (Care and Treatment) (Scotland) Act 2003	115
Duty to inquire	116
Cooperation with local authority	117
Warrants for entry	117
Medical examinations and access to records	117
Access to records	118
Choice of procedures	119
Conclusion	121
Chapter 9 – Emergencies	**122**
Adult Support and Protection (Scotland) Act 2007	122
Application to justice of the peace	122
Involving the adult	123
Temporary banning order	124
Using the emergency measures	124

Adults with Incapacity (Scotland) Act 2000 124
 Interim guardianship 125
Mental Health (Care and Treatment) (Scotland) Act 2003 126
 Removal orders 127
Police power to remove and detain 130
 Emergency detention 130
Medical treatment 131
Conclusion 133

Chapter 10 – Supporting the adult **134**
Independent advocacy 134
 Legal right to advocacy 136
 Adult Support and Protection (Scotland) Act 2007 137
 Advocacy and the principles 137
Community care services 138
 Community care assessments 138
 Carers (Scotland) Act 2016 139
 Services under Chronically Sick and Disabled Persons Act 1970 140
 Mental Health (Care and Treatment) (Scotland) Act 2003 140
 Free personal and nursing care 141
 Provision of suitable housing 141
Financial Support and advice 142
 Appointees 142
 Access to funds 143
 Management of funds in residential homes and hospitals 144
Planning for the future 146
 Advance directives 146
 Advance statements in psychiatry 147
 Statement of wishes and feelings 148
 Appointing an attorney 149
 Named person 150
Counselling and mediation 150
Criminal injuries compensation 151
Conclusion 151

Chapter 11 – Transition from child to adult protection **152**
Parental responsibility 153
Duties and powers of public bodies 154
 General powers and responsibilities of public bodies applying to children and adults 154
 General powers and responsibilities of public bodies applying to those aged over 16 156

'Adult carers' and 'young carers' 156
'Children in need' and looked after/accommodated children 157
Leaving care, continuing care and after-care 159
Local authority duties as education authority 161
School age 161
Additional support and coordinated support plans 162
Incorporation of the United Nations Convention on the Rights of the Child 164
Conclusion 167

Chapter 12 – Court measures of protection **168**
Mental health tribunals 168
Mental Health (Care and Treatment) (Scotland) Act 2003 measures 169
The sheriff court 170
Guardianship and intervention orders 171
Intervention order 172
Guardianship 172
Complaints about guardian or intervener 173
Court procedure 174
Protection orders under the Adult Support and Protection (Scotland) Act 2007 179
The adult's consent 179
Consent and incapacity 179
Undue pressure 181
Serious harm 183
Removal orders 184
Banning orders 187
Making an application for a protection order 193
Appeals 195
Antisocial behaviour orders 196
Forced marriage protection orders 197
Orders against an abuser 198
Interdict 199
Family proceedings 199
Non-harassment order 200
Vulnerable witnesses 201
Conclusion 202

Chapter 13 – Cooperation and confidentiality **203**
Impact of the Adult Support and Protection (Scotland) Act 2007 203
Duty to cooperate 203
Legal duty to share information 204

General practitioners (GPs) 205
The right to examine records 207
Mental Health (Care and Treatment) (Scotland) Act 2003 and confidentiality 209
Inquiries by local authorities 209
Disclosure of information 209
Adults with Incapacity (Scotland) Act 2000 implications 210
The independent and voluntary sector 210
Parents, informal carers, family and friends 212
Data protection 212
Legal basis for disclosure 213
Freedom of information 214
Conclusion 215

Chapter 14 – Adult protection and human rights **216**
Human rights in Scotland 217
The Human Rights Act 1998 218
The Scotland Act 1998 218
Public authorities 219
Human rights issues in adult protection 219
Protection of those at risk 219
Right to liberty 220
Respect for private and family life 232
Undue pressure and human rights 234
The UN Convention on the rights of persons with disabilities 235
Conclusion 237

Index **239**

TABLE OF CASES

[All references are to paragraph numbers]

A

A v Scottish Ministers; Anderson v Scottish Ministers 2001 SC 1, 2000 SLT 873, [2000] HRLR 450 .... 14.7
AB v CD (1851) 14 D 177 .... 13.5
A-G v Guardian Newspapers Ltd (No 2); A-G v Observer Ltd [1990] 1 AC 109, [1988] 3 WLR 776, [1988] 3 All ER 545 .... 13.3
Aberdeenshire Council v SF (No 2) [2024] EWCOP 10 .... 12.15; 14.19
Aerts v Belgium (2000) 29 EHRR 50, 5 BHRC 382, (2000) 53 BMLR 79 .... 14.7

B

Bank of Scotland v Bennett [1997] 1 FLR 801, [1997] 3 FCR 193, [1997] Fam Law 477 .... 14.26
Bostridge v Oxleas NHS Foundation Trust [2015] EWCA Civ 79, (2015) 18 CCL Rep 144, [2015] Med LR 113 .... 14.21

D

DF v Procurator Fiscal, Dundee [2023] SAC (Crim) 1, 2023 SLT (SAC) 17, 2023 SCCR 118 .... 6.13
DM, Re an application [2006] ScotSC 38 .... 5.9
Di Mascio v Mental Health Tribunal for Scotland 2008 GWD 37-559 .... 5.9

E

E v United Kingdom (Application 33218/96) [2003] 1 FLR 348, [2002] 3 FCR 700, [2002] ECHR 769 .... 14.6
Esegbona v King's College Hospital NHS Foundation Trust [2019] EWHC 77 (QB), (2019) 22 CCL Rep 155 .... 14.21
Essex CC v RF & Ors [2015] EWCOP 1 .... 5.3; 14.21

G

Glor v Switzerland (Application 13444/04) [2009] ECHR 2181 .... 14.27
Guzzardi v Italy (A/39) (1981) 3 EHRR 333, [1980] ECHR 5 .... 14.8

H

HL v United Kingdom (Application 45508/99) (2005) 40 EHRR 32, 17 BHRC 418, (2004) 7 CCL Rep 498 .... 14.8

J

JT v Stirling Council [2007] CSIH 52, 2007 SC 783, 2007 Fam LR 88 .... 6.4

Jones v Carnegie 2004 JC 136, 2004 SLT 609, 2004 SCCR 361 .... 6.11

K

K (Enduring Powers of Attorney), Re; F, Re [1988] Ch 310, [1988] 2 WLR 781, [1988] 1 All ER 358 .... 10.25
K v Argyll and Bute Council [2021] SAC (Civ) 21, 2021 SLT (Sh Ct) 293 .... 14.19
Keenan v United Kingdom (Application 27229/95) (2001) 33 EHRR 38, 10 BHRC 319, [2001] Inquest LR 8 .... 14.6

L

Litwa v Poland (Application 26629/95) (2001) 33 EHRR 53, (2002) 63 BMLR 199, [2000] MHLR 226 .... 5.8
Local Authority v Mrs D [2013] EWCOP B34 .... 14.21
London Borough of Haringey v Emile [2020] MHLO 70 (CC) 14.21
London Borough of Hillingdon v Neary [2011] EWHC 3522 (Fam), [2011] CP Rep 32, (2011) 14 CCL Rep 239 .... 14.21
London Borough of Hillingdon v Neary [2011] EWHC 1377 (COP), [2011] 4 All ER 584, [2012] 1 FLR 72 .... 14.24

M

M, Applicant 2009 SLT (Sh Ct) 185, 2009 GWD 23-378 .... 14.13, 14.24
MS v Sweden (Application 20837/92) (1999) 28 EHRR 313, 3 BHRC 248, (1999) 45 BMLR 133 .... 14.22
Moffat v McFadyen 1999 GWD 22-1038 .... 14.23
Muldoon, Applicant 2005 SLT (Sh Ct) 52, 2005 SCLR 611, 2005 GWD 5-57 . 14.13

N

Niemietz v Germany (A/251-B) (1993) 16 EHRR 97 .... 14.22

O

Osman v United Kingdom (Application 23452/94) [1999] 1 FLR 193, (2000) 29 EHRR 245, 5 BHRC 293 .... 14.6

P

P v Cheshire West & Chester Council; P v Surrey County Council [2014] UKSC 19, [2014] AC 896, [2014] 2 WLR 642 .... 14.8, 14.9, 14.10, 14.14

R

R v Bournewood Community & Mental Health NHS Trust, ex p L [1998] 2 WLR 764, [1998] 1 All ER 634, (1997–98) 1 CCL Rep 201 .... 14.8, 14.10
R (on the application of E) v Bristol City Council [2005] EWHC 74 (Admin), [2005] MHLR 83 .... 5.3
R (on the application of Greenfield) v Secretary of State for the Home Department [2005] UKHL 14, [2005] 1 WLR 673, [2005] HRLR 13 .... 11.27
R (on the application of Heather) v Leonard Cheshire Foundation (a charity) [2002] EWCA Civ 366, [2002] 2 All ER 936, [2002] HRLR 30 .... 14.5

Rabone & Anor v Pennine Care NHS Foundation Trust [2012] UKSC 2, [2012] 2 AC 72, [2012] 2 WLR 381 .... 14.6
RM & SB (as joint guardians of the adult PKM) v Greater Glasgow Health Board [2021] SAC (Civ) 33 .... 5.2

S

Smith v Donnelly 2002 JC 65, 2001 SLT 1007, 2001 SCCR 800 .... 6.11
Stankov v Bulgaria (Application 68490/01) (2009) 49 EHRR 7 .... 14.8
Storck v Germany (Application 61603/00) [2005] ECHR 406, (2005) 43 EHRR 96 .... 14.5

T

T, Applicant 2005 SLT (Sh Ct) 97, 2005 GWD 26-501 .... 5.3
Talpis v Italy (Application 41237/14) [2017] ECHR 224 .... 14.6

W

W v Edgell [1990] Ch 359, [1990] 2 WLR 471, [1990] 1 All ER 835 .... 13.3
Winterwerp v Netherlands (A/33) (1979–80) 2 EHRR 387 .... 5.8; 14.7

X

X & Y v Netherlands (A/91) (1986) 8 EHRR 235, [1985] ECHR 4 .... 14.5, 14.6

Y

YL (by her litigation friend the Official Solicitor) v Birmingham City Council; L v Birmingham City Council [2007] UKHL 27, [2008] 1 AC 95, [2007] 3 WLR 112 .... 14.5

Z

Z v Finland (Application 22009/93) (1998) 25 EHRR 371, (1999) 45 BMLR 107 .... 13.9

TABLE OF STATUTES

[All references are to paragraph numbers]

Abusive Behaviour and Sexual Harm (Scotland) Act 2016
s 2 .... 6.13
Access to Health Records Act 1990
s 4(3) 13.5
Adoption and Children (Scotland) Act 2007 .... 11.14
Adult Support and Protection (Scotland) Act 2007 .... 1.1, 1.2; 2.2–2.12, 2.16, 2.17, 2.23, 2.26, 2.34, 2.36, 2.45; 3.1, 3.11; 4.2, 4.3, 4.20, 4.21, 4.29, 4.33; 5.1, 5.2, 5.5, 5.9; 6.1, 6.2, 6.3, 6.6, 6.19; 7.2, 7.3, 7.24; 8.1, 8.2, 8.3, 8.6, 8.7, 8.8, 8.10, 8.11, 8.13, 8.14, 8.24; 9.2, 9.6, 9.10, 9.12, 9.14, 9.18, 9.19; 10.4, 10.15; 11.1, 11.3, 11.10, 11.12, 11.21, 11.24, 11.27; 12.4, 12.17, 12.18, 12.19, 12.20, 12.21, 12.22, 12.23, 12.24, 12.50; 13.2, 13.3, 13.8, 13.9, 13.10, 13.13; 14.11, 14.20, 14.26, 14.31
Pt 1 (ss 1–53) 2.2
s 1 .... 5.5
2 .... 4.33; 5.5
(b) 10.5
(f) 5.5
3 .... 6.6; 7.2; 9.2
(1) 2.3
(2) 2.3; 6.6
4 .... 2.7; 3.11; 7.3; 8.2
5 .... 4.4, 4.39; 13.2
(1) 13.2

Adult Support and Protection (Scotland) Act 2007 – *contd*
s 5(1)(g) 13.2
(2) 13.2
(3) 4.39; 13.3
6 .... 5.5; 8.2
(2) 10.4
ss 7–10 .... 2.7
s 7 .... 8.24
(1), (2) 8.3
8 .... 8.5
(1), (2) 8.5
9 .... 8.6
(2) 8.6
10 .... 4.4; 8.13; 13.8
(2), (3), (4), (6), (7) 8.13
11 .... 2.9
(1), (2) 8.7
(3) 8.11
12 .... 8.8
14(1) 12.23, 12.25
(a) 12.25
(2) 12.30
15 .... 2.9; 12.24
(1) 9.3
(2), (3) 12.27
16 .... 12.23
17(2) 12.30
(3), (4) 12.28
18 .... 8.11; 12.29
(5) 12.29
19 .... 2.9; 7.24; 12.34
(1), (2), (3), (4) 12.34
20 .... 12.32
21 .... 9.5
(4) 12.35
22 .... 9.5; 12.35
22(2) 7.24
23 .... 12.34
24 .... 12.36

Adult Support and Protection (Scotland) Act 2007 – *contd*
s 24(2) 12.36
25 .... 12.34
26, 27 .... 12.45
28 .... 12.38
29 .... 12.38
(2) 12.38
32, 33, 34 .... 12.39
35 .... 8.8; 9.18; 12.24, 12.32
(1), (2) 12.18
(3)–(6) 6.20
(3), (4), (5) 12.20
(6) 8.5; 12.20
36(1)–(4) 8.3
37(1)(a), (b) 8.4
(2) 8.4
38(1) 8.11
(2) 8.4; 9.3
39(1) 12.25
40 .... 2.11; 9.2, 12.42
(1) 8.4
(2), (7), (8) 9.3
41 .... 12.41
(2) 12.27, 12.34, 12.42
(3) 12.19
(6) 12.43
42 .... 2.10; 3.1, 3.11
(1) 3.10
(2) 3.3
(3) 3.2, 3.4
43 .... 3.7
(1) 3.10
(3) 4.5
(6) 3.6, 3.10
44 .... 3.7, 3.9
45 .... 3.4
46 .... 3.10
47 .... 3.1, 3.9
48 .... 2.34
48(5) 3.1
49 .... 4.39; 13.8
(2) 8.13
51 .... 12.46
(1) 8.12
(4) 12.46
52 .... 4.4
(2) 8.6, 8.13
53 .... 4.3, 4.33

Adult Support and Protection (Scotland) Act 2007 – *contd*
s 53(1) 2.3; 6.6; 7.2; 8.2; 11.1, 11.10
Pt 2 (ss 54–61) 2.2
s 58 .... 2.28
Pt 3 (ss 62–67) 2.2
s 64 .... 2.36
Adults with Incapacity (Scotland) Act 2000 .... 2.2, 2.4, 2.23–2.34; 4.2, 4.17, 4.19, 4.20, 4.26, 4.33, 4.34; 5.2, 5.3, 5.5, 5.9, 5.10, 5.12; 6.1, 6.5, 6.15, 6.19, 6.28; 7.3; 8.6, 8.8, 8.15, 8.24; 9.7, 9.8, 9.18; 10.17, 10.18, 10.20, 10.22, 10.24, 10.25; 11.1, 11.10, 11.12, 11.27; 12.5, 12.6, 12.9, 12.19, 12.21; 13.12; 14.11, 14.17, 14.31
s 1(1), (3) 5.3
(4) 4.33; 5.3; 13.12
(a) 10.5
(5) 5.3
(6) 2.24; 8.15; 9.8; 11.1, 11.10
2(2) 12.9
(3) 12.14
3 .... 7.18
(3) 7.12; 12.8; 14.17
(4), (5) 12.13
6 .... 2.26; 4.17
(2) 4.18; 7.18
(a) 12.8
(d) 7.3
(f) 4.19
9(1)(c), (d) 4.28
10 .... 2.26
(1)(b) 8.16
s 10(1)(c) 4.21; 8.16
(1)(d) 8.16
12(1) 8.16
(2) 8.16; 13.12
13 .... 2.34
Pt 2 (ss 15–24) 2.27
s 15 .... 2.27; 10.25
16 .... 2.27

Adults with Incapacity (Scotland) Act 2000 – *contd*
s 20 .... 7.12
(2)(e) 7.12
(4) 7.12
22A, 23 .... 7.11
24(2) 7.12
24A, 24B 10.15
Pt 3 (ss 25–33) 4.17; 10.15
s 25 .... 2.28; 7.21
26(1) 10.16
26B–26E 10.16
30(2) 10.17
31 .... 10.16
(3) 7.22
Pt 4 (ss 34–46) 2.29; 7.12, 7.26; 10.18, 10.20
s 35 .... 7.26; 10.19
(2) 10.19
37(7) 10.20
40(2) 7.26
41 .... 10.20
45(1), (6) 7.27
46 .... 10.18
Pt 5 (ss 47–52) 2.30; 9.8
s 47 .... 2.30; 9.18
(1), (1A) 9.18
(7) 9.8
(a), (c) 9.18
50(6) 12.4
Pt 6 (ss 53–79A) 4.17
s 53 .... 12.6
(3) 12.5
(7) 7.31
57 .... 9.8
(2) 7.3, 7.15; 12.5
(3) 9.8; 12.10
(6), (6A) 9.8
58(4) 12.7
(6) 7.31
64(3) 12.49
70(1), (2), (3), (4), (4A) 12.16
71 .... 12.8
(1)(a), (b), (c) 7.16
73 .... 7.17
(1), (3) 12.8
74 .... 12.8
79A 11.10
81 .... 7.31

Adults with Incapacity (Scotland) Act 2000 – *contd*
s 81A 4.18
82(1) 5.10
83 .... 6.15; 7.23
87 .... 6.19
(1) 4.33; 5.3
Antisocial Behaviour etc. (Scotland) Act 2004 .... 12.47
s 4 .... 12.47
(5), (11) 12.47
7, 9, 10, 13 .... 12.47
103, 143 .... 12.47
Carers (Scotland) Act 2016 .... 2.36; 10.8; 11.11
s 1 .... 11.11
(1) 10.8
ss 2, 3 .... 11.11
s 6 .... 11.11
(2) 10.8
9 .... 11.11
(1)(b) 10.8
12 .... 11.11
(2) 10.8
(6) 11.11
15 .... 11.11
(1)(b) 10.8
ss 19, 20 .... 11.11
s 21 .... 10.8
24 .... 11.11
31 .... 10.8
Children (Scotland) Act 1995 .... 11.27
s 1 .... 11.3
(2)(b) 11.4
2 .... 11.3
17(1), (1A) 11.15
(6) 11.14
22 .... 11.12
25 .... 11.13, 11.14
26A 11.16
29(1), (2A), (5), (5A), (5B) 11.17
30 .... 11.18
76 .... 12.51
93(2), (4) 11.12
Chronically Sick and Disabled Persons Act 1970 .... 2.37; 10.9
s 2(1) 2.37; 10.9
Chronically Sick and Disabled Persons (Scotland) Act 1972 .... 2.37; 10.9

Civil Jurisdiction and Judgments Act 1982
Sch 8 .... 12.41
Civil Partnership Act 2004
ss 104, 113 .... 12.51
Community Care and Health (Scotland) Act 2002.......... 2.36
s 1(1) 10.11
Sch 1 .... 10.11
Contempt of Court Act 1981
s 15(2)(a).......... 12.37
Courts Reform (Scotland) Act 2014.......... 12.46
s 44 .... 12.49
ss 46, 49, 50 .... 12.4
109 ....12.4, 12.14, 12.46
110 .... 12.4
Sch 1 .... 12.49
Criminal Justice and Licensing (Scotland) Act 2010
s 14 .... 7.31
s 38(1) 6.11
s 227A 7.31
Criminal Justice (Scotland) Act 2016
s 1 .... 12.47
ss 3, 4 .... 12.38
ss 38, 39, 40, 42 .... 12.38
Criminal Procedure (Scotland) Act 1995
ss 227A, 227H 7.31
s 234AA 12.47
Data Protection Act 1998 .... 7.8
s 11 .... 7.8
Data Protection Act 2018 .....13.15, 13.17
Pt 3, Ch 2 (ss 34–42) 13.15
Sch 1 .... 13.15
Disabled Persons (Services, Consultation and Representation) Act 1986 ....2.37; 10.9
Domestic Abuse (Scotland) Act 2011
ss 2, 3 .... 12.51
Domestic Abuse (Scotland) Act 2018 .... 6.20
ss 1, 2, 4, 6 .... 6.20
Education (Additional Support for Learning) (Scotland) Act 2004 .... 11.21, 11.22, 11.25, 11.27
s 1 .... 11.22
Education (Additional Support for Learning) (Scotland) Act 2004 – *contd*
s 1(1A), (1B) 11.22
4 .... 11.23
6(1A) 11.24
9 .... 11.23, 11.24
s 29(1) 11.21
Education (Scotland) Act 1980 . 11.27
s 1 .... 11.27
ss 31–33 .... 11.20
135(1) 11.21
Family Law (Scotland) Act 1985
s 1(2), (5) 11.4
4 .... 11.4
Forced Marriage etc (Protection and Jurisdiction) (Scotland) Act 2011
s 1(1) 12.48
2, 3, 4, 6–8, 9, 14 .... 12.48
Freedom of Information (Scotland) Act 2002 .... 13.17
ss 1, 25, 38 .... 3.10
Sch 1
para 21 .... 3.10
Hate Crime and Public Order (Scotland) Act 2021
s 4(1)(b) 14.1
Health and Social Care Act 2008
s 145 .... 14.5
Homelessness etc. (Scotland) Act 2003 .... 2.44
Housing (Scotland) Act 1987 ....2.44; 10.12
ss 31, 32 .... 10.12
Housing (Scotland) Act 2001 .... 2.44
Human Rights Act 1998 ....14.3, 14.17, 14.27
s 4 .... 14.3
6 .... 14.5
Local Government (Scotland) Act 1973
s 64 .... 4.3
Matrimonial Homes (Family Protection) (Scotland) Act 1981
s 1(1) 12.34
4(2) 12.51
14 .... 12.51
Mental Capacity Act 2005
s 24 .... 10.22
Mental Health Act 1983 .... 14.21

Mental Health (Care and Treatment) (Scotland) Act 2003..........2.13–2.22, 2.26, 2.34; 4.2, 4.21, 4.26, 4.33, 4.35, 4.39; 5.2, 5.3, 5.4, 5.5, 5.9, 5.11; 6.1, 6.2, 6.3, 6.4, 6.19, 6.28; 8.17, 8.18, 8.19, 8.21, 8.24; 9.9, 9.10, 9.12, 9.14, 9.17, 9.18, 9.19; 10.3, 10.4, 10.10, 10.23, 10.27; 11.9, 11.10, 11.27; 12.2, 12.3, 12.11, 12.19, 12.21, 12.23, 12.30; 13.10, 13.11; 14.7, 14.20
s 1..........5.4; 11.9
(3)..........4.33; 5.4
(a)..........5.4; 10.5
(b), (f)–(h)..........5.4
(4)..........5.4
(5)..........4.33; 5.4; 13.11
(6), (7), (8), (10)..........5.4
2..........5.4; 11.9
(4)..........5.4
3..........5.4
5..........5.11
8..........4.24
11..........4.22; 6.3
(2)..........7.3
12..........4.25
13(5)(b)..........4.26
(6)..........4.26
14(1)..........4.23
15, 16..........4.23
17..........4.26
21..........12.2
23, 24..........11.9
25..........10.10; 11.9
(2), (3)..........10.10
26..........10.10; 11.9
27..........11.9
33..........2.16; 4.21; 6.3; 8.18; 9.9
34..........2.17; 8.19; 13.10
(4)..........8.19
35..........2.16; 8.20; 9.9
(1)..........8.23
(2)..........8.20
(4), (6)..........8.21
(7), (8)..........8.22

Mental Health (Care and Treatment) (Scotland) Act 2003 – *contd*
s 35(10)–(12)..........8.23
Pt 5 (ss 36–43)..........12.3
s 36..........8.17; 12.3
(3)(b), (c)..........9.17
(4)..........12.3
(8)..........9.17
Pt 6 (ss 44–56)..........12.3
s 44..........8.17; 12.3
(4)..........12.3
46, 50..........4.35
Pt 7 (ss 57–129)..........12.3
s 63..........8.17
64(3)..........12.2
(5)..........6.4
82..........4.35
250..........4.35; 10.27
251, 253..........4.35
259..........2.13; 5.5
(1), (4), (5)..........10.3
274..........2.34
275..........2.20; 10.23
276..........10.23
(8)..........4.35
276A..........10.3, 10.23
276B..........10.23
293..........2.16; 9.10; 12.3
(1), (2)..........9.11
(3)..........9.12
(c)..........9.10
(4), (7), (8)..........9.11
294..........9.11
295..........9.15
(3), (4)–(5), (6)..........9.15
295A, 296..........9.13, 9.15
297..........9.16
300..........9.14
315..........6.15
316–318..........4.39
324(2)..........12.2
328(1)..........2.14
(2)..........2.14; 6.19
Mental Health (Scotland) Act 1984..........5.2
Mental Health (Scotland) Act 2015..........4.35; 10.3
s 22..........4.35
26..........10.23

National Health Service (Scotland) Act 1978
s 10A 4.13
10B 4.14
10C(1) 4.13
10E(1) 4.13
10J(1), (2) 4.15
10N(1) 4.15
10P 4.13
10R 4.16
Police and Fire Reform (Scotland) Act 2012
s 20 .... 11.7
Protection from Abuse (Scotland) Act 2001
s 1 .... 12.50
(1A) 12.51
4(1) 12.50
Protection from Harassment Act 1997
ss 8, 8A, 11 .... 12.52
Protection of Vulnerable Groups (Scotland) Act 2007 .... 2.41–2.43
s 1 .... 2.42
s 35 .... 2.42
94, 95 .... 2.43
Public Health etc (Scotland) Act 2008 .... 14.7
Public Services Reform (Scotland) Act 2010 .... 4.5, 4.13
s 44 .... 4.5
45 .... 4.6
47(1) 4.5
50 .... 4.7
51 .... 4.5
52 .... 4.5
53 .... 4.7
62(1) 4.11
64(1) 4.11
65(1), (2), (8) 4.12
66 .... 4.10
79(1) 4.9
80(1) 4.5
108 .... 4.13
Sch 12
para 2 .... 9.14
20 .... 10.11
Sch 14
para 21 .... 4.5
Regulation of Care (Scotland) Act 2001
s 8 .... 10.19
Scotland Act 1998 .... 14.4
s 29 .... 14.4
57(2) 14.4
Sexual Offences (Scotland) Act 2009 .... 6.13
ss 17, 46 .... 6.13
Social Care (Self-directed Support) (Scotland) Act 2013 .... 2.38; 5.6; 10.7
s 1 .... 5.6
2 .... 5.7
4 .... 2.38
6 .... 2.39
9(2) 2.39
17 .... 2.39
Social Work (Scotland) Act 1968 .... 2.36; 10.7, 10.9; 11.8; 14.11
s 12 .... 2.36; 11.7; 14.5
(1) 4.2
12A 2.36, 2.38; 10.7; 11.8
12AA 11.8
(1) 2.36
13ZA 2.36; 14.11, 14.12, 14.13, 14.14, 14.16
(3), (4) 14.11
13A 11.8; 14.5
14, 27 .... 11.8
59(1) 10.10
United Nations Convention on the Rights of the Child (Incorporation) (Scotland) Act 2024 .... 11.27, 11.28
s 1(2) 11.27
6(1), (2), (3), (4) 11.27
7(1)(a), (b) 11.27
8 .... 11.27
Sch 1 .... 11.27
para 1 .... 11.27
paras 12, 19, 23, 39 .... 11.27
Victims and Witnesses (Scotland) Act 2014
s 4 .... 4.41
Vulnerable Witnesses (Scotland) Act 2004 .... 2.35; 10.1; 12.53; 14.29
s 11(1) 12.53
12(1)–(4), (5)–(7) 12.53
19, 20, 21, 22 .... 12.53

TABLE OF STATUTORY INSTRUMENTS

[All references are to paragraph numbers]

Act of Sederunt (Sheriff Appeal Court Rules) 2021, SSI 2021/468
r 6.3(1) 12.46
Act of Sederunt (Summary Applications, Statutory Applications and Appeals etc Rules) 1999, SI 1999/929
Pt XVI (rr 3.16.1–3.16.13) 12.9
r 3.16.3 .... 12.12
3.16.4, 3.16.5 .... 12.11
3.16.6 .... 12.12
3.16.7, 3.16.8 .... 12.10
Pt XXXV (rr 3.35.1–3.35.9) 12.41
r 3.35.3 .... 12.35, 12.41
3.35.6 .... 12.45
3.35.8 .... 12.46
Sch 1
Form 23 .... 12.10
Adult Support and Protection (Scotland) Act 2007 (Restriction on the Authorisation of Council Officers) Order 2008, SSI 2008/306 .... 4.3
art 4 .... 4.3
Adults with Incapacity (Management of Residents' Finances) (No 2) (Scotland) Regulations 2003, SSI 2003/266 .... 10.18
reg 5 .... 10.20
Adults with Incapacity (Management of Residents' Finances) (Scotland) Regulations 2005, SSI 2005/610 .... 7.26; 10.19
Adults with Incapacity (Non-compliance with Decisions of Welfare Guardians) (Scotland) Regulations 2002, SSI 2002/98
regs 2, 3 .... 12.16
Adults with Incapacity (Supervision of Welfare Guardians etc. by Local Authorities) (Scotland) Regulations 2002, SSI 2002/95 .... 14.19
Aftercare (Eligible Needs) (Scotland) Order 2015, SSI 2015/156
art 2 .... 11.17
Carers (Waiving of Charges for Support) (Scotland) Regulations 2014, SSI 2014/65 .... 10.8
Community Care (Personal Care and Nursing Care) (Scotland) Amendment (No 2) Regulations 2018, SSI 2018/200 .... 10.11
Consumer Contracts (Information, Cancellation and Additional Charges) Regulations 2013, SI 2013/3134 .... 7.8
Continuing Care (Scotland) Order 2015, SSI 2015/158
arts 2, 3 .... 11.16
Council Tax Benefit (General) Regulations 1992, SI 1992/1814
reg 61(3) 7.19; 10.14
Criminal Justice (Scotland) Act 2016 (Support for Vulnerable Persons) Regulations 2019, SSI 2019/437 .... 12.38
regs 4, 6 .... 12.38
Fixed-term Employees (Prevention of Less Favourable Treatment) Regulations 2002, SI 2002/2034 .... 3.6
reg 8 .... 3.6

Forced Marriage etc. (Protection and Jurisdiction) (Scotland) Act 2011 (Application to Civil Partnerships and Consequential Provision) Order 2023, SSI 2023/194 .. 6.21
Housing Benefit (General) Regulations 1987, SI 1987/1971
reg 71(3) 7.19; 10.14
Mental Health (Advance Statements) (Prescribed Class of Persons) (Scotland) Regulations 2004, SSI 2004/387 .... 10.23
Mental Health (Form of Documents) (Scotland) Regulations 2006, SSI 2006/12 .... 8.23; 9.11
Mental Health (Recall or Variation of Removal Order) (Scotland) Regulations 2006, SSI 2006/11 ...... 9.15
Mental Health Tribunal for Scotland (Practice and Procedure) (No 2) Tribunal Rules 2005, SSI 2005/519
r 47(1) 12.2
66(1), (6) 12.2
70(3) 12.2
Registration of Social Workers and Social Service Workers in Care Services (Scotland) Regulations 2013, SSI 2013/227 .... 4.31
Self-directed Support (Direct Payments) (Scotland) Regulations 2014, SSI 2014/25 .... 7.28
reg 5 .... 7.28
8 .... 7.28
(2), (3), (4) 7.29
9 .... 2.40
(b) 7.30
11(2)(b) 7.28
Social Security (Claims and Payments) Regulation 1987, SI 1987/1968
reg 33 .... 7.19, 7.20; 10.14
Social Security Information-sharing (Scotland) Regulations 2021, SSI 2021/178 .... 13.9
Social Security Information-sharing (Scotland) Regulations 2024, SSI 2024/8 .... 13.9

TABLE OF CONVENTIONS

[All references are to paragraph numbers]

Convention for the Protection of Human Rights and Fundamental Freedoms (Rome, 4 November 1950) 11.27; 13.15; 14.2, 14.3, 14.4, 14.5, 14.7, 14.17, 14.22, 14.27
art 3 ..... 14.1, 14.6
4 ..... 14.6
5 ..... 14.7, 14.15, 14.17, 14.21, 14.26
(1) 14.7
(e) 14.7
(5) 14.7
8 ..... 13.9, 13.15; 14.1, 14.21, 14.22, 14.23, 14.25
10 ..... 14.1

United Nations Convention on the Rights of Persons with Disabilities (New York, 30 March 2007) 14.27–14.30
preamble (e) 14.28
art 1 ..... 14.28
12 ..... 14.29, 14.30
(3) 7.10
(4) 14.26
14, 19, 22, 23 ..... 14.29

United Nations Convention on the Rights of the Child (New York, 20 November 1989) 11.27, 11.28

Universal Declaration of Human Rights (New York, 10 December 1948) 14.2, 14.27

Chapter 1

THE DEVELOPMENT OF ADULT PROTECTION LAW IN SCOTLAND

1.1 Since the introduction of the Adult Support and Protection (Scotland) Act 2007 there have been changes in both policy and practice. There have also been developments in the international legal framework and the introduction of terms such as 'Human Rights Enablement' which require a person-centered and rights-based approach.

The language around harm and protection has also changed. Increasingly, rather than looking to concepts of 'benefit' or 'best interests' to guide decisions, those involved are required to respect and implement the adult's own will and preference where that is a viable option. There is a recognition of the need to use and develop models of supported and autonomous decision making instead of appointing proxy decision makers. We have become more nuanced in the way we differentiate between a lifestyle choice and an adult who is in fact unable to take action to make sure their living situation is safe. We know more about coercive control and the impact this can have on decision making.

Practitioners have an increased understanding of what constitutes harm, what makes people vulnerable and the context in which harm happens. Technology has introduced new challenges. For example, historically the law has provided remedies designed to keep those causing harm physically distant from vulnerable adults. However, orders which exclude those individuals from a particular geographic area or place will not prevent harm on social media.

While changes in law and practice are positive, they also present challenges. Decisions about when to take action, and what action to take, are not always clear-cut and practitioners need to be supported and enabled to exercise their professional judgement appropriately.

As at 31 March 2021, there were an estimated 33,353 residents aged 18 years and over in care homes.[1] Recent projections suggest that by 2043, 22.9% of Scotland's population will be of pensionable age, compared with

1 Public Health Scotland: Care home census for adults in Scotland.

19% in 2018. It is further projected that the number of people aged 90+ will double between 2019 and 2043.[2] Our ageing population will continue to create increasing demands on adult protection resources.

This chapter aims to put what follows into a wider context and highlight some of the tensions inherent in any system of adult protection. Subsequent chapters explain the current legal position in Scotland, as well as highlighting some of the practical issues faced in adult protection today.

INTRODUCTION TO ADULT PROTECTION

1.2 Adult protection is a general term covering the laws, policies and procedures that dictate and influence the response in a situation where it is suspected, or known, that an adult is experiencing harm or abuse. It deals with situations where harm is inflicted by a third party, as well as self-harm and neglect. It is also relevant where harm is unintended, for example where it occurs as a result of a carer struggling financially or with the physical and emotional side of caring.

The Adult Support and Protection (Scotland) Act 2007 was initially seen as an extension of mental health and adult incapacity legislation. The three acts were often grouped and taught together. While there remain strong links and interactions between these laws, the definition of 'adult at risk' has been applied broadly. Many adult support referrals will relate to people who are at risk of harm primarily due to factors such as being homeless, having a dependency on alcohol or drugs, dealing with an eating or hoarding disorder or being subject to coercive control in a relationship.

The range of situations those involved in adult protection can face means that the legislation needs to be flexible and provide appropriate responses. However, this also means that professionals, and particularly social workers, are required to use their judgement about the most appropriate way to proceed. As a result, it has become essential that those involved understand the legal framework within which they are operating, and how best to utilise the various laws to achieve an acceptable outcome. They also need the confidence and support to make decisions.

Adult protection is not just about protecting adults from harm. It is also about providing support, as reflected in the title of the legislation. This means avoiding making assumptions about what is best for an individual. It also creates the need to look beyond simply avoiding harm and instead

[2] National Record of Scotland: projected Population of Scotland (2020-based) (updated January 2023).

provide the support and help that people need to make their own choices about their lives.

SCOPE OF LEGISLATION

1.3 The system of adult protection does not automatically apply to all adults in Scotland. Instead, each piece of legislation applies to a defined group of adults, who are generally viewed as being more 'vulnerable' than the general population. This might be because they have a disability or are in poor physical or mental health.

The idea of a person being more inherently vulnerable than another is controversial. We will all find ourselves feeling vulnerable at points in our lives due to external situations, attitudes and power imbalances. For example, when getting results of medical tests or when alone at night in an unfamiliar area. Vulnerability is often viewed as a negative feeling, but being 'vulnerable', or at a higher risk of harm, can actually add excitement and quality to life. This is why so many people enjoy extreme sports. There is much merit in the idea that situations create vulnerability rather than a person's inherent characteristics.

BALANCING RISK AND PROTECTION

1.4 Adult protection can involve balancing rights and duties that appear to be in conflict. This tension often arises because adults have rights to make their own decisions about how they live their lives, provided they act within the law. However, society also has an obligation to provide an appropriate level of protection to those experiencing harm and abuse, particularly where they are less able to make decisions or protect their interests.

In some cases, decisions by local authorities and other organisations about when to intervene will be very clear. In a situation where an adult who lacks capacity is being physically or sexually abused, there will be an overwhelming consensus that an intervention should take place swiftly.

However, those involved in adult protection will know that cases are not always so straightforward, especially where close, and often complicated, personal relationships are involved.

For example, an older person, who was previously very careful with money, might begin gifting large sums of money to another person. To the outsider, the relationship might seem exploitative. However, there may be aspects of the relationship that the adult values. They might enjoy attention and affection, friendship, social contact or even receive physical care and support. Regardless of what anyone else thinks, the adult might view these benefits as outweighing the negatives, and in such cases the decision about if, when and how to intervene is more difficult.

Complex issues can also emerge where other people consider an individual's living arrangements unacceptable. Where conditions have deteriorated as a direct result of illness or disability, it may be appropriate to intervene. However, where the living conditions are long established, the position becomes less clear. Careful consideration will need to be given to whether this is the genuine choice of a capable adult or an individual who is unable to take the steps to maintain their home in a way that would generally be thought of as acceptable.

Of course, robust mechanisms are needed to allow public authorities to stop harm or abuse. However, most adults take for granted the right to make their own decisions about their lives, even if they know those choices are unwise or increase the risk of harm. Taking risks, and experiencing the outcomes of choices, helps people find out what they want and is part of what makes life interesting and meaningful. It is important that those involved in adult protection can justify any action to remove or limit a person's right to personal autonomy and self-determination.

THE WIDER CONTEXT

1.5 One of the big issues for those involved in adult protection is achieving long-term success. Legislation can provide clear powers to intervene and, in particular, to remove an adult from an abusive situation in the short-term. However, unless the adult has real alternatives, any intervention may have limited success. If the adult has no access to emotional support, counselling, alternative housing, advice about money and other appropriate services then they may well decide that returning to their original living situation is the best option.

There is a real need to view adult protection in this wider context and think seriously about what is available in terms of housing, support and community care services, as well as access to advice and advocacy. These services are explored further in Chapter 10 and will inform decisions about when and how to intervene.

CONCLUSION

1.6 While the law provides a range of powers and duties, it does not necessarily offer a straightforward answer to individual situations. Cases continue to be challenging and involve difficult decisions about intervention. While there will often be an element of discretion involved, those working in adult protection must be aware that their powers and duties are part of a definite legal framework which requires them to operate within set rules and apply specific principles to decisions. Using the principles underlying the legislation will, in many cases, help resolve the complex ethical issues underlying adult protection practice.

Chapter 2

THE LEGAL FRAMEWORK

2.1 This chapter introduces the main legislation relevant to adult protection and provides a foundation for later chapters. Some of the legislation overlaps, and in individual cases, more than one legal remedy or approach may be available. This will mean a decision is required about which route, or combination of routes, is the most appropriate. In other cases, it might be difficult to make any formal intervention.

The focus of this book is on provisions of direct relevance to adult support and protection. However, given the diverse range of individuals who might fall within the definition of 'adults at risk' there will be cases where other legislation is used. Where possible, reference has been made to other sources for further information. It is always necessary to have due regard to the general principles of each piece of legislation. These are set out and discussed in Chapter 5.

ADULT SUPPORT AND PROTECTION (SCOTLAND) ACT 2007

2.2 The Adult Support and Protection (Scotland) Act 2007[1] was based on a Vulnerable Adults Bill proposed by the Scottish Law Commission in 1997.[2] The legislation was initially seen as an extension of existing mental health and incapacity legislation. It was generally acknowledged that there were individuals experiencing harm who required interventions but, because they fell outwith the definitions of existing legislation, practitioners found it very difficult to act. At that point, there were concerns that the law did not provide appropriate options where someone was considered to have capacity but was also vulnerable and thought to be experiencing harm. This was particularly the case with older people. However, there was a reluctance to include age as a characteristic that

1 For full text of the legislation see www.legislation.gov.uk: Adult Support and Protection (Scotland) Act 2007 (ASP(S)A 2007).

2 *Report on Vulnerable Adults* (Scottish Law Commission No 158, 1996).

might automatically imply vulnerability. Therefore, the definition sought to include them by referencing adults who are vulnerable as a result of 'physical or mental infirmity'. Since then we have seen the categories of adults at risk of harm widen greatly. For example, to potentially include those affected by modern slavery, homelessness, hoarding, eating disorders, alcohol and drug addiction. The broad types of harm are covered more fully in Chapters 6 and 7.

The Act was designed to make sure that the relevant authorities had the powers they needed to allow them to intervene to prevent harm or abuse. As a result, much of the focus in the Act is on formal court orders. However, in practice the Act is often considered a 'gateway' to putting in place appropriate support. The vast majority of cases do not result in any formal protective measures. Generally, adults are supported on a consensual basis or diverted to other legislative options, eg an application for guardianship is made.

The focus in this book is on Part 1 of the Act, which came into force on 1 October 2008. Parts 2 and 3 amend other laws and are largely outside the scope of this book.[3]

Adults covered by Act

2.3 The legislation uses the term 'adults at risk'. These are adults who:

- are unable to safeguard their own well-being, property, rights or other interests;
- are at risk of harm; and
- because they are affected by disability, mental disorder, illness or physical or mental infirmity, are more vulnerable to being harmed than adults who are not so affected.[4]

An adult might be at risk where another person's conduct is causing, or is likely to cause, harm. However, situations where the adult is causing, or is likely to cause, harm to themselves are also covered.[5] Adults under this Act are defined as being individuals over the age of 16.[6] Local authorities may have additional duties to young adults and these are covered in Chapter 11.

[3] Parts 2 and 3 amended community care legislation and the Adults with Incapacity (Scotland) Act 2000, respectively.

[4] ASP(S)A 2007, s 3(1).

[5] ASP(S)A 2007, s 3(2).

[6] ASP(S)A 2007, s 53(1).

The definition has often been referred to as the 'three-point test'; although, 'three-point criteria' is now more used, to avoid the perceived negative connotations of the word 'test'. An adult must meet all three of the criteria to fall within the definition of 'adult at risk'. It is generally helpful to apply the definition as widely as possible, so that adults are not excluded from getting help or support.

If an adult is considered not to meet the three criteria, the local authority is still expected to consider all the options available to protect that person from harm.[7]

The concept of 'capacity' and the Act

2.4 The definition of 'adult at risk' was debated at length before the final version found in the legislation was agreed. Specifically, it was intended to be broad enough to cover those with capacity but who are more vulnerable to abuse. Some individuals are covered by the Adult Support and Protection (Scotland) Act 2007 but not the Adults with Incapacity (Scotland) Act 2000. This means that action and interventions may be appropriate even where someone appears to have, or has been assessed as having, capacity. Clearly, there may be practical difficulties where such adults are resistant to discussing their situation or accepting support. However, attempts should still be made to fully assess a situation and all actions should be fully documented.

Local authorities have legal duties to those adults who are at risk of, or experiencing, harm, but are deemed to have capacity. The Code of Practice states:

> 'While someone who lacks capacity may be unable to safeguard their own well-being, property, rights or other interests, it should never be assumed that an adult who has capacity is able to do so, nor should any decision made, regarding whether an adult is an adult at risk, ever be delayed for an assessment of capacity to be undertaken'.[8]

'Unwilling or unable'

2.5 One aspect of the definition that has been challenging to apply in practice is establishing what constitutes an adult being 'unable to

7 *Adult Support and Protection (Scotland) Act 2007 Code of Practice* (ASP(S)A 2007 Code of Practice) (July 2022), p 20

8 ASP(S)A 2007 Code of Practice, p 19.

safeguard their own well-being, property, rights or other interests'. The Code of Practice provides some interesting discussion on the distinction between being 'unable to safeguard' and 'unwilling to safeguard'. In simple terms, an adult who is able but unwilling to safeguard their own interests is said not to be an adult at risk.

However, it is also clear that some adults might initially present as being unwilling to safeguard their interests, but further inquiries will reveal they are actually unable to do so. Therefore, it is important to take time to evaluate the reasons for a decision rather than concluding the adult is making a 'lifestyle choice'. There are many factors that will impact someone's ability to safeguard their interests. For example, those who have experienced trauma, adverse childhood experiences, abusive relationships and/or coercive control may appear to be making a lifestyle choice, when actually they are unable to remove themselves from a harmful situation.[9]

These are cases when balancing autonomy with protection is challenging. It will be important that detailed assessments are made involving all relevant individuals and agencies.

Scope of Act

2.6 The duties, powers and responsibilities contained in the Act are explored in detail throughout this book. In very broad terms, the provisions cover the following areas:

Inquiries and investigatory powers

2.7 Historically, many local authority procedures make a distinction between an inquiry and an investigation as if they are two different processes. However, the Act does not make such a distinction. The specific legal duty is on local authorities to 'make inquiries' in cases where it believes an adult at risk is experiencing, or is likely to experience, harm.[10] The powers that might then be used to gather information are the 'investigatory powers' which allow the local authority to carry out visits and interviews, consider medical examinations and recover records.

9 ASP(S)A 2007 Code of Practice, pp 20–22 contains guidance on Trauma Informed Practice.

10 ASP(S)A 2007, s 4.

There are also powers of entry to facilitate investigations where access is likely to be an issue.[11]

Cooperation

2.8 Specific public bodies are required to cooperate on matters of adult protection. Currently, these are the Mental Welfare Commission, the Care Inspectorate, Healthcare Improvement Scotland, the Public Guardian, local authorities, the chief constable of Police Scotland and health boards. There is provision for Scottish Ministers to specify other public bodies in regulations. As at September 2024 this power had not been exercised and there were no proposals for regulations.

Court orders

2.9 The legislation provides for a range of orders to deal with harmful or abusive situations. These are granted by a court and allow the local authority to properly carry out inquiries into harm, remove an adult at risk or ban an alleged abuser from a specific place. The orders are called assessment orders,[12] removal orders[13] and banning orders[14] and are dealt with in more detail in subsequent chapters. An application for a banning order can also be made by the adult or someone living in the same house as the adult. Applications for orders will generally be submitted to the sheriff court, but justices of the peace can grant orders in an emergency.

Adult Protection Committees

2.10 Local authorities are required to operate multidisciplinary adult protection committees to oversee adult protection.[15] The role of these committees is explored in more detail in Chapter 3.

Potential use of Act

2.11 When a local authority becomes aware that there is an adult at risk in its area, it has a duty to make inquiries. However, this rarely results

11 ASP(S)A 2007, ss 7–10.
12 ASP(S)A 2007, s 11.
13 ASP(S)A 2007, s 14.
14 ASP(S)A 2007, s 19.
15 ASP(S)A 2007, s 42.

in the granting of a formal order. The adult may be accepting of support which removes or reduces the risk of harm. Sometimes an intervention under other legislation might be more appropriate. There will be cases made subject to ongoing monitoring and review and in some instances the decision will be that no further action is needed.

However, in some cases an application for a court order will be necessary. Local authorities might use a formal order where:

- harm is suspected but the individual involved has the capacity to make decisions and is not able to accept any interventions or support. In such cases, the local authority might act if it believes the adult is being unduly pressured into not cooperating;[16]
- a third party appears to be obstructing the local authority's inquiries. For example, repeatedly advising that the adult is unavailable or insisting on being present during meetings. If this happens, the local authority can apply for a court order to gain access and carry out an interview;
- there is real risk of harm if an adult at risk is not immediately removed from a situation. In this situation, the local authority can apply for an urgent removal order.[17]

Information needs of adults, relatives and carers

2.12 The majority of families, carers, friends and adults will not need to know the provisions of the legislation unless they are part of a specific investigation. However, a general awareness about some of the signs of harm and abuse is important.[18] As is the confidence that concerns about the welfare or finances of an adult who could fall within the legislation should be reported and will be taken seriously. It may also be useful for individuals to know that:

- local authorities have a duty to inquire regarding suspected abuse and may have the power to intervene even if the adult has capacity and is refusing to cooperate. This can happen if someone else is unduly pressuring the adult;

16 See paras **12.20**, **12.21** and **14.26** for further discussion on consent and undue pressure.

17 ASP(S)A 2007, s 40.

18 This is explored further in Chapters 6 and 7.

- no one can be detained, compelled to cooperate with an interview or forced to have a medical examination against their will under this Act. That said, it may be concerning if someone close to the adult strongly encourages the adult to refuse to cooperate;
- adults must always have their views taken into account;
- adults should receive information about what is happening and can ask to see any court order; and
- legal representation is available.

MENTAL HEALTH (CARE AND TREATMENT) (SCOTLAND) ACT 2003

2.13 The Mental Health (Care and Treatment) (Scotland) Act 2003 was designed to modernise and improve the use of compulsory measures in mental health care. It reflects the general move towards care and treatment in the community rather than in hospitals or other residential settings. The title was debated at length and the words 'care' and 'treatment' were deliberately included to reflect the philosophy behind the legislation.

The Act was also an opportunity to improve patient focus, and in some instances provides for support even when compulsory measures are not being used. An example of this approach is the inclusion of a right to access independent advocacy services.[19]

It also contains mechanisms for dealing with offenders who have a mental disorder and so interacts with the criminal justice system. However, the details of these aspects of the legislation are not within the scope of this book.[20]

People covered by Act

2.14 The Mental Health (Care and Treatment) (Scotland) Act 2003 covers individuals who are defined as having a 'mental disorder'. This term includes mental illness, personality disorder and learning disability.[21] Certain behaviours or characteristics do not, in isolation, indicate a mental

[19] Mental Health (Care and Treatment) (Scotland) Act 2003 (MH(CT)(S)A 2003), s 259.

[20] Hilary Patrick and Jill Stavert, *Mental Health, Incapacity and the Law in Scotland* (2nd edn, Bloomsbury Professional, 2016, new edn forthcoming 2025).

[21] MH(CT)(S)A 2003, s 328(1).

disorder. These include sexual deviancy, drug or alcohol dependence or the failure to act as a prudent person would in any particular situation.[22] Unlike the adult protection and incapacity legislation, there is no prescribed age in the Act.

Scope of Act

2.15 In basic terms, the Mental Health (Care and Treatment) (Scotland) Act 2003 provides for the protection of people with a mental disorder in a hospital or community setting. The main provisions relate to the following areas:

Investigation of harm

2.16 The local authority is under a duty to investigate if it believes that a person aged 16 or over[23] has a mental disorder and may be suffering ill treatment, neglect or another deficiency in care and treatment.[24] The duty also applies where there is a risk of financial abuse or loss of the patient's property.

The similarity to the duty found in the Adult Support and Protection (Scotland) Act 2007 means the local authority may be obliged to look into an individual case under both pieces of legislation. The local authority has the power to apply for a court order requiring entry for the purposes of an investigation.[25] It can also take emergency action where necessary.[26]

Cooperation

2.17 Specific public bodies are required to cooperate with the local authority in any investigation of harm.[27] This is similar to the duty contained in the Adult Support and Protection (Scotland) Act 2007 and currently covers the Mental Welfare Commission, the Public Guardian, Healthcare Improvement Scotland, the Care Inspectorate and health boards.[28]

22 For a complete list see the MH(CT)(S)A 2003, s 328(2).
23 This particular duty only applies to adults. There is a different system for child protection.
24 MH(CT)(S)A 2003, s 33.
25 MH(CT)(S)A 2003, s 35.
26 MH(CT)(S)A 2003, s 293.
27 MH(CT)(S)A 2003, s 34.
28 The role and responsibilities of these organisations are explored further in Chapter 4.

Detention

2.18 The Act provides for various measures to allow an individual to receive medical care and treatment on a compulsory basis. These include emergency and short-term detention in hospital, as well as longer orders. Some treatment orders can be community based. These options are not covered in any detail in this book but other comprehensive resources are available.[29]

Mental health tribunals

2.19 The Act established mental health tribunals with a number of functions, including considering applications for orders and appeals against orders.

Advance statements

2.20 The Act provides for advance statements, which allow individuals to set out in advance how they want, and do not want, to be treated for a mental disorder.[30] The importance of such statements is explored further at paras **10.22** to **10.24**.

Relevance to adult protection

2.21 The local authority, or in many cases a health professional, is likely to consider using the Act in adult protection cases where the adult has a mental disorder and is at risk of harm. Such situations could include:

- where a person needs treatment for a mental disorder and is suffering harm. This could be where an individual is not able to take care of their personal well-being or property, because of a mental illness, and appropriate treatment would prevent the harm continuing;
- where someone is already subject to a compulsory treatment order. For example, the adult might be in breach of a condition that they take prescribed medication or attend medical appointments; or

[29] Patrick and Stavert, *Mental Health, Incapacity and the Law in Scotland* (2016).
[30] MH(CT)(S)A 2003, s 275.

- someone has a mental disorder and needs to be detained for their own protection or the protection of others. This covers situations where the primary reason for detention is protection rather than treatment.

Information needs of adults, relatives and carers

2.22 Most people will not find themselves subject to a compulsory intervention. However, it is helpful to be aware that:

- local authorities have a duty to investigate harm and abuse;
- when action is taken under this Act individuals have clearly defined legal rights to be heard and represented, as well as to appeal decisions;
- families, carers and friends may also have an independent right to be heard as the nearest relative or named person;
- people with a mental disorder have the right to access independent advocacy services;
- any individual can write an advance statement that expresses their views about how they want to be treated; and
- the Mental Welfare Commission can investigate concerns.

ADULTS WITH INCAPACITY (SCOTLAND) ACT 2000

2.23 The Adults with Incapacity (Scotland) Act 2000 regulates how decisions are made for individuals who lack capacity in relation to an aspect of their welfare, property, financial affairs or medical treatment. It created the office of Public Guardian, which has a major role in both monitoring and regulating interventions under the Act.[31]

The Act was designed to provide an individual approach to decision making and to recognise that, as far as possible, people should have autonomy and be able to control their lives. The ability to make specific decisions should only be transferred to someone else where this is justified and necessary in all the circumstances.

In terms of adult protection, the Adults with Incapacity (Scotland) Act 2000 contains a range of options to deal with situations of harm and abuse,

[31] See para **4.17** for more information about the Public Guardian.

where the adult involved lacks capacity. It can provide a longer-term solution and, even if not used immediately, may be useful after an initial intervention under another piece of legislation. For example, following an adult's removal under the Adult Support and Protection (Scotland) Act 2007, it may become apparent that they are unable to make their own decisions and it is necessary to appoint a guardian.

Adults covered by Act

2.24 The Adults with Incapacity (Scotland) Act 2000 applies to individuals over the age of 16 who lack the legal capacity to make some, or all, decisions about their lives. 'Incapacity' is defined in the Adults with Incapacity (Scotland) Act 2000 as including those who are unable to:

- act;
- make decisions;
- communicate decisions;
- understand decisions; or
- retain a memory of decisions.[32]

The definition could include some people with learning disabilities or mental illness, as well as those who have impaired capacity for another reason, for example, following a head injury or because of an illness such as dementia.

Scope of Act

2.25 The Adults with Incapacity (Scotland) Act 2000 is a wide-ranging piece of legislation containing options that can be used in individual cases. In basic terms, it includes provisions on the following:

Investigation of harm

2.26 The responsibility for investigating depends on the type of harm involved. The local authority is under a duty to investigate harm where the personal welfare of an adult seems to be at risk or where there are complaints about a welfare attorney or guardian or a person authorised

32 Adults with Incapacity (Scotland) Act 2000 (AWI(S)A 2000), s 1(6).

under a welfare intervention order.[33] The Public Guardian investigates any circumstances where the property or financial affairs of an adult who might lack capacity seem to be at risk.[34]

The duties overlap with those in both the Adult Support and Protection (Scotland) Act 2007 and the Mental Health (Care and Treatment) (Scotland) Act 2003. This means a local authority might have a duty to investigate a single case under all three pieces of legislation. In practice, only one investigation is likely to take place.

PRINCIPLES AND PRACTICE

The decision about which piece of legislation should be used is important, given there are differences in not just the duties and powers, but also the approach. The local authority should be clear which legislation it is acting under in any case, as this will affect the procedure it operates. For example, under the Adult Support and Protection (Scotland) Act 2007 an individual being interviewed should be advised that they do not need to cooperate. This is not the case under other adult protection legislation.

Attorneys

2.27 An individual can appoint an attorney to take decisions if, in the future, they become unable to make these decisions themselves. Attorneys can be appointed to make financial decisions or welfare decisions or both.[35] It is possible for financial powers to start immediately even if the individual retains capacity. This must be specified in the power of attorney. Welfare powers are only activated when the adult loses capacity. If the intention is the attorney will continue to act after the adult loses capacity, then they must be appointed in accordance with the procedure set out in the legislation.[36] The attorney can be anyone the person chooses, provided they are over the age of 16. There is a legal requirement that the attorney formally accepts the position and, for this reason, it is important to check that a potential attorney is prepared to take on this role. Powers of attorney are explored further in Chapter 10.

33 AWI(S)A 2000, s 10.
34 AWI(S)A 2000, s 6.
35 AWI(S)A 2000, ss 15 and 16.
36 AWI(S)A 2000, Part 2.

Managing bank accounts

2.28 The Act allows an individual or organisation[37] to apply to the Public Guardian for authority to manage an existing bank account, or open and manage a new bank account, for an adult who lacks capacity. This system is designed to deal with normal living expenses and is usually used by families or organisations providing support. More information about managing bank accounts can be found at para **10.15**.

Managing residents' finances

2.29 This allows managers of residential accommodation to manage funds for residents and can be useful for adults with incapacity living in, or moving to, residential accommodation.[38] This power is only available to managers of services that are registered with the Care Inspectorate. More information about the scheme can be found at para **10.18**.

Making medical decisions

2.30 The Adults with Incapacity (Scotland) Act 2000 regulates decisions about medical care and treatment.[39] Medical practitioners are responsible for assessing an individual's capacity to make a specific decision about medical care or treatment. If the individual involved has capacity, their decision about whether or not to have any treatment offered must be respected. If they lack capacity, a statutory certificate is completed detailing the nature of the treatment needed.[40]

Intervention and guardianship orders

2.31 Intervention orders and guardianship orders are mechanisms for making decisions for those who lack capacity (in whole or in part). The application process for both is very similar, although the purpose of each order is different. An intervention order is used to make a one-off decision, while a guardianship order is an ongoing order used where someone will need a number of decisions made over a period of time. Both orders can be used for financial and/or welfare decisions. More information about these orders can be found in Chapter 12.

[37] AWI(S)A 2000, s 25 (as amended by the ASP(S)A 2007, s 58).
[38] AWI(S)A 2000, Part 4.
[39] AWI(S)A 2000, Part 5.
[40] AWI(S)A 2000, s 47.

Relevance for adult protection

2.32 Consideration of the Act is likely in most adult protection cases where the adult involved appears to lack capacity. The types of situation where a local authority might use the Act include:

- where an individual's personal welfare, finances or property are at risk and they lack capacity to make their own decisions. The local authority must consider if any further action is necessary;
- in cases where a guardian or attorney has already been appointed with the power to make decisions to prevent harm. For example, another person might already have the power to decide where the adult should live. The local authority also monitors guardians to make sure they carry out their role properly;
- where there is financial abuse or an individual is having difficulties managing their money. There are a number of options in such cases, explored further in Chapters 7 and 10.

Information needs of adults, relatives and carers

2.33 As the population ages, more and more people will have to navigate the provisions of this Act. In specific cases, more detailed advice will be necessary, but it may be helpful for individuals to know that:

- local authorities have a duty to investigate suspected harm and abuse;
- everyone should think about granting a power of attorney to provide for the possibility they might lose capacity at some point in the future;
- a range of options are available if an adult becomes, or is likely to become, unable to make decisions.

CODES OF PRACTICE

2.34 Codes of practice supplement the Adults with Incapacity (Scotland) Act 2000, the Mental Health (Care and Treatment) (Scotland) Act 2003 and the Adult Support and Protection (Scotland) Act 2007.[41]

[41] Under provisions in the AWI(S)A 2000, s 13, MH(CT)(S)A 2003, s 274 and ASP(S)A 2007, s 48.

Whilst such codes of practice are not legally binding, they are statutory documents, and in any legal challenge or complaint about a person's performance of their functions under the legislation, their failure to have regard to the relevant code of practice could be relevant.

OTHER RELEVANT LEGISLATION

Vulnerable Witnesses (Scotland) Act 2004

2.35 The Vulnerable Witnesses (Scotland) Act 2004 was designed to provide additional support for certain accused, victims and witnesses to help them give their best evidence in court. It recognises that, while giving evidence is a difficult experience for everyone, certain people face additional barriers. The Act introduced a range of measures to assist witnesses including the use of screens, supporters and giving evidence from a remote location via a weblink. Other measures, such as giving evidence in a closed court, may be available on request. These adjustments may be of benefit where an adult who is considered vulnerable is involved in criminal or civil court proceedings. The civil court provisions are discussed in more detail at para **12.53**.

Social Work (Scotland) Act 1968

2.36 The Social Work (Scotland) Act 1968 sets out the duties of local authorities to provide social care and support for their areas. Local authorities have a duty to promote social welfare in their area by making available advice, guidance and assistance to those in need, as appropriate.[42]

A local authority has a legal duty to make a formal assessment of the needs of anyone within its area appearing to require community care services.[43] This involves carrying out a community care assessment identifying the person's needs, and then recording how it proposes to meet those needs. Where an intervention is made in an adult protection case there will often be a need to carry out a formal assessment of need. Carers have a right to a separate assessment.[44] There is more information about these assessments in Chapter 10.

42 Social Work (Scotland) Act 1968 (SW(S)A 1968), s 12.

43 SW(S)A 1968, s 12A.

44 SW(S)A 1968, s 12AA(1) (added by the Community Care and Health (Scotland) Act 2002). Carers (Scotland) Act 2016.

The Adult Support and Protection (Scotland) Act 2007 amended this Act in an attempt to clarify local authorities' powers to help incapable adults benefit from social services.[45] This amendment allows a local authority to take steps to move an incapable adult to residential accommodation without a guardianship order, intervention order or the consent of an attorney. However, there has been discussion about the human rights implications of this amendment. This is discussed further at para **14.11**.

Chronically Sick and Disabled Persons Act 1970

2.37 Under the Chronically Sick and Disabled Persons Act 1970, if the local authority thinks that a disabled person in its area needs specific services it must arrange to provide these.[46] These services are listed in the Act and include practical help at home, meals, telephone equipment, home adaptations and help with transport to services. In adult protection cases, where the adult has a disability, a formal assessment under this Act will often be necessary.

Social Care (Self-directed Support) (Scotland) Act 2013

2.38 The Social Care (Self-directed Support) (Scotland) Act 2013 was introduced to provide a wider range of choice and control to individuals in terms of how they receive support. There was a general recognition that the uptake of direct payments (payments made to individuals to enable them to purchase their own care) was low and that other options needed to be made available to give people more control, without necessarily having to take over full financial management of the budget. Local authorities are now under a duty to offer anyone assessed as needing care and support[47] four options. These are:

- Option 1 – Making a direct payment to the supported person for the provision of support. This means that the supported person receives a monetary payment and arranges their own support.
- Option 2 – The supported person decides what support they need but this is arranged and paid for by the local authority. This

[45] ASP(S)A 2007, s 64 inserted s 13ZA to the SW(S)A 1968.

[46] Chronically Sick and Disabled Persons Act 1970, s 2(1) as amended by the Chronically Sick and Disabled Persons (Scotland) Act 1972 and the Disabled Persons (Services, Consultation and Representation) Act 1986.

[47] Under the SW(S)A 1968, s 12A.

option should allow more control over support without having the responsibility of actually managing the money directly. Someone using this option is often described as having an 'individual budget' or 'individual service fund'.

- Option 3 – The local authority decides what support is needed and arranges and pays for this. This is the more traditional method of delivering support.
- Option 4 – A combination of Options 1, 2 and 3 for different aspects of support. For example, the supported person might ask the local authority to arrange a day service but request a monetary payment for the respite element of their support.[48]

2.39 The local authority is under a duty to explain the nature and effect of each of the options and provide information about the help and support available to manage support.[49] Consideration must also be given to providing information about independent advocacy services which can help. Where someone appears to need assistance in deciding between the options and there is no welfare guardian, welfare attorney or intervener with relevant powers, the local authority is under a duty to identify someone who can provide that support.[50]

2.40 Providing individuals who receive care and support with more control over how this happens is a positive step. However, it does mean that the local authority may have less control over how support is provided and this could have implications for adult protection. The local authority will still owe duties of care to those using services and will require to be satisfied that any arrangements are appropriate. Where someone lacks capacity and has not appointed an attorney, a guardianship order will normally be required before a decision can be made on which option to use. Guardians, attorneys and interveners who make decisions on self-directed support are not permitted to be paid for any caring responsibilities using direct payments.[51]

48 Social Care (Self-directed Support) (Scotland) Act 2013 (SC(SdS)(S)A 2013), s 4.
49 SC(SdS)(S)A 2013, s 9(2).
50 SC(SdS)(S)A 2013, ss 6 and 17.
51 Self-directed Support (Direct Payments) (Scotland) Regulations 2014, reg 9.

Protection of Vulnerable Groups (Scotland) Act 2007

2.41 The Protection of Vulnerable Groups (Scotland) Act 2007 created a Protection of Vulnerable Groups Scheme intended to make sure that those individuals who are unsuitable to work with children or certain 'protected' adults are identified and removed from the workforce. The scheme is operated by Disclosure Scotland.[52]

2.42 The scheme is designed to be continually updated with new information. This was viewed as an improvement on the existing disclosure checks which simply showed someone had no convictions at a particular point in time. If information comes to light after a person is initially registered, employers and other relevant parties will be notified of this. For example, if an individual is convicted of a criminal offence after they have taken up employment or is suspended from another job for misconduct then all employers will be notified that this has happened.

Where new information is made available, the employer may have some discretion to decide whether or not it is appropriate for an individual to continue in a particular role. However, some offences or circumstances may mean a person cannot be considered fit to work with protected adults. In such cases, they will be added to the list held by Disclosure Scotland of individuals barred from particular roles.[53] It is an offence to employ someone on this list in a role which involves work with protected adults.[54]

2.43 Any person carrying out any paid or unpaid work[55] in relation to 'protected adults' must be a member of the scheme. A protected adult is defined as someone over the age of 16 who receives one or more care, health or welfare services.[56] The definition is different to those seen elsewhere in adult protection legislation. It is service based and so an individual is covered because they receive a service rather than because they have a particular condition.

52 For more information see www.disclosurescotland.co.uk.
53 Protection of Vulnerable Groups (Scotland) Act 2007 (PVG(S)A 2007), s 1.
54 PVG(S)A 2007, s 35.
55 PVG(S)A 2007, s 95.
56 PVG(S)A 2007, s 94.

Housing (Scotland) Act 1987

2.44 The local authority is under a legal duty to provide housing and has particular duties to those who may be considered homeless in terms of the legislation.[57] Housing law is not covered in any detail in this book but adult protection cases may involve consideration of long- and short-term housing options, for example, where it is unreasonable for an adult to return home.

CONCLUSION

2.45 The Adult Support and Protection (Scotland) Act 2007 covers a range of individuals with diverse support needs and is often seen as a gateway to services. Often interventions will happen with the adult's approval or other legislation will be used. Most inquiries will not result in a formal court order under the Act. However, they remain an important tool for practitioners.

57 Housing (Scotland) Act 1987 as amended by the Housing (Scotland) Act 2001, and the Homelessness etc. (Scotland) Act 2003.

Chapter 3

ADULT PROTECTION COMMITTEES

3.1 Even before the introduction of the Bill that would become the Adult Support and Protection (Scotland) Act 2007, many local authorities had created committees with specific responsibility for coordinating adult protection efforts across local agencies. Although some concern was voiced during the debates on the Bill as to whether making such arrangements compulsory would simply be another bureaucratic burden on local authorities, the measures passed into law without significant amendment. As a result, since 28 October 2008 all local authorities have been required to establish and operate adult protection committees.[1]

The legal requirements regarding adult protection committees, as set out in the 2007 Act, are brief. Over time, there has been significant development of committees' role across Scotland. This is now reflected in separate guidance that has been issued by the Scottish Government.[2] There are also references to adult protection committees in various other guidance that has been produced and will be referred to in the remainder of this chapter. Committees must have regard to the guidance, insofar as it relates to their statutory functions.[3] Likewise, councils, council officers and health professionals must have regard to guidance issued concerning their functions under the 2007 Act, where relevant.[4]

A duty to, 'have regard to', guidance does not, however, equate to a requirement to follow guidance in all circumstances. Committees, councils and the officers and professionals mentioned therefore have to consider the particular circumstances they might be presented with and decide whether or not there is good reason to depart from the guidance.

1 Adult Support and Protection (Scotland) Act 2007 (ASP(S)A 2007), s 42.
2 *The Adult Support and Protection (Scotland) Act 2007 Guidance For Adult Protection Committees* (Scottish Government, July 2022) (APC Guidance).
3 ASP(S)A 2007, s 47.
4 ASP(S)A 2007, ss 47 and 48(5).

ROLE AND FUNCTIONS OF ADULT PROTECTION COMMITTEES

3.2 Adult protection committees play an important strategic role in coordinating adult protection work within their area. They are multi-agency committees with representation from various public bodies.[5] The core functions of committees are:

- keeping local adult protection practices and procedures under review (in particular, those relating to inter-agency cooperation);
- providing information, advice and suggestions to public bodies and office holders on the exercise of their functions locally;
- improving information and skills across local agencies; and
- such other functions (relating to the safeguarding of adults at risk) as may be specified by an order of the Scottish Ministers.

To date, no further functions have been specified.

3.3 In addition, committees, in carrying out their functions, 'must have regard to the desirability of improving co-operation between [the relevant public bodies] for the purpose of assisting those bodies … to perform functions in order to safeguard adults at risk present in the council's area'.[6] The improvement of cooperation between public agencies is thus an all-pervading function of committees.

It seems clear that the functions identified are not intended to be read restrictively, so that, should a committee or the constituent agencies feel that committee involvement in other areas of adult protection is appropriate, this may take place.[7] One example of this is in efforts to raise awareness of adult protection issues among the public at large.[8] Many committees have taken a role in this, although it is not a function listed in the legislation itself.

3.4 The following agencies are specifically referred to as having a key role in adult protection committees and safeguarding adults at risk:

5 ASP(S)A 2007, s 42(3).
6 ASP(S)A 2007, s 42(2).
7 APC Guidance, p 9 states: 'Local Terms of Reference may therefore go beyond the statutory requirements of the Act, or allow APCs to address some matters not fully falling within the terms of the Act, if so approved by the APC'.
8 APC Guidance, p 14.

- the local authority;
- the Care Inspectorate;
- Healthcare Improvement Scotland;
- the relevant health board;
- the Police; and
- any other public body or office holder as the Scottish Ministers may by order specify.[9]

It is clearly intended that these bodies will work with their local committee voluntarily in supporting it to perform its functions. There is no specific duty placed on agencies to cooperate with committees, beyond a duty to provide information reasonably required to carry out its functions.[10] In particular, it is worth noting that there is no statutory requirement to follow advice or proposals issued by an adult protection committee, even where these are in regard to its core functions (for example, committees cannot require agencies to amend their procedures). Nonetheless, it is likely that local governance arrangements will ensure a commitment to the work of the committee and some means of resolving any disagreement as to its carrying it out (see the section on governance and accountability below).

Membership

3.5 In establishing the adult protection committee, the local authority must appoint a convener and certain statutory members.

Convener

3.6 The convener must not be a councillor or employee of the local authority making the appointment.[11] There is no restriction on councillors or employees of other local authorities being appointed. Guidance indicates that the convener should also be independent of those organisations that are represented on the committee and the local authority, health board

9 ASP(S)A 2007, s 42(3). (No such order has been made, at the time of writing.)

10 ASP(S)A 2007, s 45. This duty also extends to the Mental Welfare Commission and the Public Guardian.

11 ASP(S)A 2007, s 43(6).

and police, in particular.[12] It further suggests that, although only the local authority has statutory responsibility for the appointment of the convener, it should be done, 'after an open recruitment process involving an interview with the three Chief Officers [ie of the local authority, health board and police] or their nominees'.[13]

No legislative provision is made, or guidance provided as to the remuneration, period of office or other contractual terms of the convener's appointment. Given the requirement that they produce a biennial report, it would seem appropriate that terms of office last for at least that two-year period. Guidance suggests that the convener's appointment should be for a fixed term, with an option for renewal, linked to ongoing approval from the Chief Officers and subject to appraisal.[14]

Statutory members/attendees

3.7 The relevant health board(s), Police Scotland and Healthcare Improvement Scotland must nominate at least one representative to sit on the local adult protection committee. The Care Inspectorate may nominate a representative, if it chooses to do so. The local authority must appoint these nominees to its committee.[15]

The committee must also allow certain other bodies to send a representative to meetings as they consider appropriate. These are the Mental Welfare Commission, the Public Guardian and the Care Inspectorate (if it has not nominated a permanent member to the committee).[16]

Despite being required to by the legislation, Healthcare Improvement Scotland does not have permanent representation on any committee, at the time of writing. It is however represented at the Adult Support and Protection Conveners' Scotland Group and the National Strategic

12 APC Guidance, p 5.

13 APC Guidance, p 19.

14 APC Guidance, p 19. It is notable that no reference is made in the guidance to the terms of the Fixed-term Employees (Prevention of Less Favourable Treatment) Regulations 2002 (SI 2002/2034), and, in particular, reg 8, which operates to make fixed-term employees automatically become permanent employees in many circumstances, after four years. A full consideration of the status and rights of conveners in employment law is beyond the scope of this book. (See also note 30, below.)

15 ASP(S)A 2007, s 43. There is a power to make regulations to add to the list of those entitled to nominate a representative.

16 ASP(S)A 2007, s 44.

Forum.[17] The Care Inspectorate had permanent representation on many committees at their inception, but its strategic link inspectors and relationship managers now attend on a less regular basis.[18]

The Office of the Public Guardian does not attend committees on a regular basis, though it does attend if invited to provide specific input. The Mental Welfare Commission has taken the same approach but from 2024 intends to attend each committee annually as a minimum. It will continue to attend when invited or where a topic of relevance is being discussed, eg new guidance or the outcome of an investigation.

Further members/attendees

3.8 In addition to statutory members, local authorities may invite anyone they consider to have relevant knowledge and skills to be part of the committee or attend any particular meeting. There are usually local authority officers who sit as members of the committee, as well as further representatives from the statutory member organisations, although there is no requirement that any more than one nominee from each such agency be appointed a member. Some committees include elected members of the local authority. Again, this is not a statutory requirement, and it is not referred to in the guidance. Fire and rescue and ambulance services are also often represented, as are trading standards and financial institutions. The APC Guidance suggests that wider involvement and engagement may also be carried out by inviting non-APC members to sit on sub-committees. In that regard, it proposes possible beneficial links with:

- services for adults, children and families;
- other council services including housing, education, consumer protection, trading standards and community safety;
- health services including GP General Practices, allied health professionals, acute and psychiatric hospitals and community health services;
- third and independent sector organisations, eg care providers and carer groups;

[17] HIS FOI response, 9 May 2024. The Conveners' Group and Forum are not statutory bodies, but have been set up to allow discussion of national-level issues and share good practice. The latter is chaired by a Scottish Government minister.

[18] Care Inspectorate FOI response, 15 April 2024. The Care Inspectorate does not hold searchable records of its attendance at adult protection committees, so was unable to confirm the specific frequency.

- the financial sector;
- independent advocacy organisations.[19]

Aside from the statutory appointees, whether a particular service or sector is represented directly at the level of the committee, or by input into subject-specific sub-committees or working groups, is likely to depend on local circumstances and the particular priorities of the committee itself.

In regard to contact with representatives of the independent care sector and with service user and carer organisations, identifying the appropriate representative of such groups may pose difficulties. Biennial reports show that representation of users and carers is one of the areas that is often identified as needing further work, and it is common to see local advocacy organisations fulfilling this role. Some committees have formed sub-groups intended to try and capture the views of service users and carers. The precise format of engagement is very variable across Scotland. No doubt this is due, at least in part, to the difficulty in balancing lay involvement with the high-level strategic role of the committee and the technical aspects of its work.

Due to the unrestrictive approach to membership adopted by the legislation, and as is suggested by the above, there is wide variation locally as to representation. Committees tend to range in size from 12–30 members.[20]

Procedures

3.9 The way committees operate is not set down by statute and each committee is responsible for formulating its own procedures.[21] They must have regard to guidance issued by Scottish Ministers about how they operate.[22]

The vast majority of committees cover just one local authority area. However, there are two examples of joint adult protection committees being established.[23] Many local authorities hold joint training events or create cross-authority working groups.

19 APC Guidance, pp 6–7.

20 A detailed review of the 2010–12 biennial reports – Ekosgen (January 2013): www.gov.scot/Resource/0041/00418395.pdf.

21 ASP(S)A 2007, s 44.

22 ASP(S)A 2007, s 47.

23 The East and Midlothian Public Protection Committee (which encompasses the adult protection committee function for those areas) and the Forth Valley APC which did cover Clackmannanshire, Falkirk and Stirling, but has more recently been split into its constituent councils).

Guidance suggests that links with other public protection committees (child protection committees and Multi-Agency Public Protection Arrangements) should be established to allow proper communication and coordination of work.[24]

Governance and accountability

3.10 Although there is multi-agency membership and there is no requirement for elected member representation, the adult protection committee is a committee of the local authority (or local authorities) who form it. This is clear from the fact that the responsibility to establish the committee lies squarely with the local authority[25] and is reinforced in the language used in the provision regarding appointments to the committee, which states, 'It is for the council to appoint the convener and the other members of *its* Adult Protection Committee'.[26]

Nonetheless, a committee which was run only at the behest of the local authority would be unlikely to achieve the multi-agency functions required of it. For that reason, it is made clear in the guidance that lines of accountability not just to the local authority, but to the health board and police will be required. A corollary of that is that proper authority to bind their organisations to decisions of the committee will either have to be given to those representatives sitting on it, or be obtainable by some other procedure. All adult protection committees report directly to their local Chief Officers Group, which will include Chief Executive and Director level members from the local authority, NHS and Police Scotland, and major decisions may require ratification by that group.[27]

Two points of note flow from the fact that the adult protection committee is a committee of the local authority. Firstly, information held by the committee is potentially recoverable in terms of a freedom of information request, opening the potential for direct public scrutiny of its work.[28] The guidance suggests that minutes of meetings might be made

24 APC Guidance, p 6.

25 ASP(S)A 2007, s 42(1).

26 ASP(S)A 2007, s 43(1) (emphasis added).

27 APC Guidance, p 18.

28 Freedom of Information (Scotland) Act 2002 (FOI(S)A 2002), s 1, Sch 1 para 21. There are many exceptions to the general requirement to disclose information, including where such information is personal or sensitive personal information, or is already published (FOI(S)A 2002, ss 25 and 38). A full consideration of the law relating to freedom of information is beyond the scope of this book.

publicly available, subject to redaction of any sensitive or confidential information.[29]

Secondly, unless it enters into another local arrangement, ultimate responsibility for the oversight of the work of the independent convener lies with the local authority. In the event that any disciplinary action is required (assuming the absence of any other local arrangement), it would fall to the local authority to carry out an appropriate process of investigation and sanction.[30] It may be considered that this contradicts the requirement that the convener may not be an officer of the local authority.[31] It is suggested that, in order to make sense of this contradiction, the requirement must be interpreted to mean that the convener may not be an officer of the local authority, other than in their capacity as convener of the adult protection committee.

Adult protection committees are not directly accountable to the Scottish Government, although oversight is maintained by requiring a report to be produced for Scottish Ministers every two years by the independent convener.[32] This should report on the general work of the committee in the preceding two years in the furtherance of its functions (statutory or otherwise) and is copied to the bodies represented on the committee, the Mental Welfare Commission, the Public Guardian and the Care Inspectorate (where it is not a member of the committee). The biennial reports for each committee were originally made available online by the Scottish Government. A summary report was produced and published in regard to the 2012–14 reports. Both practices appear now to have fallen into disuse.[33] However, each local authority does publish its own biennial reports on its website.

29 APC Guidance, p 11.

30 The precise employment status and rights of an independent convener is likely to be a complicated question and may depend on what arrangements are made locally regarding remuneration, terms and conditions of engagement and where these latter are set out. This is ultimately an employment law matter and beyond the scope of this book.

31 ASP(S)A 2007, s 43(6).

32 ASP(S)A 2007, s 46.

33 https://www.gov.scot/publications/apc-biennial-reports-2012-14-summary-report/pages/1/. Search of the Scottish Government website on 14 July 2024 for 'biennial report' found no other hits.

LEARNING REVIEWS AND LARGE SCALE INVESTIGATIONS

3.11 A learning review, in the context of adult protection, is defined by the Scottish Government as: 'a means for public bodies and office holders with responsibilities relating to the protection of adults at risk of harm to learn lessons from considering the circumstances where an adult at risk has died or been significantly harmed.'[34] Since their inception, adult protection committees have taken responsibility for overseeing such processes (albeit, perhaps, under different names). While there is no explicit mention of committees having this responsibility in the legislation, it can readily be inferred from the core functions that are set out in the Adult Support and Protection (Scotland) Act 2007, s 42. In particular, such reviews contribute to their oversight of local procedure and practice; allow them to give advice on safeguarding functions; and help to improve skills and knowledge of local officers working in this field. The Scottish Government has separate statutory guidance as to how such reviews should be conducted, which aims to harmonise practice across different public protection disciplines and across Scotland.[35] That guidance and the general guidance for committees are clear that adult protection committees, on behalf of their Chief Officers Groups, should have responsibility for commissioning and overseeing learning reviews.[36] It is also stipulated that the Care Inspectorate should be informed of a decision to initiate, or not to initiate, a review. A copy of the final report from any review, suitably anonymised, should be sent to the Care Inspectorate in order to allow it to communicate learning across Scotland.[37] Large scale investigations (LSIs) are another area in which adult protection committees have taken an interest, but which are not specifically referred to in the 2007 Act. Various guidance documents now refer to these explicitly.[38] While it would perhaps require a creative reading of the core functions set out in the Act to say

[34] *National Guidance for Adult Protection Committees Undertaking Learning Reviews* (Scottish Government, May 2022), p 4.

[35] *National Guidance for Adult Protection Committees Undertaking Learning Reviews* (Scottish Government, May 2022), p 2.

[36] APC Guidance, p 13.

[37] *National Guidance for Adult Protection Committees Undertaking Learning Reviews* (Scottish Government, May 2022), p 17.

[38] See for example the *Adult Support and Protection (Scotland) Act 2007 Code of Practice* (ASP(S)A 2007 Code of Practice) (July 2022), pp 65–68; the APC Guidance, p 14; *Adult Support and Protection (Scotland) Act 2007 Guidance for General Practice* (Scottish Government, July 2022), pp 19–20.

there is a specific statutory role for committees in these investigations, if the public bodies who do have duties to investigate harm (in particular the local authority) consider it useful to coordinate their efforts through the adult protection committee, there is no reason why that cannot be agreed in local procedures.

In general, LSIs are appropriate where there are a number of adults at risk in circumstances which appear to be linked in some way. Such a situation may indicate that they are subject to a similar source of harm, perhaps at a systemic level. It follows that proper inquiry or investigation of the individuals' affairs under the Adult Support and Protection (Scotland) Act 2007, s 4, will have to take the broader picture into account. Where there is concern in relation to a particular care service, the contract for the service will also usually provide a legal basis for an LSI. The Scottish Government suggest the following situations should trigger an LSI:

- 'an adult protection referral is received that involves 2 or more adults living within or cared for by the same service;
- a referral is received regarding one adult, but the nature of the referral raises queries regarding the standard of care provided by a service;
- where more than one perpetrator is suspected;
- institutional harm is suspected;
- a whistle-blower has made serious allegations regarding a service;
- there are significant concerns regarding the quality of care provided and a service's ability to improve. These concerns could come from a regulatory body such as the Care Inspectorate;
- an adult or adults are living independently within the community but are subject to harm from a perpetrator or group of perpetrators, or it is strongly suspected that more than one adult is subject to such harm;
- concerns regarding an adult are raised following their admission to hospital or discharge. This may include concerns about a care service that are evidenced by an admission to hospital, or concerns regarding an NHS service area;
- concerns are raised via a complaint to the Care Inspectorate, NHS Board, or the local Council or Health and Social Care Partnership;

- concerns are raised by General Practices, District Nurses, Dentists, Allied Health Professionals etc. who attend a service.'[39]

CONCLUSION

3.12 Adult protection committees perform an important strategic role in the promotion of multi-agency working and the oversight of procedure and practice within their area. They are given great freedom by central government to determine how they perform their statutory functions and to reach beyond these, as seems appropriate to their local circumstances. While they are committees of their local authority, the involvement of other partner agencies and their remit require them to be run on a multi-agency basis and, in that respect, they should be an example of good practice for those working at an operational level.

[39] ASP(S)A) 2007 Code of Practice, p 66.

Chapter 4

KEY ORGANISATIONS AND INDIVIDUALS

4.1 This chapter looks at some of the key organisations and individuals involved in adult protection cases, including local authorities, health care providers, protective bodies and those involved in the criminal justice system. The role of adult protection committees is covered in Chapter 3.

LOCAL AUTHORITIES

4.2 Local authorities have a lead role in adult protection with several legal duties under the Adult Support and Protection (Scotland) Act 2007. Their role and responsibilities are introduced here and discussed more fully throughout this book. The legislation places a duty on them to investigate where a person may be at risk. Community care law requires them to assess people's needs for support and organise, or pay for, services where appropriate. They have additional important obligations under the Adults with Incapacity (Scotland) Act 2000 and the Mental Health (Care and Treatment) (Scotland) Act 2003.

Local authorities have a general duty to promote social welfare in their area, by providing advice, guidance, assistance and such facilities as they consider suitable and adequate.[1] They may provide services themselves, arrange for another organisation to provide them or provide funding so that the individual can arrange their own.

One of the most important changes brought about by the Adult Support and Protection (Scotland) Act 2007 was to set out very clearly the key role of the local authority in protecting adults at risk of harm.[2]

Anyone concerned that an adult may be at risk should contact the local authority's social work department. If the person appears to be seriously mentally unwell, it might be appropriate to contact a medical practitioner or telephone 111 for advice. If the person has a mental health

1 Social Work (Scotland) Act 1968, s 12(1).
2 Adult Support and Protection (Scotland) Act 2007 (ASP(S)A 2007).

officer, then they may be able to assist. Mental health officers are specialist social workers with additional training and experience in mental illness, dementia and learning disabilities. They carry out certain functions under mental health and incapacity legislation.

Council officers

4.3 The Adult Support and Protection (Scotland) Act 2007 defines a council officer as someone appointed by a council under the Local Government (Scotland) Act 1973, section 64.[3]

Recognising that many disciplines can have a role in adult protection, councils may appoint registered social workers, nurses and occupational therapists to act in an investigatory role under the Adult Support and Protection (Scotland) Act 2007. Social service workers registered with the Scottish Social Services Council[4] may also support social workers to carry out this role. All these professionals must have at least 12 months' post-qualifying experience of identifying, assessing and managing adults at risk.[5] The Council can withdraw the authority of a council officer if the individual no longer meets the relevant requirements.

A social service worker who is not a qualified social worker cannot be responsible for initiating an assessment order, a removal order, moving an adult at risk or protecting the property of an adult moved under adult protection law.[6]

HEALTH CARE PROVIDERS

4.4 A number of health care providers are involved in adult protection in Scotland. These include General Practitioners (GPs) who provide primary health care, health boards which run hospitals and integrated health and social care corporate bodies.

Other health professionals who may be involved with adults at risk include nurses (both hospital-based and those working in the community), physiotherapists, health visitors and occupational therapists.

The relevant health board, and those working for it, must cooperate with a local authority making inquiries into any case involving an adult at

3 ASP(S)A 2007, s 53.

4 www.sssc.uk.com

5 The Adult Support and Protection (Scotland) Act 2007 (Restriction on the Authorisation of Council Officers) Order 2008 (SSI 2008/306).

6 SSI 2008/306, art 4.

risk. They must also cooperate with the other relevant parties to any adult protection investigation.[7] Health professionals may be asked to carry out medical assessments where a local authority is investigating a case. In some cases, the rules of patient confidentiality will not apply and a health professional can be required to hand over health records for the purposes of an inquiry.[8] However, any inspection of those records should only be carried out by another health professional. At the time of writing, the term 'health professional' includes doctors, nurses and midwives, but Scottish Ministers could extend the rules to cover, for example, occupational therapists and psychologists.[9] For more details on patient confidentiality and the position of GPs, see Chapter 13.

SOCIAL CARE AND SOCIAL WORK IMPROVEMENT SCOTLAND ('THE CARE INSPECTORATE')

4.5 Social Care and Social Work Improvement Scotland (normally referred to as 'the Care Inspectorate') was established by the Public Services Reform (Scotland) Act 2010.[10] It was set up to help streamline the number of government and regulatory agencies in Scotland and replaced the Care Commission,[11] the Social Work Inspection Agency (SWIA) and the child protection unit of His Majesty's Inspectorate for Education (HMIe).

Care services in Scotland are not allowed to operate unless they are registered with the Care Inspectorate. There are currently around 11,300 registered services in Scotland. This includes all types of residential care home, nurse agencies, childcare services, care at home and housing support services.[12] The Care Inspectorate's functions are carrying out inspections, supporting improvement, dealing with complaints and enforcement action. It can take action to force services to improve and close down services if necessary.[13] The Care Inspectorate also provides and publishes information to the public about the availability and quality of social services[14] and can nominate a representative to attend adult protection

7 ASP(S)A 2007, s 5.
8 ASP(S)A 2007, s 10.
9 ASP(S)A 2007, s 52.
10 Public Services Reform (Scotland) Act 2010 (PSR(S)A 2010), s 44.
11 PSR(S)A 2010, s 52.
12 PSR(S)A 2010, s 47(1).
13 Subject to the decision of a sheriff.
14 PSR(S)A 2010, s 51.

committees (although it does not attend as a standing member).[15] It is a criminal offence to provide a registrable service while not registered with the Care Inspectorate.[16]

4.6 The legislation sets out some general principles which the Care Inspectorate must apply when exercising its functions. These are:

- the safety and well-being of all persons who use, or are eligible to use, any social service are to be protected and enhanced;
- the independence of those persons is to be promoted;
- diversity in the provision of social services is to be promoted with a view to those persons being afforded choice; and
- good practice in the provision of social services is to be identified, promulgated and promoted.[17]

Inspections

4.7 Under Public Services Reform (Scotland) Act 2010, s 53, the Care Inspectorate can inspect any social work service or organisation providing such a service.[18] All services in certain categories, including care homes for older people or other adults, can expect, as a minimum, one annual unannounced visit. Other service types are inspected according to an agreed frequency framework. As well as this programme of regular inspections, additional, or more focussed, inspections can be carried out where necessary. This might happen following a complaint or incident raising cause for concern. Reports of these investigations are available on the Care Inspectorate's website.[19] The Care Inspectorate uses National Care Standards to check the quality of care.[20]

4.8 The inspection reports grade services in relation to specified categories, on a scale from six (excellent) to one (unsatisfactory). These categories include care and support, physical environment and quality of

[15] ASP(S)A 2007, s 43(3), as amended by PSR(S)A 2010, Sch 14, para 21.

[16] PSR(S)A 2010, s 80(1).

[17] PSR(S)A 2010, s 45.

[18] The Care Inspectorate carried out 4,068 individual inspections in 2022/23. *Annual report and accounts 2022–23* (www.careinspectorate.com).

[19] www.careinspectorate.com

[20] PSR(S)A 2010, s 50.

staff. A report may also contain both recommendations and requirements and is available to the public. A recommendation is a suggestion about what the care provider should do to deliver best practice. Failure to comply does not result in enforcement action. A requirement is a statement setting out what a service provider must do to improve outcomes for people using the service. The care provider will be expected to comply with a requirement and enforcement action may be taken if they fail to do so.

All services have to formally notify the Care Inspectorate of particular events, including any allegations of abuse or other accidents, and injuries to anyone using a care service.

Complaints

4.9 Anyone concerned about a care service can make a complaint to the Care Inspectorate.[21] While it is usually preferable for the complainer to be identified, anonymous complaints will be considered. The types of complaint that can be investigated are those involving any action (or lack of action) by a service or about the actual standard of the service. Complaints will only be considered if they are made within six months of the incident complained about. This time limit can be waived in exceptional circumstances. It is important to be aware of this deadline, particularly if the care provider's, or local authority's, own complaints procedure has been initiated. A referral to the Care Inspectorate might need to be made before the outcome of an internal complaint is known, so that the matter is not time barred. The Care Inspectorate is unable to consider complaints about deaths in care homes or their pricing policies.

4.10 Where a complaint is upheld the Care Inspectorate might make recommendations, require improvements or order an action plan to be implemented. The service could be regraded or receive a formal improvement notice. Its conditions of registration could also be varied with options to change or remove a condition as well as imposing an additional condition.[22]

21 PSR(S)A 2010, s 79(1).
22 PSR(S)A 2010, s 66.

Enforcement

4.11 Where the Care Inspectorate has sufficient concerns about a service it can issue a formal Improvement Notice.[23] In the year 2022/23, 45 such notices were issued. This requires the service to make improvements within a specified timescale. A failure to improve could result in cancellation of registration.[24]

4.12 Where the Care Inspectorate feels that immediate action is needed, it may require the care provider to take emergency measures. Where concerns are very serious and risk is significant, the ultimate sanction is an application to the sheriff court for emergency cancellation of registration and the closure of the service. If the Sheriff is satisfied that, unless the order is made, there will be a serious risk to the life, health or well-being of individuals, they may grant the application. The Sheriff can also make any relevant interim order.[25] Any decision of the Sheriff can be appealed to the Sheriff Appeal Court within 14 days.[26]

HEALTHCARE IMPROVEMENT SCOTLAND (HIS)

4.13 Healthcare Improvement Scotland (HIS) was established in 2010 by the Public Services Reform (Scotland) Act 2010. This organisation took over the functions of the Care Commission relating to independent health care provision and replaced NHS Quality Improvement Scotland.[27] HIS has a number of responsibilities including supporting, ensuring and monitoring the quality of health care provided or secured by the health service.[28] It also provides information to the public about the availability and quality of independent health care services.[29] Services providing independent health care must be registered with HIS.[30]

Anyone concerned about an independent health care service can complain directly to HIS, which may consider an inspection or enforcement

23 PSR(S)A 2010, s 62(1).
24 PSR(S)A 2010, s 64(1).
25 PSR(S)A 2010, s 65(1), (2).
26 PSR(S)A 2010, s 65(8).
27 National Health Service (Scotland) Act 1978 (NHS(S)A 1978), s 10A as amended by the PSR(S)A 2010, s 108.
28 NHS(S)A 1978, s 10C(1).
29 NHS(S)A 1978, s 10E(1).
30 NHS(S)A 1978, s 10P.

action. Additional information about the complaints procedure and the role and responsibility of HIS is available on its website.[31]

4.14 The legislation sets out some principles that HIS must apply when carrying out its functions. These are:

- the safety and well-being of all persons who use services provided under the health service and independent health care services are to be protected and enhanced;
- good practice in the provision of those services is to be identified, promulgated and promoted; and
- the provision of services in a manner which takes appropriate account of guidance and other information (including evidence) published or endorsed by HIS is to be promoted and encouraged.[32]

Inspections

4.15 HIS may inspect any independent care service to evaluate the effectiveness of the service, encourage improvement or investigate any incident.[33] Inspections may be carried out in relation to the organisations providing the care service. Inspection reports are provided and are available to the public.[34] HIS also inspects the care of older people and the environment in NHS hospitals.

Enforcement

4.16 HIS has similar powers to the Care Inspectorate in terms of the options available when enforcement action is necessary. An Improvement Notice can be issued requiring an independent health care service to take particular action within a set timescale.[35] Failure to comply with an Improvement Notice might result in cancellation of registration, meaning the service can no longer operate. HIS may also apply to the Sheriff for emergency cancellation of a service's registration.

31 www.healthcareimprovementscotland.scot
32 NHS(S)A 1978, s 10B.
33 NHS(S)A 1978, s 10J(1), (2).
34 NHS(S)A 1978, s 10N(1).
35 NHS(S)A 1978, s 10R.

PUBLIC GUARDIAN

4.17 The Public Guardian has important duties and powers in relation to adults who, due to incapacity, may be unable to manage all or part of their property or financial affairs or safeguard or promote their interests or rights.

The Public Guardian maintains the registers of powers of attorney and appointments and interventions under the Adults with Incapacity (Scotland) Act 2000. They also monitor and supervise people appointed under Adults with Incapacity (Scotland) Act 2000, Parts 3 and 6 to manage the financial or property affairs of adults who are unable to do so for themselves.

The Public Guardian can intervene if an adult is at risk of financial abuse or is otherwise unable to manage financial or property matters. The Public Guardian must investigate if they become aware that the property or financial affairs of an adult appear to be at risk.[36] The Public Guardian may initiate or take part in any legal proceedings needed to safeguard the affairs of an adult whose finances are at risk. Safeguards include freezing bank accounts or income and other action taken could include applying for the removal of an attorney or guardian, an application for a guardianship order to appoint a new guardian, or reporting fraud or dishonesty to the police.

There is helpful information on the Public Guardian's website[37] and the office can be approached by anyone needing information or advice.

Investigations

4.18 The Public Guardian must investigate any complaint about a financial attorney, a financial guardian, a financial intervener or a person operating an access to funds account.[38] In the course of carrying out an investigation, the Public Guardian may require anyone with financial powers to provide any relevant records and information about how these powers have been used. They may also require anyone who holds, or has held, funds belonging to an adult to hand over records and other information.[39] This might include banks, other financial institutions or the Department of Work and Pensions.

[36] Adults with Incapacity (Scotland) Act 2000 (AWI(S)A 2000), s 6.
[37] www.publicguardian-scotland.gov.uk
[38] AWI(S)A 2000, s 6(2).
[39] AWI(S)A 2000, s 81A.

4.19 If a person with powers under the Adults with Incapacity (Scotland) Act 2000 misuses those powers and/or the adult's property or financial affairs seem to be at risk, the Public Guardian may take any steps thought necessary to safeguard those affairs. This might involve making an application to the Sheriff for any order deemed necessary. They will also involve the police if criminal activity is suspected. The office will consult with any relevant local authority and the Mental Welfare Commission if they have a potential interest in the case.[40]

Overlap with other bodies

4.20 The Adults with Incapacity (Scotland) Act 2000 authorises the Public Guardian to investigate financial or property concerns about an adult with mental incapacity. The Adult Support and Protection (Scotland) Act 2007 gives local authorities a duty to investigate financial harm. The Public Guardian reports any report of harm or abuse to the local authority, which will often start its own inquiries. This has the potential to result in duplication of investigations.

When the Public Guardian undertakes an investigation they will advise the relevant local authority to see if it has had any contact with the adult or other persons involved. Where the Public Guardian concludes an adult is at risk but is not incapable in terms of the Adults with Incapacity (Scotland) Act 2000, the local authority will normally be required to investigate instead.

Where appropriate, following an investigation, the Public Guardian has specific legal powers to commence proceedings to safeguard the property or financial interests of an adult unable to do this for themselves. The local authority also has a duty to apply to the court for financial powers in particular situations (see Chapter 7) but it does not have the power to take as wide-ranging proceedings as the Public Guardian.[41]

There can be overlap with the role of both the Care Inspectorate and HIS where issues of financial abuse occur in registered care settings or in independent health care provision.

[40] AWI(S)A 2000, s 6(2)(f).

[41] See Adrian Ward's comments on the Public Guardian in *Adults with Incapacity Legislation* (W. Green, 2008).

MENTAL WELFARE COMMISSION

4.21 The Mental Welfare Commission ('the Commission') is an independent organisation working to protect and promote the rights and welfare of everyone (children as well as adults) in Scotland who has a mental illness, learning disability, dementia or other related condition. It has various statutory duties which it seeks to carry out by focussing on five broad areas of work. These are visiting people, monitoring the legislation, carrying out investigations, providing information/advice and influencing/challenging. It has a wide remit and may be involved in a number of settings, including prisons, residential care, hospitals and day services.

As well as a formal role in monitoring the operation of mental health and incapacity legislation, it can become involved in individual cases where adults are or have been at risk. Such cases may come to its attention either on one of its regular visits or following a referral. In many instances, some initial advice might be given and the concerned individual will be signposted to the appropriate organisation. However, it may investigate itself, ask the local authority to investigate or, in some cases, hold a formal inquiry.[42]

The Commission should be notified of deaths in specified circumstances including where the adult was subject to compulsory treatment or there is a significant concern regarding an aspect of the care and treatment prior to the patient's death. It also expects to be notified of significant investigations under key legislation,[43] and any protection orders granted under the Adult Support and Protection (Scotland) Act 2007.

The Commission has considerable experience in issues relating to the protection of adults with mental disorders. It provides a wide range of advice and guidance to both professionals and members of the public. More information is available on its website.[44]

Investigations

4.22 The Commission has legal powers to carry out investigations as it considers appropriate where it believes that someone with a mental disorder may be (or has been) at risk. The risk could be:

42 Mental Health (Care and Treatment) (Scotland) Act 2003 (MH(CT)(S)A 2003), s 12.

43 These are investigations under the MH(CT)(S)A 2003, s 33 and AWI(S)A 2000, s 10(1)(c).

44 www.mwcscot.org.uk

- that the person is unlawfully detained in hospital;
- ill-treatment, neglect or inadequate care or treatment, either currently or in the past;
- that someone who appears to live alone or without care is unable to look after themselves or their property or finances;
- loss or damage to a person's property because of their mental disorder, or the risk of such loss in the future.[45]

4.23 The Commission may need to interview the adult, carers or others who have raised concerns. A member of the Commission staff can be authorised to interview that person, in private, where this is considered appropriate.[46] A medical professional or appropriately trained member of the Commission's staff can carry out a medical examination of the adult.[47] A person authorised by the Commission can also inspect any relevant records.[48] The Commission will not be able to investigate every case that comes to its attention. However, it is a useful source of independent advice.

4.24 The Commission publishes the outcome of its formal investigations.[49] It can make recommendations to a body if it considers it appropriate, including Scottish Ministers, local authorities, health boards, care homes, individual social workers, doctors and the police.[50]

Inquiries

4.25 In addition to its ability to investigate any case, the Mental Welfare Commission can carry out a formal inquiry. This is a semi-judicial process, with witnesses being required to attend and give evidence on oath.[51] To date, the Commission has not found it necessary to use these formal powers.

45 MH(CT)(S)A 2003, s 11.
46 MH(CT)(S)A 2003, s 14(1).
47 MH(CT)(S)A 2003, s 15.
48 MH(CT)(S)A 2003, s 16.
49 See the 'Publications' section of the Mental Welfare Commission for Scotland website (www.mwcscot.org.uk).
50 MH(CT)(S)A 2003, s 8.
51 MH(CT)(S)A 2003, s 12.

Visits

4.26 The Commission has wide powers to visit people subject to compulsory orders under the Mental Health (Care and Treatment) (Scotland) Act 2003 and the Adults with Incapacity (Scotland) Act 2000. It can also visit people with a mental disorder in any other setting, including hospitals (in both the NHS and independent sector), care homes, secure accommodation, local authority services and prisons, to inspect the service and facilities. Such visits may be pre-arranged but can be unannounced.[52] The organisation being inspected is under a duty to give all the help that is necessary to enable the Commission to carry out its functions.[53] The Commission categorises visits as local visits, themed visits,[54] welfare guardianship visits and other visits. Local visits are made to individuals in local services including specific hospital wards, prisons or care homes. In the year, 2023–24 they visited 149 locations and reviewed the care of 1,019 individuals.[55]

During the course of its visits the Commission should offer those using the service the opportunity to have a private meeting with Commission staff and discuss any concerns.[56] The Commission also seeks the views of family members and others who visit the adults involved.

4.27 The Commission visits people who are subject to welfare guardianship orders, welfare intervention orders and welfare powers of attorney. This will often involve visiting people in their own homes. In the year 1 April 2023 to 31 March 2024, 329 such visits were carried out.

Overlap with other bodies

4.28 Some of the Mental Welfare Commission's duties are very similar to those of local authorities, although there are significant differences. For example, the Commission does not have a duty to investigate where a

52 MH(CT)(S)A 2003, s 13(6).
53 MH(CT)(S)A 2003, s 17.
54 For example in 2023, the themed visits focussed on out of NHS care placements and compulsory treatment for mental illness in the community.
55 Statistics are taken from the *Mental Welfare Commission Report 2023–24*. See the 'Publications' section of the Mental Welfare Commission for Scotland website (www.mwcscot.org.uk).
56 MH(CT)(S)A 2003, s 13(5)(b).

person's mental disorder poses a risk to others. This is the responsibility of the local authority, through its mental health officers.

Where the local authority has an overlapping role, the Commission may ask the local authority to take the lead and advise the Commission of the results of any investigation. Depending on the outcome, the Commission may then decide to carry out its own investigation.

Where there is a complaint about a welfare attorney, welfare guardian or a person with welfare powers under an intervention order and the Commission is not satisfied with the local authority's investigation, or there has been no investigation, the Commission can receive and investigate the complaint.[57] It should also consult with the Public Guardian and any relevant local authority which has a common interest in the case.[58]

The duties of the Commission overlap with those of the Care Inspectorate and the Public Guardian. These organisations have memorandums of understanding explaining how they deal with overlapping functions. For example, while the Commission has a duty to investigate where property is at risk it will usually leave such matters to the Public Guardian.

Where there is any doubt about which organisation is primarily considered responsible for investigating, it is sensible to report concerns to all the bodies with a statutory duty. It is for them to consider how best to fulfil their role and whether to rely initially on another organisation carrying out an investigation. The Scottish Government has recognised that there is a need for a clearer investigative structure and, at the time of writing, is consulting on how this might be achieved.[59]

CARE PROVIDERS

4.29 While local authorities and health boards provide some welfare and support services, these are often delivered by voluntary, charitable and private agencies. These include support services, employment projects, day care services, advice agencies, and independent advocacy organisations.

All care providers must have appropriate adult protection policies and are often contractually bound to report any matters of concern to the local authority. An employee of an independent organisation could also report any concerns to the Care Inspectorate, Public Guardian or Mental Welfare

57 AWI(S)A 2000, s 9(1)(d).

58 AWI(S)A 2000, s 9(1)(c).

59 The Adults with Incapacity Amendment Act Consultation (July 2024) (www.gov.scot), p 15.

Commission. When a local authority carries out inquiries into possible risk to an adult, an independent agency may be legally required to hand over some, or all, of its records for examination. More information about this is found in Chapter 13.

PROFESSIONAL REGULATORS

4.30 Most health and social care professionals are regulated by a professional body. In relation to medical staff the General Medical Council regulates doctors, the Nursing and Midwifery Council regulates nurses and the Health Professions Council regulates allied professionals, including occupational therapists, psychologists and speech and language therapists. More information is available from the individual websites.[60]

4.31 The Scottish Social Services Council (SSSC) is responsible for the registration of social care workers, including social workers and care and support staff. Social care workers cannot be employed unless they are registered.[61] From 3 June 2024, anyone starting a role that requires registration has three months to apply. In order to maintain registration, all individuals need to complete an annual online declaration. The SSSC produces detailed standards and codes of practice as well as publishing the outcome of any investigations. More information is available from the SSSC website.[62]

4.32 All professional regulators have different powers to investigate issues around fitness to practice. These powers may include removing a person unfit to carry out their duties or imposing restrictions on their ability to practise. Anyone concerned about a care professional can make a complaint directly to the regulator.

INDIVIDUALS SUPPORTING AN ADULT

4.33 A family member, carer, friend or other individual may have concerns that an adult is at risk, either from a third person(s), or from self-harm or neglect. For example, they may see a deterioration in the physical appearance or mental health of a neighbour.

[60] www.gmc-uk.org, www.nmc.org.uk, www.hcpc-uk.org

[61] The Registration of Social Workers and Social Service Workers in Care Services (Scotland) Regulations 2013 (SSI 2013/227).

[62] www.sssc.uk.com

It may be possible to contact the person's general practitioner or other relevant health professional. Anyone concerned about an adult can also contact the local authority social work department, which has overall responsibility for making the appropriate inquiries. If a crime may have been committed, anyone with information or concerns should contact the police.

Involvement of family and carers is a key principle of all adult protection legislation.[63] The Adults with Incapacity (Scotland) Act 2000, the Adult Support and Protection (Scotland) Act 2007 and the Mental Health (Care and Treatment) (Scotland) Act 2003 all require those intervening to take account of the views of relevant parties.[64] The Mental Health (Care and Treatment) (Scotland) Act 2003 also requires consideration of the needs and circumstances of carers and of the importance of providing information to carers.

Unfortunately, the legislation does not contain a single definition of carers. The Adults with Incapacity (Scotland) Act 2000 requires the involvement of the 'primary carer'. This is the person, paid or unpaid, who is primarily involved in caring for the adult. In some cases, this might be the manager of the care home in which the adult resides.[65]

The Mental Health (Care and Treatment) (Scotland) Act 2003 excludes paid carers and volunteers employed by voluntary organisations from its definition of carers, and the Adult Support and Protection (Scotland) Act 2007 also uses this definition.[66] A paid carer or volunteer will not be considered the primary carer under these Acts, even if they provide most of the care for the adult.

However, arrangements made under these Acts could still be discussed, where appropriate, with paid carers or volunteers. Where care packages are being devised for people at risk, local authorities will have to establish what help is available to the adult from all sources, and all carers' input will remain valuable.

Attorneys, guardians and people authorised under intervention orders

4.34 Under the Adults with Incapacity (Scotland) Act 2000, an individual may sign a power of attorney appointing someone to manage

[63] See Chapter 5 for information about the general principles.
[64] AWI(S)A 2000, s 1(4), ASP(S)A 2007, s 2, MH(CT)(S)A 2003, s 1(3), (5).
[65] AWI(S)A 2000, ss 1(4), 87(1).
[66] ASP(S)A 2007, s 53.

matters should they be unable to act on their own behalf in the future. The person appointed is called an attorney. The power of attorney may give the attorney power to manage money and property, and/or to have a role in welfare decisions, such as medical matters or where the person should live. More details about powers of attorney are in Chapter 10.

Similarly, if someone becomes unable to take decisions and there is a need to protect their interests, the sheriff court may appoint a guardian to take financial or welfare decisions or both. If a one-off decision is required, for example, to end a tenancy or sell a car, the court may make an intervention order to authorise the transaction. For more details on guardianship and intervention orders, see Chapter 12.

Any attorney, guardian or person with a relevant intervention order should be involved in adult protection procedures as appropriate.

Named person

4.35 The Mental Health (Care and Treatment) (Scotland) Act 2003 provides anyone over the age of 16 can nominate a named person who will have the right to be informed and consulted about the care of the person making the nomination.[67] This is done in accordance with a set procedure. Those responsible for the person's care and treatment must take account of the views of the named person, unless it is unreasonable or not practical to do so. The role of the named person is to represent and safeguard the adult's interests. The other rights of a named person include:

- to be consulted when certain things happen, including where a short-term detention or an application for a compulsory treatment order is being considered;[68]
- to be notified of changes to the adult's circumstances, including where a short-term detention is revoked;[69]
- to receive copies of certain records or information which are given to the adult, including details regarding decisions or treatment conflicting with an advance statement;[70]

67 MH(CT)(S) A 2003, s 250 (as amended).
68 MH(CT)(S)A 2003, ss 46 and 60.
69 MH(CT)(S)A 2003, s 82.
70 MH(CT)(S)A 2003, s 276(8).

- to make applications or appeals to the Tribunal, and to be heard and give or lead evidence at a hearing.

Under the original legislation, where there was no nomination, the primary carer was automatically the named person. Where there was no primary carer the nearest relative would act. However, this was changed by the Mental Health (Scotland) Act 2015 and there is now no default position, meaning where there is no nomination there will be no named person.[71]

The named person and the adult can act independently of each other. This means that situations can, and do, arise where they disagree about what should happen. If the adult feels it is necessary, they can revoke the appointment and either not have a named person at all or appoint another named person. The role of the named person is distinct and different from the role of an independent advocate.

The Mental Welfare Commission has produced guidance on the role of a named person.[72]

Independent advocacy

4.36 Independent advocacy is a way of helping people express their own wishes and needs and make their own decisions. Advocacy workers can help people speak up for themselves or can speak on behalf of them if necessary. They can also help with communication, although in some cases technical or other aids to communication may also be necessary. For more information about advocacy and legal rights, see Chapter 10.

CRIMINAL JUSTICE SYSTEM

4.37 Where an adult at risk may be experiencing harm that could constitute a criminal offence it is essential to consider the need to report concerns to the police. The police can be informed whether or not the adult consents, although in practice, it can be difficult to investigate without the alleged victim's cooperation. However, according to guidance issued by the Crown Office and Procurator Fiscal Service 'where there is sufficient evidence and the crime was perpetrated because of the perceived or

[71] Mental Health (Scotland) Act 2015, s 22 repeals MH(CT)(S)A 2003, ss 251 and 253.

[72] 'Mental Health Law in Scotland: A Guide to Named Persons' (www.mwcscot.org.uk).

actual vulnerability based on their age or perceived age, there is a strong presumption in favour of prosecution'.[73] Common crimes include physical or sexual assaults, harassment, fraud and theft. It is sensible to report any suspicions to the police even if you are not sure whether a particular act constitutes a criminal offence.

The police

4.38 Responsibility for investigating crime in Scotland rests with the police and so they may be involved in inquiries into possible risk to an adult. They might be the first people with whom a vulnerable person comes into contact, where there are reports of a disturbance at a person's home or where someone is found in a disorientated state. The police might also need to be involved where there is considered a risk to investigating staff. For example, a council officer might need to be accompanied when carrying out inquiries.

4.39 There are various offences under the Mental Health (Care and Treatment) (Scotland) Act 2003, including helping a person abscond, making false statements and obstruction.[74] Adult protection legislation also contains specific offences, including refusing to hand over records to an authorised council officer or obstructing anyone acting under an adult protection order or warrant without reasonable excuse.[75]

The police are key members of the local adult protection committee and are, like the other relevant bodies, under a legal duty to cooperate in relevant inquiries.[76]

If an adult protection issue comes to the police, for example from a member of the public, they must report this to the relevant local authority.[77] In many areas, the majority of referrals under the Act have been made by the police, and local protocols for managing investigations will apply.

Crown Office Procurator Fiscal Service

4.40 The Crown Office and Procurator Fiscal Service is responsible for the prosecution of crime in Scotland. It also investigates any sudden or

[73] COPFS 'Older Persons Policy' (June 2023), published on www.copfs.gov.uk

[74] MH(CT)(S)A 2003, ss 316–318.

[75] ASP(S)A 2007, s 49.

[76] ASP(S)A 2007, s 5.

[77] ASP(S)A 2007, s 5(3).

suspicious deaths (with a view to a possible fatal accident inquiry) and complaints against the police. The head of the service is the Lord Advocate, the principal law officer in Scotland.

Where a crime may have been committed, the police carry out an initial investigation and then submit a report to the local prosecutor, who is known as the procurator fiscal.

Procurators fiscal deal with all investigations into crimes and carry out all prosecutions in the sheriff and district courts. The procurator fiscal decides if a prosecution would be in the public interest and whether or not there is sufficient evidence to prosecute. The Crown Office Prosecution Code explains the type of considerations prosecutors take into account, including the seriousness of the crime, its effect on the victim, any mitigating circumstances and the effect of any possible prosecution on the alleged victim.[78] The police and procurator fiscal will work closely in any future inquiries and the procurator fiscal may give the police instructions on how to conduct an inquiry.

4.41 In cases that could lead to a jury trial, a procurator fiscal interviews witnesses and reviews the evidence. They then report to the Crown Office, where an Advocate Depute (sometimes referred to as Crown Counsel), will review the case. Advocate Deputes are senior lawyers employed in the Crown Office. They generally conduct prosecutions in the High Court and make the decision whether to prosecute sheriff and jury cases (although sheriff court cases are conducted by depute procurators fiscal).

Even where the decision is taken not to prosecute there are alternatives to prosecution, such as a fine, a warning or diversion from prosecution into a support or treatment programme.

Victims often find it difficult to accept that the prosecution service will not divulge the reasons for its decision not to prosecute, but there could be good reasons for this, such as protecting confidential information or preserving evidence for a future prosecution. A victim has the right to ask for reasons and a review of a decision not to prosecute. The request for a review should be made as soon as possible and ideally no later than one month after the decision.[79]

The Crown Office and local prosecution services attend local adult protection committee meetings where appropriate to discuss criminal justice matters.

78 This Code is available from www.copfs.gov.uk. See 'Prosecution Code' on the COPFS website.

79 See 'Victims' Right to Review' on the COPFS website.

CONCLUSION

4.42 The local authority and adult protection committees have the primary role under adult support and protection legislation. However, many other individuals and organisations have an important role, particularly since support and care is now normally arranged using private providers. The cooperation of all those involved is vital for adult protection legislation to work appropriately and effectively.

Chapter 5

PRINCIPLES IN ADULT PROTECTION LAW

5.1 The Adult Support and Protection (Scotland) Act 2007, in common with other key legislation in this field, contains a set of principles which are set out in the initial sections. These principles have a crucial impact on how the law should work in practice. This chapter looks at the principles and examines their legal and practical effect.

The inclusion of principles in Scottish legislation is a relatively new development. The principles place a legal duty on practitioners to consider decisions from a variety of perspectives. This is vital where a law deals with complex ethical issues affecting the rights of the individual.

BACKGROUND TO PRINCIPLES

5.2 Both the Adults with Incapacity (Scotland) Act 2000 and the Mental Health (Care and Treatment) (Scotland) Act 2003 are considered to be values-based laws. Those proposing reform had a clear view of the principles they felt should underlie the legislation.[1] The principles set out the ethical basis for the powers granted under the legislation and the values underpinning it. These principles clearly influenced the development of the Adult Support and Protection (Scotland) Act 2007.

Principles can also influence the content of legislation. For example, the importance of respect for the wishes of the patient gave rise to the right to access independent advocacy in the Mental Health (Care and Treatment) (Scotland) Act 2003.

The principles are not simply statements of good practice and have an ongoing day-to-day importance for the way people exercise statutory powers. Everyone acting under the legislation should have regard to the principles in relation to any decision. For example, a court should not

1 *Report on Incapable Adults* (Scottish Law Commission, 1995), paras 2.47–2.73. *New Directions: Report on the Review of the Mental Health (Scotland) Act 1984* (2001), Ch 3.

grant guardianship under the Adults with Incapacity (Scotland) Act 2000 unless it is satisfied that this is the least restrictive option necessary to protect the adult's interests. A doctor deciding about the use of compulsory medication under the Mental Health (Care and Treatment) (Scotland) Act 2003 must have proper regard to the patient's wishes.

The principles inform practical decision making and give those operating the relevant legislation guidance on how it should work. The principles cannot be applied mechanically, and it is not unusual for principles to conflict. For example, in mental health cases, a person may not want medical treatment, but there may be clear evidence this would benefit them.[2] Those intervening will have to balance the different principles. This often involves very difficult questions of judgement.

PRINCIPLES AND PRACTICE

Balancing benefit and risk in individual cases can be extremely difficult. A common example is where someone appears to be at risk but is adamant they do not need help. In such circumstances, the impact of intervening against their will could reduce any benefit to them.

Perhaps the person may be prepared to accept a less restrictive alternative, and this may reduce some risks, but not all. However, the benefit to them of not having arrangements imposed, may outweigh these risks.

PRINCIPLES IN ADULTS WITH INCAPACITY (SCOTLAND) ACT 2000

5.3 The Adults with Incapacity (Scotland) Act 2000 contains a clear statement of principles. These principles apply to any intervention in the life of an adult who is unable to take one or more decisions about financial, health or welfare matters. Anyone taking action under the Act has a legal duty to implement the principles.[3]

2 See *RM & SB (as joint guardians of the adult PKM) v Greater Glasgow Health Board* [2021] SAC (Civ) 33 for further discussion (www.scotcourts.gov.uk/media/mkapbs0q/sheriff-appeal-court-judgement-rm-and-sb-as-joint-guardians-of-the-adult-pkm-against-greater-glasgow-health-board-09-november-2021.pdf).

3 Adults with Incapacity (Scotland) Act 2000 (AWI(S)A 2000), s 1(1).

This applies both to interventions and to decisions not to intervene.[4] This means a Sheriff may decide not to grant an order if they conclude that the benefit to an adult would not be sufficient to justify overruling the adult's wishes.

There are five key principles:

- **Benefit:** There should be no intervention under the Act unless the person intervening or authorising the intervention is satisfied that this will benefit the adult, and that this is the only reasonable way of achieving the benefit. For example, where someone could remain at home with extra help, it may not be reasonable to move the person to residential care against their will.

  The use of the term 'benefit' was deliberate. The Scottish Law Commission recommended that the principle be expressed as 'benefit' rather than 'best interests', which it regarded as too paternalistic in questions of adult welfare. The Commission did not think 'best interests' gave enough emphasis to the wishes and feelings of the adult.[5]

PRINCIPLES AND PRACTICE

The concept of benefit has been fairly widely interpreted. In the case of *T, Applicant*,[6] an Intervention Order was granted to correct an unforeseen and unfair consequence of the wording of an adult's will. In his decision, the Sheriff recognised that the concept of benefit went beyond financial gain '...the nature of the "benefit" here, for the adult, is to allow the regulation of her affairs in accordance with her previously stated wishes'.

- **Least restrictive option:** Any intervention should be the least restrictive option in relation to the freedom of the adult necessary to achieve the purpose.[7]

4 See Adrian Ward, *Adult Incapacity* (W Green, 2003), para 4.3.

5 *Report on Incapable Adults*, para 2.50.

6 2005 SLT (Sh Ct) 97

7 AWI(S)A 2000, s 1(3).

PRINCIPLES AND PRACTICE

In the English case of *Essex CC v RF & Ors*[8] the local authority was criticised for a decision to move a man, aged 91, into a care home. The judge commented that there was 'no evidence that consideration was given to the less restrictive option of supporting him at home in accordance with his wish to remain there'.

- **Ascertaining views of adult:** Anyone deciding whether to intervene, and if so, how, should consider the present and past wishes and feelings of the adult.[9]

  All reasonable means should be used to find out the adult's views and feelings, past and present. This may involve using communication or interpretation facilities, including advocacy. Inquiries should be made to establish whether the adult has expressed a view on the matter or has made an advance statement or living will.

  The duty to show respect for the adult's present wishes and feelings applies even when an adult is unable to take a decision. This is an important safeguard against a person being bound by past statements that may no longer reflect their position.[10] If the use of communication facilities reveals that the person can take the relevant decision, then the Adults with Incapacity (Scotland) Act 2000 cannot be used.

PRINCIPLES AND PRACTICE

Even people with significantly impaired capacity can communicate what they want, feel or think, by behaviour, facial expression, or gestures. Their preferences should be taken into account even if they are unable to make a decision.

In some cases, for example, it might be clear from behaviour and mood that someone is more content in one location than another. It might be appropriate to take this as an expression of the adult's wishes and factor this into a decision made about where they should live.

8 *Essex CC v RF* [2015] EWCOP 1.

9 AWI(S)A 2000, s 1(4).

10 Adrian Ward, *Adults with Incapacity Legislation* (W. Green, 2008).

- **Respect for views of significant others:** The views of the adult's nearest relative,[11] named person and primary carer[12] must be taken into account, if this is reasonable and practicable. In addition, the views of any guardian or attorney with relevant powers and of any other person with an interest in the adult's welfare or the proposed intervention should be sought and considered.[13]

  The requirement to have respect for the views of significant others does not necessarily mean that these people should receive confidential information where the adult does not want this to happen. The courts in England have said that it may not be 'practicable' to consider another's views where the adult has said they do not want them involved.[14] Similar arguments could be advanced in such cases in Scotland.

- **Encouraging use and development of skills:** A guardian, attorney, or person managing a resident's funds must encourage the adult to exercise whatever skills they have in connection with property, financial or personal welfare matters and to develop new skills, so far as reasonable and practicable.[15]

The current principles have parity, so no principle is seen as more important than the others. At the time of writing, the Scottish Government is consulting on changes to the wording and hierarchy of the principles.[16] This is in response to concerns that the current principles do not do enough to make sure the rights of those subject to the Act are upheld.[17] The consultation suggests a new rebuttable principle that effect is given to the adult's reasonably ascertainable will and preferences. This would have priority over the other principles.

[11] As defined in the Mental Health (Care and Treatment) (Scotland) Act 2003 (MH(CT)(S)A 2003).

[12] That is, the person or organisation primarily caring for the adult. This could include a paid carer. AWI(S)A 2000, s 87(1).

[13] AWI(S)A 2000, s 1(4).

[14] *R (E) v Bristol City Council* [2005] EWHC 74 (Admin).

[15] AWI(S)A 2000, s 1(5).

[16] The Adults with Incapacity Amendment Act Consultation (July 2024) (www.gov.scot), p 13.

[17] See the Scottish Mental Health Law Review and Scottish Government Response for further discussion: *Scottish mental health law review: our response* (www.gov.scot).

MENTAL HEALTH (CARE AND TREATMENT) (SCOTLAND) ACT 2003 PRINCIPLES

5.4 The principles contained in the Mental Health (Care and Treatment) (Scotland) Act 2003 apply to everyone exercising functions under the Act[18] (other than the patient and those representing the patient[19]) and require them to have regard to the following:

- **Participation**: The need to take account of the patient's wishes and feelings, past and present.[20] Those involved must take appropriate means to establish the patient's views.[21] People should consider how to enable the patient to participate as fully as possible in decisions, and should bear in mind the need to give the patient information and support.[22]
- **Respect for views of significant others**: The importance of considering the views of the named person, any carer and any welfare guardian or attorney, provided it is reasonable and practicable to do so.[23]
- **Respect for carers**: The Mental Health (Care and Treatment) (Scotland) Act 2003 is the only adult protection law to include, as far as reasonable and practicable, considering the needs of any carer and the importance of giving a carer the information needed to help care for the person.[24] (This principle could conflict with the principle of respect for the patient's wishes where a patient does not wish a carer to receive information. On the other hand, a carer may need certain information to be able to care.)
- **Least restrictive alternative**: Duties under the Act should be carried out in the least restrictive manner necessary in the circumstances, bearing in mind the other principles, the needs of any carer, the duty of reciprocity (below) and any other considerations.[25]

[18] MH(CT)(S)A 2003, ss 1–3.

[19] That is the patient's named person or primary carer, any independent advocate or lawyer representing the patient, a curator *ad litem*, guardian or welfare attorney of the patient. MH(CT)(S)A 2003, s 1(7).

[20] MH(CT)(S)A 2003, s 1(3)(a).

[21] MH(CT)(S)A 2003, s 1(8).

[22] MH(CT)(S)A 2003, s 1(3), (10).

[23] MH(CT)(S)A 2003, s 1(3)(b).

[24] MH(CT)(S)A 2003, s 1(5).

[25] MH(CT)(S)A 2003, s 1(4).

- **Benefit**: The importance of providing the maximum benefit to the patient.[26]
- **Child welfare**: If the patient is a child or young person under 18, the need to intervene in the way that will best secure their welfare.[27]
- **Non-discrimination and respect for diversity**: The need to ensure the patient's treatment is no worse than what someone who is not a patient would receive in a similar situation, unless this is justified in the circumstances.[28] (This somewhat obscurely worded principle stems from the Millan Committee principle of equality, which said that powers under the Act should be exercised without any direct or indirect discrimination on grounds of age, sex, race, disability etc.[29])

  The person's abilities, background and characteristics, including their age, sex, sexual orientation, religious persuasion and cultural and ethnic background should be taken into account.[30]

  Effectively, this means not discriminating, treating people fairly and making positive attempts to meet people's individual needs.
- **Reciprocity**: The importance of providing appropriate services to a person subject to compulsory measures, including providing continuing care when the person is no longer subject to such measures.[31]

ADULT SUPPORT AND PROTECTION (SCOTLAND) ACT 2007

5.5 The Adult Support and Protection (Scotland) Act 2007 principles adapt the principles of the Adults with Incapacity (Scotland) Act 2000 and the Mental Health (Care and Treatment) (Scotland) Act 2003, taking elements of both.

There is one overarching 'general principle'. This states that a person should intervene, or authorise an intervention under the Act, only if they are satisfied that the intervention will provide a benefit to the adult not

26 MH(CT)(S)A 2003, s 1(3)(f).
27 MH(CT)(S)A 2003, s 2(4).
28 MH(CT)(S)A 2003, s 1(3)(g).
29 *New Directions* (above), recommendation 3.3(3).
30 MH(CT)(S)A 2003, s 1(3)(h).
31 MH(CT)(S)A 2003, s 1(6).

reasonably obtainable without the intervention *and* that the proposed intervention is the least restrictive option available.[32]

Any public body or office holder authorising any intervention or performing a function under the Act must have regard to this general principle (insofar as it is relevant)[33] and to the following:

- **The adult's wishes and feelings (past and present), insofar as these are ascertainable:** There is no explicit duty to make all reasonable efforts to ascertain the adult's views (although this is clearly good practice) but there is a duty to consider the importance of providing independent advocacy services.[34] People with a mental disorder have an entitlement to advocacy services under the Mental Health (Care and Treatment) (Scotland) Act 2003.[35]

- **The views of relevant other parties insofar as these are known:** The list includes the adult's nearest relative or primary carer,[36] any guardian or attorney and any other person with an interest in the adult's well-being or property known to the person carrying out the function. This could include a named person appointed under the Mental Health (Care and Treatment) (Scotland) Act 2003 or any other person who has been involved in helping the adult.

- **Participation:** The importance of the adult participating as fully as possible in any decisions and of giving them such information and support as is necessary to facilitate this.

- **Non-discrimination:** The importance of ensuring that the adult is not, without justification, treated less favourably than the way in which any other adult who is not at risk might be treated in a similar situation.

- **Respect for diversity:** The adult's abilities, background and characteristics must be respected. This includes age, sex, sexual orientation, religious persuasion, racial origin, ethnic group and cultural and linguistic heritage.[37]

  The code of practice confirms that the principles only apply to a public body or office holder authorising any intervention or carrying

[32] Adult Support and Protection Act 2007 (ASP(S)A 2007), s 1.
[33] ASP(S)A 2007, s 2.
[34] ASP(S)A 2007, s 6.
[35] MH(CT)(S)A 2003, s 259.
[36] As defined in the MH(CT)(S)A 2003.
[37] ASP(S)A 2007, s 2(f).

out a function in terms of the Act. This means that other relevant parties, including the adult, primary carer, independent advocate, a guardian or an attorney, are not bound by the principles, although a guardian or attorney will be bound by the principles of the Adults with Incapacity (Scotland) Act 2000.[38]

SOCIAL CARE (SELF-DIRECTED SUPPORT) (SCOTLAND) ACT 2013

5.6 The Social Care (Self-directed Support) (Scotland) Act 2013 sets out some general principles. These are worded differently from those contained in previous legislation and focus on making sure that individuals who receive services are involved in making decisions. The general principles are:[39]

- **Involvement:** The person must have as much involvement as they wish in relation to the assessment of their need for services and the provision of those services.
- **Assistance:** The person must be provided with any assistance reasonably required to enable them to express views about the options for self-directed support.
- **Collaboration:** The local authority must collaborate with a person in relation to the assessment of their needs for support or services and the provision of those services.

5.7 Further general principles state that in carrying out its functions the local authority must take reasonable steps to facilitate the following general principles:

- that the right to dignity of the person is to be respected; and
- that the person's right to participate in the life of the community in which the person lives is to be respected.[40]

[38] *Adult Support and Protection (Scotland) Act 2007 Code of Practice*, p 12.
[39] Social Care (Self-directed Support) (Scotland) 2013 (SC(SDS)A 2013), s 1.
[40] SC(SDS)A 2013, s 2.

Table 5.1 – The principles compared

Principle	ASP Act	MH(CT) Act	AWI Act
Benefit	✓	✓	✓
Least restrictive option	✓	✓	✓
Find out and consider the adult's views	✓	✓	✓
Consider the views of significant others	✓	✓	✓
Encourage use and development of skills			✓
Involving carers		✓	
Child welfare		✓	
Non discrimination	✓	✓	
Reciprocity		✓	
Respect for diversity	✓	✓	
Support adult to participate in decisions	✓	✓	

HUMAN RIGHTS CONCEPTS

5.8 Chapter 14 looks at how human rights law deals with adult protection issues. Human rights law includes important concepts that supplement the principles in the Scottish legislation and can usefully aid decision making.

The human rights approach starts by setting out specific rights: to liberty, respect for family life etc. Any interference with those rights must be *lawful*. It must also be *necessary*. There must be no less restrictive alternative, and the risks must be such that the intervention is appropriate.[41]

[41] See, for example, *Litwa v Poland* (26629/95) (2001) 33 EHRR 53, (2002) 63 BMLR 199, [2000] MHLR 226, para 78, ECHR 2000-III.

Similarly, any intervention must be *proportionate*, that is, it must be appropriate for the risk posed.[42] Decision takers must weigh up the relevant risks and benefits to the person at risk and others, and their response should be a balanced response to these risks and benefits.

LEGAL IMPACT OF PRINCIPLES

5.9 The principles in the Adults with Incapacity (Scotland) Act 2000 are clearly stated and impose binding legal obligations. These principles direct the way in which bodies must carry out their duties under the law. For example, a Sheriff cannot grant an order unless they are satisfied that it will benefit the adult and is the least restrictive option.[43]

Some people have argued that the Mental Health (Care and Treatment) (Scotland) Act 2003 principles are less clearly stated. Those involved must only 'have regard' to the principles. However, the courts will require evidence that those intervening have considered the principles.[44] It also appears that, in practice, the mental health tribunal gives serious consideration to the principles when it reaches decisions.

Anyone concerned that those intervening have not given due consideration to the principles could challenge this by means of judicial review.

The Adult Support and Protection (Scotland) Act 2007 principles are like the Adults with Incapacity (Scotland) Act 2000 principles in that they are clearly stated, but, like Mental Health (Care and Treatment) (Scotland) Act 2003 principles, the duty is only to 'have regard' to the principles.

The nature of the principles in each of the Acts reflects the complex issues raised in individual cases. We have seen that the principles may need to be balanced one against another, and the law recognises this.

Adults with Incapacity (Scotland) Act 2000 indemnity

5.10 The Adults with Incapacity (Scotland) Act 2000 specifically protects people acting in accordance with its principles. Where someone acting under the Act can show that their actions were reasonable, in good faith and in accordance with the principles, they will not be liable for any

42 See *Winterwerp v Netherlands* (A/33) (1979-80) 2 EHRR 387.

43 As, for example, in *DM, Re an application* [2006] ScotSC 38. This is available on www.scotcourts.gov.uk

44 See Judgment of Sheriff Principal James A Taylor in *Di Mascio v Mental Health Tribunal for Scotland* 2008 GWD 37-559.

breach of duty of care.[45] A person who has not acted in accordance with the principles does not have the benefit of this limitation of liability. This protection is unique to that Act.

Promoting the principles

5.11 The Mental Health (Care and Treatment) (Scotland) Act 2003 gives the Mental Welfare Commission a legal duty to promote the principles of that Act, as part of its general duty to promote best practice in relation to the Act.[46]

CONCLUSION

5.12 The principles contained in adult protection legislation are often said to represent good practice. While this is the case, they are also about much more than good practice or including people in decisions. Anyone making a decision under adult protection legislation should be able to evidence how they considered and applied the principles. Otherwise, that decision may be open to challenge. Human rights law principles add an extra dimension.

Balancing the different principles and applying them to individual circumstances is a question of judgement. The principles require different emphasis in different situations. For example, the risks to an adult may be so serious that it is appropriate to overrule their wishes. Similarly, there may be situations where taking account of the views of a carer or relative may cause an adult grave distress.

The principles should help professionals making difficult decisions involving balancing human rights and risk, by providing a framework for decision taking. Adrian Ward has said, in connection with the Adults with Incapacity (Scotland) Act 2000, that 'reference to the principles will usually assist – often decisively – in resolving points of difficulty in the application of the Act's provisions to particular circumstances, or of interpretation'.[47]

[45] AWI(S)A 2000, s 82(1).
[46] MH(CT)(S)A 2003, s 5.
[47] Ward, *Adult Incapacity*, para 4.2.

Chapter 6

HARM AND ABUSE

6.1 This chapter looks at the legal definition of harm and its relevance to the Mental Health (Care and Treatment) (Scotland) Act 2003, the Adults with Incapacity (Scotland) Act 2000 and the Adult Support and Protection (Scotland) Act 2007. It also provides an introduction to the common types of harm and abuse encountered in adult protection cases. Financial abuse is considered in more detail in Chapter 7.

Abuse and harm can take place in a variety of settings and concerns may become apparent in a number of ways. It is vital that the response is effective and proportionate. The need to protect an individual must always be balanced with their right to make their own decisions about their life – even when others might think those choices are not in their best interests. The most appropriate approach in individual cases will need careful consideration and adequate support must be provided.[1]

LEGAL DEFINITIONS OF HARM AND ABUSE

6.2 The three principal adult protection statutes apply to adults with different types of support needs, but are all fundamentally focussed on preventing harm. The words used to express this in each Act differ and, in some cases, differing thresholds of severity of harm are imposed before certain action may be taken. These differences will be examined in order, from the most narrowly focussed legislation (the Mental Health (Care and Treatment) (Scotland) Act 2003) to the Act with the widest application (the Adult Support and Protection (Scotland) Act 2007).

It is worth noting that most forms of harm and abuse inflicted by one person on another will also constitute crimes of some description. Reference is made to particular crimes throughout this chapter. Financial crimes are discussed in Chapter 7.

[1] Supporting the adult is covered in Chapter 10.

Mental Health (Care and Treatment) (Scotland) Act 2003

6.3 The Mental Health (Care and Treatment) (Scotland) Act 2003 imposes a duty on local authorities to investigate situations where an adult subject to a mental disorder:

- may be, or may have been, subject, or exposed, at some place other than a hospital to ill-treatment, neglect or some other deficiency in care or treatment;
- may be suffering, or may have suffered, loss or damage to property, or be at risk of such loss or damage;
- may be living alone or without care and unable to look after themselves or their property or financial affairs; or,
- is not in hospital and, because of the mental disorder, the safety of some other person may be at risk.[2]

The decision as to whether or not any of these conditions is in place will rest on the local authority employee who encounters the situation. In addition, where the Mental Welfare Commission suspects that these circumstances apply, it may carry out its own investigation.[3]

The word 'harm' is therefore not used explicitly in this Act. Nonetheless, terms such as 'ill-treatment', 'neglect', 'deficiency in care or treatment', 'unable to look after' and 'safety' are not specifically defined, and in such circumstances, the words should be given their ordinary and natural meaning, as it appears from the words themselves and their context. In effect, then, the first three criteria above are describing situations where an adult with a mental disorder is at risk of harm, as 'risk of harm' would be interpreted in the Adult Support and Protection (Scotland) Act 2007. The difference in focus between the two Acts is in which adults they protect from that harm: those with a mental disorder in the case of the Mental Health (Care and Treatment) (Scotland) Act 2003, and those 'at risk' in that of the Adult Support and Protection (Scotland) Act 2007.

The final criterion focusses on the risk of harm to another person (in other words, the 'victim' of the harm could be anyone). Perhaps for that reason, it would appear that the types of harm envisaged are more limited, by the use only of the word 'safety'. It is suggested that this would not include financial harm or harm to property alone, but would be limited to

2 Mental Health (Care and Treatment) (Scotland) Act 2003 (MH(CT)(S)A 2003), s 33. For further details on the duty to investigate, see Chapter 8.

3 MH(CT)(S)A 2003, s 11.

harm to physical or emotional well-being, arising directly, or, perhaps, as a direct consequence of financial or property harm.

6.4 A higher threshold is imposed where compulsory measures are sought. These may only be used where there is a significant risk to an individual's health, welfare or safety or to the safety of others.[4] The observations above on the interpretation of 'safety' are equally relevant here. It is also notable that the term 'harm' is again not used; but it is clear that the significant risk referred to is a significant risk of harm to the attributes identified.

The decision as to what is a 'significant risk' is a matter for the clinical judgement of doctors and other health professionals. Where longer-term detention is being considered the mental health tribunal will need to be satisfied the risk is significant before granting a compulsory treatment order. The tribunal can also look at the issue of risk when it hears appeals.

However, there is no specific definition of 'significant risk' in the Mental Health (Care and Treatment) (Scotland) Act 2003, or in the various codes of practice published by the Scottish Government to accompany it. As has already been noted, in these circumstances, the words should be given their ordinary and natural meaning, as it appears from the words themselves and their context. It has been observed by the Inner House of the Court of Session, applying that test, that the word 'significant':

> 'is a word which has shades of meaning, depending on the context. Reference to the Oxford English Dictionary shows that at one end of the scale it can mean no more than "not insignificant" ... and at the other "important" or "notable". It can at least be said with some confidence that, by including this word, the Scottish Parliament intended to add an emphasis to the provision which it would lack if the word were omitted. In our view, this emphasis is best recognised by construing "significant" as importing more than "not insignificant"'.[5]

This observation was made in the context of rather different legislation, but it is suggested that similar considerations apply and that the risk identified must be more than merely 'not insignificant' to qualify as significant.

Against that background, usual practice in risk assessment would indicate that both the likelihood of the harm occurring, and the severity

4 Eg MH(CT)(S)A 2003, s 64(5).

5 *JT* v *Stirling Council* [2007] CSIH 52, 2007 SC 783, p 793, para 23.

of harm should be taken into account in deciding whether a risk is significant. A lower risk of very serious harm may constitute a significant risk: as may a high risk of less serious harm. A negligible risk of harm, or risk of negligible harm, is unlikely ever to constitute a 'significant' risk.

The immediacy of the potential harm is therefore only of relevance in that immediate harm may be foreseen with more assurance (and may therefore represent a higher risk – perhaps approaching certainty). Where enough is known to provide a level of confidence as to how a situation will progress, early intervention may be a better strategy than waiting in hope of an alternative development. For example, an intervention may be possible where a person's illness has recurred and there is evidence that early compulsory intervention will prevent a serious deterioration in their health.

Adults with Incapacity (Scotland) Act 2000

6.5 The Adults with Incapacity (Scotland) Act does not specifically refer to harm but instead refers to situations where an adult's finances, property or welfare seem to be at risk. In such cases, the Public Guardian (in the case of risk to finances or property) or the local authority (in the case of welfare) has a duty to investigate.[6] It will be the responsibility of the member of staff from the organisation receiving the information to assess whether there seems to be a risk and trigger an investigation.

The word 'risk' is unqualified for these purposes and would therefore appear to be intended to be broadly interpreted. All and any risk to the adult's finances, property or welfare thus requires investigation. Again, the word 'harm' is not used explicitly, but it is clear that it is the risk of harm to finances, property or welfare that triggers the relevant duty.

Adult Support and Protection (Scotland) Act 2007

6.6 The Adult Support and Protection (Scotland) Act 2007 provides for the support and protection of 'adults at risk'. An important part of the definition of 'adult at risk', is that the adult is at risk of harm.[7] 'Harm' is defined in the Act as all harmful conduct and, in particular, includes:

- conduct that causes physical harm;

[6] For further information about investigations, see Chapter 8.

[7] Adult Support and Protection (Scotland) Act 2007 (ASP(S)A 2007), s 3. See further para **2.3** on the definition of an 'adult at risk'.

- conduct that causes psychological harm (for example: by causing fear, alarm or distress);
- unlawful conduct that appropriates or adversely affects property, rights or interests (for example: theft, fraud, embezzlement or extortion); and
- conduct that causes self-harm.[8]

An adult is considered 'at risk of harm' where:

- another person's conduct is causing (or is likely to cause) the adult to be harmed; or
- the adult is engaging (or is likely to engage) in conduct that causes (or is likely to cause) self-harm.[9]

A local authority is under an obligation to investigate where it thinks an adult is at risk of harm. Other public bodies are under a duty to report the circumstances of adults at risk of harm to the local authority.[10] The initial responsibility to assess whether an adult is at risk of harm is therefore on the member of staff from the local authority or other public body encountering the situation, in the first instance.

It is clear from the definitions of 'harm' and 'risk of harm' that these terms are to be interpreted widely. The definition of 'harm' is rather circular and is clearly not only limited to the specific examples provided, encompassing, 'all harmful conduct'. This suggests that anything that could ordinarily and naturally be described as harmful fits within this term. In defining 'risk of harm' the way it does, the Act arguably extends what may be termed the ordinary meaning of the phrase, since it specifically includes situations where an adult is actually being harmed and not only those where there is the potential for such harm.

It is also worth noting the emphasis in the definition of 'harm' on conduct *causing* harm. This suggests that whether the conduct is *intended* to cause harm is not relevant to the definition. It is the actual effect on the individual adult that is important. Conduct that may not be harmful for the 'average person', may well cause harm to an adult with a specific condition. For example, providing an inappropriate diet for an adult diagnosed with diabetes would constitute harmful behaviour.

8 ASP(S)A 2007, s 53(1).
9 ASP(S)A 2007, s 3(2).
10 For a full list of those bodies required to make such referrals, see Chapter 4. For further information about investigations, see Chapter 8.

The Act also refers to a 'risk of serious harm' as a basic requirement for the granting of a protection order. Where an application for an order is made, it will be for the Sheriff hearing the case to decide whether this higher threshold is met. Further consideration of what 'serious harm' means is dealt with at para **2.22**.

COMMON CATEGORIES OF HARM AND ABUSE

6.7 Given the wide definition of 'harm' used in legislation, no definitive list of all types of harmful conduct can be compiled. The following consideration of common categories of reported harm, and the types of conduct they may encompass, is intended to provide a starting point for practitioners. In almost all situations involving abuse of one person by another, there will also be criminal justice implications.

Physical abuse

6.8 Physical abuse normally involves deliberately inflicting pain or suffering on another individual. This can include behaviour such as punching, slapping, hitting, kicking, shaking, burning, scalding or forcing an individual to take substances that are likely to cause harm. Female genital mutilation would be classified as physical abuse.

It includes providing support or assistance in a way that causes physical injury. For example, where a carer is rough and causes injury when helping an adult in or out or the bath. Inappropriate medication, sedation for the convenience of a carer or administering covert medication without proper authority, can also be classed as physical abuse.

6.9 Any deliberate attack or attempted attack on another person is an assault, whether there is injury resulting or not. Threatening gestures can also amount to an assault. Making serious threats to life or limb or to damage a person's property or reputation is also a crime. Other threats may constitute a breach of the peace (see para **6.11** below).

Psychological abuse

6.10 Abuse can also take the form of threats, taunts, name-calling and otherwise belittling, undermining or bullying an individual. For example, a carer or relative may use derogatory terms to refer to someone and make threats that they will be moved into a hospital ward or care home if they fail to comply or complain. This type of abuse can be hard to identify, due to lack of physical evidence, but is extremely damaging for those experiencing it.

6.11 As well as being an adult protection matter, conduct likely to place someone in a state of fear and alarm might also constitute a breach of the peace under the common law.[11] A breach of the peace can occur even if the victim is not actually alarmed, provided a reasonable person would be. While a breach of the peace was originally a public order offence, it may also now be relevant even where the behaviour takes place in private, provided there is a realistic risk of it being discovered.[12] There is also a statutory offence (often referred to as 'statutory breach of the peace') committed if a person behaves in a threatening or abusive manner, likely to cause a reasonable person to suffer fear or alarm, and the person intends that, or is reckless as to whether that will be the effect.[13]

Sexual abuse

6.12 Generally, sexual abuse is any sexual activity to which an individual has not consented, or cannot consent. It covers a variety of behaviours, including non-consensual touching or penetration, exposure, showing another individual sexually explicit material or publishing sexually explicit material involving a person without consent.

6.13 Sexual abuse is a criminal offence. The Sexual Offences (Scotland) Act 2009 sets out sexual crimes, including rape, sexual assault, sexual coercion, communicating indecently and coercing someone into looking at a sexual image. These offences occur where the person does not give free consent. There are specific provisions stating that a person with a mental disorder cannot consent if they are unable to understand the proposed conduct, make a decision as to whether to engage in it or whether it should take place, or communicate that decision.[14] It is also a specific criminal offence for a care worker to have a sexual relationship with someone with a mental disorder whom they support.[15] This is the case even if the relationship is apparently consensual, as this is considered

11 For discussion of the cases see *Smith v Donnelly* 2002 JC 65, 2001 SLT 1007.
12 *Jones v Carnegie* 2004 JC 136.
13 Criminal Justice and Licensing (Scotland) Act 2010, s 38(1).
14 Sexual Offences (Scotland) Act 2009 (SO(S)A 2009), s 17.
15 SO(S)A 2009, s 46.

an abuse of a position of trust. However, spouses and partners who are also carers are excluded from these provisions. Publication of intimate film or images, with the intention of causing fear, alarm or distress (or being reckless as to that effect), where the film or images were not already in the public domain, is an offence. The offence is also committed where publication is only threatened.[16]

Neglect by a third party

6.14 Neglect describes an ongoing lack of appropriate care and attention. As with all forms of harm, it can be intentional or unintentional and includes a lack of stimulation, safety, nourishment or nutrition, warmth or medical attention. Neglect can happen in any setting in which an adult is dependent on someone else for care and attention, including family homes and formal care settings.

6.15 Where a person neglects an adult to whom they owe a duty of care and the adult suffers injury or death, they may be guilty of a common law crime. Common law crimes include culpably and recklessly causing injury and culpable homicide. In addition, anyone exercising powers under the Adults with Incapacity (Scotland) Act 2000 who ill-treats or wilfully neglects the adult with incapacity commits an offence.[17] This would include guardians, attorneys, those acting under an intervention order or anyone who has been delegated welfare powers. It is also an offence for a provider of care services (paid or unpaid) to ill-treat or wilfully neglect anyone with a mental disorder.[18]

Self harm, neglect or abuse

Self neglect

6.16 Self-neglect happens when an individual does not take appropriate care of their physical and mental health or needs. It can include behaviour such as a failure to wash clothes, maintain personal hygiene, eat properly or keep their home in a reasonable condition. This may be the result of a

[16] Abusive Behaviour and Sexual Harm (Scotland) Act 2016, s 2. This offence is often called 'revenge porn' colloquially; though it is not limited to such situations (*DF v Procurator Fiscal, Dundee* [2023] SAC (Crim) 1, 2023 SCCR 118).

[17] Adults with Incapacity (Scotland) Act 2000, s 83.

[18] MH(CT)(S)A 2003, s 315.

physical difficulty or a mental disorder or illness. In particular, hoarding behaviour may be symptomatic of a diagnosable mental disorder. If so, this may broaden the formal legal avenues open to public authorities in intervening in such cases. Nonetheless, hoarding, as with other forms of self-neglect, continues to raise complicated questions as to the extent to which the individual engaging in the harmful behaviour can be said to be unable, rather than merely unwilling, to act differently.

PRINCIPLES AND PRACTICE

Cases of self-neglect can be challenging, as they involve the need to balance individuals' rights to choose how they live with the protection of those who are unable to cope due to a mental impairment or illness. In every case, consideration about how an individual will respond to any intervention will be necessary before a decision is made on how to proceed. Consideration of duties towards others, such as neighbours affected by the adult's behaviour, must also be taken into account. Local authorities may have duties to take action where property is not maintained to an acceptable standard.[19]

Self-harm or injury

6.17 Self-harm or injury occurs when an individual causes a direct physical injury to themselves. Injury can be inflicted in a number of ways, including cutting, burning, scalding, hair pulling, using blunt objects or interfering with wounds healing. Self-harm or injury is a complex topic and any intervention requires to be carefully managed.

Eating disorders

6.18 Eating disorders are often indicated when an individual's eating patterns or behaviours cause them significant physical or mental harm. Common examples are bulimia and anorexia. Some eating disorders will amount to, or be a symptom of, mental disorder. As with the issues around self-harm, dealing with eating disorders is complicated and the benefits of any action need careful consideration. Direct intervention is a serious step

[19] For example, under environmental health legislation. Contact the local environmental health department for further information.

and must be balanced with the individual's right to make decisions about their body. It might be appropriate to use the legislation in serious or life threatening cases in a similar way to situations of self-harm or neglect.

Alcohol and drug abuse

6.19 Alcohol and drug dependency or abuse is specifically excluded from the definition of 'mental disorder' in the Mental Health (Care and Treatment) (Scotland) Act 2003[20] and that definition is also used in the Adults with Incapacity (Scotland) Act 2000.[21] The Adult Support and Protection (Scotland) Act 2007 uses the term, but does not specifically import the definition from the Mental Health (Care and Treatment) (Scotland) Act 2003.

The *Adult Support and Protection (Scotland) Act 2007 Code of Practice* recognises that drug or alcohol misuse may, in many situations, be the cause, symptom and/or trigger of a mental disorder.[22] Similarly, the use of drugs or alcohol may interfere with the effectiveness of medication prescribed to treat a mental disorder. Substance misuse can be a catalyst for a lack of self-care and may cause physical harm in itself, or equally be a symptom of self-neglect. It is therefore not the case that, simply because drug or alcohol misuse is a factor, or even the primary factor, in a harmful situation, the Acts described above do not apply. In applying the criteria for intervention, careful consideration must be given to the ordinary and natural meaning of the words used, bearing in mind that the only term alcohol and drug dependency or abuse is specifically excluded from is 'mental disorder'.

Domestic abuse and 'coercive control'

6.20 In general terms, domestic abuse normally describes any type of abuse that happens between two people in a relationship (or who have been in a relationship together in the past). It is an extremely complex problem and may particularly include aspects of physical, sexual and psychological abuse, as well as other types of harm mentioned here.

20 MH(CT)(S)A 2003, s 328(2).

21 AWI(S)A 2000, s 87.

22 *Adult Support and Protection (Scotland) Act 2007 Code of Practice* (ASP(S)A 2007 Code of Practice) (July 2022), pp 22–23.

For the purposes of the criminal law, the offence of, 'Abusive behaviour towards partner or ex-partner', is committed where:

- a person engages in a course of behaviour which is abusive of their partner or ex-partner,
- a reasonable person would consider the course of behaviour to be likely to cause the partner or ex-partner to suffer physical or psychological harm (including fear, alarm and distress), and
- either the person intends by the course of behaviour to cause their partner or ex-partner to suffer harm of that type or is reckless as to whether it does so.[23]

Note that all three criteria need to be satisfied for the offence to be established.

Regarding the first of these criteria, 'abusive behaviour' includes:

- behaviour directed at the partner or ex-partner that is violent (including sexual violence), threatening or intimidating; and,
- behaviour directed at the partner or ex-partner, their child (under 18), or at another person, that either has as its purpose (or among its purposes) one or more of the relevant effects or would be considered by a reasonable person to be likely to have one or more of those effects.[24]

The relevant effects are of:

- making the partner or ex-partner dependent on, or subordinate to, the perpetrator;
- isolating the partner or ex-partner from friends, relatives or other sources of support;
- controlling, regulating or monitoring the partner or ex-partner's day-to-day activities;
- depriving the partner or ex-partner of freedom of action (or restricting it);
- frightening, humiliating, degrading or punishing the partner or ex-partner.[25]

[23] Domestic Abuse (Scotland) Act 2018 (DA(S)A 2018), s 1.
[24] DA(S)A 2018, s.2
[25] DA(S)A 2018.

It is not necessary for the partner or ex-partner actually to suffer harm or any of the relevant effects in order for the offence to have been committed.[26] It is a defence for a person accused to show that the course of behaviour was reasonable in the particular circumstances.[27]

When this offence was first created it was linked to the concept of 'coercive control';[28] although it is notable that this phrase is not used (or defined) anywhere in the legislation itself. The Code of Practice offers a definition of coercive control (which it describes as 'illustrative') as: 'A pattern of acts of assault, threats, humiliation and intimidation or other abuse that is used to harm, punish, or frighten their victim'.[29] This tends to suggest a wider ambit than only domestic abuse situations. That impression is reinforced by the use of the terms within the Code of Practice in reference to the distinction between an adult being unwilling and unable to protect their interests, and in financial harm situations.[30] In the former case, it is referred to alongside 'undue pressure', perhaps suggesting the concepts are to be taken to be analogous. That could be somewhat confusing, as the term 'undue pressure' only appears in the 2007 Act in the context of overriding an adult's refusal to consent to a protection order being granted or enforced.[31]

It is suggested that it is not helpful, in the context of assessing whether an adult is at risk of harm, to become overly concerned as to whether a particular behaviour fits a definition of 'coercive control', in the context of either domestic abuse or otherwise. In all cases, it is the effect of the behaviour on the adult, and whether that effect (or potential effect) may be properly considered as 'harmful' in the ordinary sense of the word, that is of importance. If controlling behaviour is being exercised that does fit the more rigorous definition set out in the Domestic Abuse (Scotland) Act 2018, then the police should be informed, as with any suspected criminal offence.

26 DA(S)A 2018, s 4.

27 DA(S)A 2018, s 6.

28 Eg by Emma E Forbes, *The Domestic Abuse (Scotland) Act 2018: the whole story?* (2018) 22(3) Edin L Rev 406–411. Humza Yousaf, then First Minister, stated, when the Act came into force: 'The Domestic Abuse Act makes absolutely clear that coercive and controlling behaviour is domestic abuse and a crime', www.gov.scot/news/domestic-abuse-act-in-force/

29 ASP(S)A 2007 Code of Practice, p 99.

30 ASP(S)A 2007 Code of Practice, pp 16 and 23.

31 ASP(S)A 2007, s 35(3)–(6). 'Undue pressure' in this context is discussed at paras **12.19** and **12.20**.

Forced marriage

6.21 The Scottish Government defines forced marriage as: 'A marriage in which one or both parties do not (or, in the case of some adults with learning or physical disabilities, cannot) consent to the marriage and duress is involved.'[32] 'Duress' encompasses both threat of physical force and emotional pressure. A distinction must be noted between forced and arranged marriage. In the latter, both parties give their full and free consent to the marriage.

As well as criminal sanctions, forced marriage protection orders may be sought by various individuals and public authorities through the civil courts, to help protect adults in forced marriage situations.[33] These protections have also been extended to persons forced to enter into civil partnership.[34]

Human trafficking

6.22 The trafficking of human beings is a form of harm in itself, because of the fundamental impact it has on a person's dignity and security of person. It will usually be accompanied by other forms of abuse. There is a gender-specific aspect to human trafficking, in that men and women will tend to be trafficked for different purposes: men more frequently for the purpose of forced labour; women for the purpose of forced prostitution or other sexual exploitation.

Financial abuse

6.23 Financial abuse involves an inappropriate use of an individual's money or other property without their agreement or consent. A wide range of activity can constitute this type of harm and the means of responding to it are, in many cases, rather different from other types of harm listed here. Such abuse may also be a criminal offence.[35]

[32] *Forced Marriage Statutory Guidance* (revised 2014). www.gov.scot/Topics/People/Equality/violence-women/forcedmarriage

[33] See para **12.48**.

[34] Forced Marriage etc. (Protection and Jurisdiction) (Scotland) Act 2011 (Application to Civil Partnerships and Consequential Provision) Order 2023 (SSI 2023/194).

[35] See para **7.23**.

RECOGNISING HARM OR ABUSE

6.24 Harm and abuse can become apparent in a number of ways and because reactions vary from person to person, it is important to take any disclosures, allegations, concerns, injuries or changes in behaviour seriously and investigate in an appropriate manner.

Disclosure by adult

6.25 In some cases, an adult may report abuse or harm directly, by telling a social worker, carer, family member, support staff or the police. Those who become aware of harm may be under a legal duty to disclose that information to the appropriate authority. The issues around the disclosure of information are looked at in detail in Chapter 13.

Disclosure by a third party

6.26 Information about abuse or harm can come to light because a third party has witnessed the abuse or has been abused by the same person or in the same institution or setting.

Concerns raised following behaviour changes

6.27 A person who knows the adult well and who has noticed significant changes may report concerns. This could be a relative, friend, neighbour, teacher, colleague or support worker worried about an adult's appearance, lack of funds, increasing debts or changes in behaviour and mood.

Other indicators can be disrupted sleeping patterns or frequent nightmares, a loss of personal modesty, a fear of being alone, or someone becoming prone to angry and aggressive outbursts. There may also be the development of psychological difficulties, including depression, obsessive behaviour, a loss of confidence or panic attacks. Such changes can be a way of communicating emotions and as such should be taken seriously and investigated.

Medical care and treatment

6.28 The adult may have unexplained physical injuries, such as cuts, bleeding or bruising, that indicate abuse. In some cases, urgent action might be necessary to make sure the individual gets the medical care and treatment they need.

Where the adult refuses to cooperate, and lacks capacity, consideration might be given to using the powers under the Adults with Incapacity (Scotland) Act 2000. Otherwise, any care or treatment against the wishes of a competent adult can constitute an assault, unless it is covered under the common law doctrine of necessity or the Mental Health (Care and Treatment) (Scotland) Act 2003.[36] Issues around medical treatment are examined in Chapter 9.

Abuse may also become apparent when an adult with reduced capacity becomes pregnant or is diagnosed with a sexually transmitted disease.

CONCLUSION

6.29 Although different Acts use different terminology, all are fundamentally focussed on preventing 'harm' and differ ultimately only in the groups of adults to which they apply. The definition of harm is a wide one, encompassing many different types of treatment and may, correspondingly, be uncovered in many different settings.

[36] Note that this can authorise treatment only for mental disorder.

Chapter 7

FINANCIAL HARM AND ABUSE

7.1 The financial abuse of adults is a major national issue and can take many forms. It might involve misuse of benefits, using the adult's details to take out loans or making unauthorised bank account withdrawals.[1] It can also extend to commercial debt, where adults who are clearly vulnerable are inappropriately sold products or find themselves targeted by fraudsters.

In August 2012, financial harm was announced as one of the five National Adult Support priorities, and a team was established to produce recommendations for future work and changes. The resulting report highlighted some of the recognised factors that increase a person's vulnerability to financial harm.[2] These include living alone, increased dependency on external support and reduced capacity to understand and manage financial affairs.[3] The report concluded that over the next 20 years or so, given the ageing population 'we clearly face a national challenge on an unprecedented scale'.[4] Many adult protection committees have since established financial harm sub-groups to achieve a coordinated approach.[5]

This chapter focusses on the types of financial harm and the challenges in using the legislation to deal with it. It also provides practical steps to help protect against financial harm.

LEGAL DEFINITIONS OF FINANCIAL HARM AND ABUSE

7.2 The defnition of an 'adult at risk' in the Adult Support and Protection (Scotland) Act 2007 refers to those who are unable to safeguard their own

1 For a list of the types and indicators of abuse and harm see www.scie.org.uk: Types and indicators of abuse: Safeguarding adults – SCIE.

2 Summary of the achievements and recommendations from the five national priority projects (Scottish Government, 2 July 2014).

3 Project review and closure report (Scottish Government, 31 March 2014).

4 Project Review and Closure Report: National Adult Support Priorities, p 1, Section 2.

5 *Adult Support and Protection (Scotland) Act 2007 Code of Practice* (July 2022), p 23.

property, rights or other interests and are at risk of harm.[6] Financial 'harm' is defined as covering 'unlawful conduct which appropriates or adversely affects property, rights or interests (for example: theft, fraud, embezzlement or extortion)'.[7] This could include anything from persuading the adult to transfer the title of their house to keeping the change from a weekly shop. Not all adults experiencing financial harm will fall under the definition of an adult at risk. However, some of the suggestions in this chapter could be used with the adult's consent to reduce the risk of harm.

It is important that the opportunity is taken to report misappropriation on any scale. Where the adult is on a low income, being deprived of relatively small amounts of cash can leave them short of money for essential items and so cause harm. In addition, it is common for misappropriation to escalate, where the frequency and amount increases over time.

7.3 Under the Adult Support and Protection (Scotland) Act 2007, local authorities are under a duty to inquire where they know or believe the property or affairs of an adult covered by the legislation may be at risk.[8] Other legislation also refers to financial harm in terms of the responsibilities of particular organisations. Under the Adults with Incapacity (Scotland) Act 2000 the Public Guardian has the duty to investigate any circumstances where the property or financial affairs of an adult seem to be at risk.[9] However, the local authority should also be notified of any concerns. It is common for financial abuse to happen alongside other types of harm or abuse, and there may be additional concerns about the adult's personal welfare, for example, where the adult has insufficient funds to pay for food, utilities or to replace clothing. In addition, the local authority may have a duty to act to make sure that the person's finances are protected. Where further information is needed, there are powers available allowing a council officer to require any person holding financial records that relate to an adult believed to be an adult at risk to provide copies.[10] This allows access to bank statements or loan agreements. The local authority also has a duty to apply for the appointment of a financial guardian where this is necessary to protect the adult's financial affairs.[11] The Mental Welfare Commission also has a duty to investigate in a range of circumstances including where the person is under a compulsory order or where it

6 Adult Support and Protection (Scotland) Act 2007 (ASP(S)A 2007), s 3.
7 ASP(S)A 2007, s 53(1).
8 ASP(S)A 2007, s 4.
9 Adults with Incapacity (Scotland) Act 2000 (AWI(S)A 2000), s 6(2)(d).
10 ASP(S)A 2007, s 10. For further discussion see para **8.13**.
11 AWI(S)A 2000, s 57(2).

considers someone's property is at risk because of a mental disorder.[12] They can also investigate where the patient is living alone, or without care and is unable to look after their property or financial affairs.

COMMON CATEGORIES OF FINANCIAL HARM AND ABUSE

7.4 There are many types of financial abuse and harm. These are often divided into cases where the harm involves those close to the adult and cases where it is perpetrated by a stranger. In most cases, the person causing the harm will be a family member, friend or carer. However, increasingly financial harm is happening at a distance with sophisticated scams and the prevalence of electronic transactions.[13]

Misuse of formal authority

7.5 Financial abuse or harm may be caused by someone who has been formally appointed to manage the adult's finances. This is a particular risk where a financial attorney or benefits appointee is involved. Cases involving financial guardians are more likely to be identified as there is formal monitoring by the Public Guardian. For example, a failure to submit the annual account or respond to requests for information will alert the Public Guardian to possible issues. Where there are concerns about any such individuals, these can be reported to the Public Guardian, the Mental Welfare Commission, or the local authority. It should be sufficient to report concerns to one of these organisations who will then refer to other interested parties where necessary. However, the person reporting may want to refer to all the relevant organisations and let them decide who is most appropriate to investigate further. The Department of Work and Pensions should also be informed, so that action can be taken to make sure benefit income is protected and paid to a responsible third party (even in the short term) until issues are investigated. Anyone holding a formal appointment has legal duties to manage money properly and apply the principles of the legislation. The procedure for removing an attorney, guardian or appointee is set out later in this chapter.

12 Mental Health (Care and Treatment) (Scotland) Act 2003, s 11(2).

13 'Nature of fraud and computer misuse in England and Wales' (Office for National Statistics) (www.ons.gov.uk).

Harm by individual with no formal role

7.6 Financial harm or abuse may be caused by those without a formal role in the adult's life, such as relatives, friends or acquaintances. These are often people that the adult trusts and on whom the adult has a degree of dependence. Even when the adult does have concerns, they may be worried about the consequences of challenging or upsetting those involved. They may fear that if the help provided by that individual is withdrawn then the only option will be residential care. There have been cases of individuals befriending someone they view as vulnerable and then misappropriating funds. They might offer to collect benefits, pay bills or pick up shopping as a way of getting access to an adult's bank account.

These cases can be difficult, particularly where the adult is vulnerable but considered to have capacity. Where someone close to the adult is involved, the adult may understandably want the financial harm to stop but the relationship to continue. This will make remedies such as banning orders less workable. Where an adult remains at home, it is difficult to effectively monitor contact. The adult might not view themselves as having suffered harm or may not want to acknowledge or accept an unwise decision. Similarly, the perpetrator may seek to justify their actions as being in line with the adult's wishes or representing reasonable recompense for the services they provide. However, there are a range of options which should be considered and are set out below.

Harm by companies or strangers

7.7 Financial harm or abuse can be caused by people not previously known to the adult. Vulnerable individuals are commonly targeted by those trying to steal or extort money through false marketing, doorstep crimes or pressure sales. Common examples are where someone claims to be from the police, local authority or a utility company to gain access to a house. They may also pose as genuine workmen and convince the adult that work needs to be carried out. The work is either then not done or is substandard. Fraudulent schemes often work from a distance, through unsolicited mail, emails, telephone calls or text messages. These are becoming increasingly convincing, often including personal details. In some cases, the adult's details may be sold on to other companies and the same people are then repeatedly targeted. The adult may not realise they have been the victim of a crime or may be embarrassed about having been deceived and reluctant to report what has happened.

7.8 Where there are concerns that someone has been the victim of, or targeted by, someone seeking to commit financial harm, the police and trading standards[14] should be notified immediately. It is difficult to eliminate this type of harm. However, there are ways to reduce the risk to a particular individual. These include:

- Contacting the local authority where any work is required. Most have 'Trusted Trader' lists to allow people to find reliable tradesmen.[15]
- Returning letters unopened and marked 'unsolicited mail, please return to sender'.
- Joining the mailing preference service which companies should check before sending letters.[16] This should stop junk mail and generic advertising but will not prevent scams where the mail is addressed to an individual by name.
- Joining the Royal Mail opt-out service. This will stop unaddressed advertising leaflets and flyers being delivered by the Royal Mail, though it will not stop delivery by others eg local businesses.[17]
- Placing a redirect on the adult's mail so it is delivered to another address. This allows an appropriate third party to monitor mail and ensure that the adult only sees legitimate correspondence.
- Enforcing the individual's right to stop their information being used for direct marketing purposes. Where a particular company targets them, a notice under the Data Protection Act 1998 can be sent.[18] If the company does not cease contacting the adult, the Information Commissioner for Scotland can take further action.[19]
- Registering with the telephone preference service. This can significantly reduce unsolicited telephone calls. The service extends to mobile numbers as well as landlines.[20]

14 www.tsscot.co.uk

15 See the 'Traders vetted by Trading Standards' section of the Scotland Trusted Trader website (www.trustedtrader.scot).

16 www.mpsonline.org.uk

17 www.royalmail.com

18 Data Protection Act 1998, s 11.

19 www.ico.org.uk

20 www.tpsonline.org.uk. To prevent calls to mobile phones you can either register online or text TPS and an email address to 85095.

- Using call blocking options. Many mobile phones will identify calls as 'spam' so they can be ignored. Most major providers have opt-in services which can divert nuisance calls to a junk voicemail box or silence calls from unknown numbers. There are also many call blocking apps and devices available.
- Using the 'cooling off period' that applies to many contracts. This means the contract can be cancelled within 7 or 14 days. Individuals have a right to be advised of this period at the time the contract is concluded.[21]
- Installing video doorbells. These work as a deterrent and can provide useful evidence of any inappropriate interactions. They alert a third party to callers in real time and most allow audio interactions.
- Improving online security. Many people have weak passwords containing significant names or dates and use the same passwords for multiple logins. Installing a password manager to create and recall unique strong passwords can help reduce risk. It is also important that anti-virus software is up to date.
- Using two factor authentication where possible so that transactions need to be verified using a code sent by text or email.
- Encouraging the shredding of paperwork containing personal details.

Some of these suggestions are significant interventions and would need the adult's informed consent. If the adult lacks capacity to consent, then an attorney or guardian with a relevant power would need to make the decision after having regard to the principles.

Finally, note that where an adult lacked the capacity to enter into an agreement or contract in the first place, it will be unenforceable.

REMEDIES

Appointment or removal of financial attorney

7.9 Where the adult still has capacity, they may want to appoint someone they trust on a formal basis as their financial attorney. The attorney would be able to assist the adult with their financial affairs

[21] The Consumer Contracts (Information, Cancellation and Additional Charges) Regulations 2013 (SI 2013/3134) .

immediately. This can be a sensible solution where the adult is suffering harm and there is someone close to them they trust and want to take on this role. The formal appointment of a suitable attorney may also deter anyone looking to exploit the adult.

7.10 Many people decide to grant a power of attorney when they begin to experience symptoms, or receive a diagnosis, of a progressive illness. It is very common for a family member to suggest their relative grants a power of attorney. That family member may even make an appointment with a solicitor. In most cases, this is not inappropriate. However, the Mental Welfare Commission issued a significant report in 2013 highlighting some of the dangers and risks involved.[22] This involved a couple with learning disabilities who were exploited by the family member they had appointed as their attorney.

As a result of this report, the Law Society of Scotland issued 'Vulnerable Clients Guidance', which all solicitors are required to follow.[23] This applies where a solicitor is, or reasonably ought to be, aware that a client is or may be vulnerable. A solicitor has an obligation to support clients to exercise legal capacity.[24] This may involve adjustments to allow an individual to provide proper instructions. For example, use of communication aids or meeting in a place where the client feels most comfortable. However, the solicitor still needs to assess the client's capacity and the quality of their instructions. Some clients will be vulnerable to pressure from others and the guidance sets out how solicitors should approach such cases. For example, where possible the client should be seen alone and anyone providing support should be neutral. There may be increased scope for undue pressure where video calls are used to take instructions. It is harder to read body language and even if the client appears alone, others may be able to listen in or influence responses.

7.11 Appointing an attorney is a private contractual arrangement and there is an assumption that adults will choose someone they trust as their attorney. As a result, attorneys are not subject to regular supervision and do not routinely report to the Public Guardian or local authority. Where

[22] *Powers of Attorney & their safeguards – Mr and Mrs D* (Mental Welfare Commission, February 2013).

[23] 'Guidance related to Rule B1.5: Vulnerable Clients Guidance' (Law Society of Scotland).

[24] Also see the obligations of State Parties to provide support to exercise legal capacity under Article 12.3 of the UN Convention on the Rights of People with Disabilities.

there are concerns about the actions of a financial attorney who has been appointed there are several options available. In some circumstances, the adult will retain capacity but may have appointed a financial attorney to act because they are struggling physically or emotionally or in the early stages of an illness. If this is the case, it is open to the adult to revoke the power of attorney and either manage their affairs on their own or appoint someone else instead. There is no set style to revoke a power of attorney but it must be accompanied by a certificate completed by a medical professional confirming the adult has capacity to make the decision.[25] The attorney might also be persuaded to resign if they are made aware that other action is likely to be taken.[26]

7.12 Unfortunately, in some cases the adult will be under a lot of pressure from the attorney to continue the arrangement. They may feel unable to revoke the appointment, despite the attorney's actions. A progressive condition may mean the adult now lacks capacity to revoke an appointment and choose someone else to act. In such cases, formal court action may be necessary. The options available are:

- An order that an attorney is formally supervised by the Public Guardian.[27] This can be on any conditions that the Sheriff considers proper. For example, the attorney might be required to submit regular accounts to the Public Guardian. The attorney can appeal against any limitation of their powers, although there is no appeal against a supervision or reporting requirement.[28]
- A Sheriff can give anyone acting under the legislation, including an attorney, a specific direction on how to exercise their powers.[29] This could include a direction on the circumstances in which a house is sold, who is consulted about decisions or the appropriateness of a proposed gift.
- An application can be made for the appointment of a financial guardian. If granted, this would supersede any existing power of attorney.[30] If the intention is to revoke the power of attorney, then a specific crave must be added to this effect. Otherwise, any powers

25 AWI(S)A 2000, s 22A.
26 AWI(S)A 2000, s 23.
27 AWI(S)A 2000, s 20.
28 AWI(S)A 2000, s 20(4).
29 AWI(S)A 2000, s 3(3).
30 AWI(S)A 2000, s 24(2).

not granted in favour of the financial guardian would remain in the remit of the attorney.

- The Sheriff could simply be asked to revoke the power of attorney without any further appointment being made.[31] This might be appropriate where money can be managed using a different option such as appointeeship or the management of residents' finances provisions set out in Part 4 of the Act.[32]

7.13 The remedies outlined above are not restricted to local authorities. A family member, friend or interested party can also apply for an attorney to be supervised, removed or replaced.

Appointment or removal of financial guardian or intervener

7.14 The process of appointing a financial guardian or intervener is more robust than that for appointing a financial attorney. This is due to the level of external scrutiny. The appointment of a financial guardian or intervener involves a court application. Interested parties (including the adult) can comment, make objections and have their views considered. There is more information about this in Chapter 12. The application includes an independent professional report looking at the applicant's ability and qualifications to perform the role. It is served on those with an interest in the adult's financial affairs including, where appropriate, care providers and close family members. There are also more safeguards in place than for attorneys, such as requirements that annual reports are submitted to the Public Guardian for approval and that financial advice is taken where appropriate. The level of scrutiny often deters individuals causing financial harm from making an application.

7.15 Where an adult already lacks the capacity to manage their finances, the appointment of a financial guardian may be a sensible option. The local authority has an important role here. If an application for financial guardianship is necessary, and no one else is prepared to apply, the local authority must apply for the appointment of a financial guardian.[33] There

31 AWI(S)A 2000, s 20(2)(e).

32 At the time of writing the Scottish Government are consulting on removing Part 4 as an option: see the Adults with Incapacity Amendment Act Consultation (July 2024) (www.gov.scot), p 39.

33 AWI(S)A 2000, s 57(2).

is a clear distinction between the duty to apply for appointment of a financial guardian and who can take on that role. The local authority can make the application but the chief social worker cannot act as the financial guardian. Most local authorities have a panel of individual solicitors they invite to take on such work.

7.16 Inevitably cases do arise where guardians have not carried out their duties appropriately. They may have acted contrary to the principles or failed to properly manage the adult's money. Many of these may be identified by the Public Guardian in annual reviews. In cases where formal intervention is required then the adult, Public Guardian, local authority or any other interested party, including friends or family members, can apply to the Sheriff and request that:

- A guardian is replaced by another more appropriate individual. [34] The Public Guardian may suggest a professional to take on this role.
- A guardian is removed.[35] The Sheriff can only remove a guardian where satisfied either that there is a substitute guardian who can start acting or that a joint guardian is appropriate to continue as the sole guardian.
- The guardianship order is recalled.[36] The Sheriff can recall a guardianship order where they are satisfied it is no longer needed, for example because the adult has regained capacity, or that the adult's finances can be safeguarded in another way.

7.17 The Public Guardian also has authority to recall the powers of a guardian relating to property or financial matters if it appears that the grounds for appointment of a guardian are no longer fulfilled and the adult's interests could be satisfactorily safeguarded or promoted in another way.[37] An example would be that the adult has regained capacity, or the funds can be better managed using other provisions. This might happen where the adult's resources have been depleted by the payment of debts and now the only income is benefits which can be managed by an appointee.

34 AWI(S)A 2000, s 71(1)(a).
35 AWI(S)A 2000, s 71(1)(b).
36 AWI(S)A 2000, s 71(1)(c).
37 AWI(S)A 2000, s 73.

7.18 Where a one-off decision needs to be made, a financial intervener might be appointed. Common examples are cases where a parent has died and there is a legal rights claim or where an adult has moved into residential care and a tenancy agreement requires to be terminated. As with guardianship, the court application procedure is robust. In addition, as an intervention order is usually time limited and for a specific action, there is less likelihood of abuse. That said the Public Guardian has power to investigate the actions of an intervener and take action where necessary.[38] It is also possible to apply to the Sheriff for an intervener to be directed on how to exercise their powers.[39]

Appointment or removal of appointee

7.19 Where someone lacks capacity to manage their own finances, the person or organisation who wants to take over can ask to be made a Department of Work and Pensions (DWP) Appointee.[40] This is useful where there is an appropriate third party who can take over claiming and managing benefit income. Before an appointment is made, the DWP needs to be satisfied that the person entitled to the benefits is not able to manage money on their own and that the proposed appointee is suitable. There is more information about this scheme in Chapter 10. A DWP appointeeship will only provide authority to manage state benefits, so where there is other income, for example a private pension, another option may need to be considered as well or instead.

7.20 Where there are concerns about the actions of an appointee, the DWP should be notified immediately. The DWP do not routinely monitor how appointees are operating or require accounting records and so there is potential for abuse. However, the DWP can remove an appointee who is not acting in the adult's best interests.[41] If a claimant becomes able to manage benefits, the appointment can be cancelled. Problems can arise where an appointeeship is revoked without an appropriate alternative being identified. In such cases, the adult's benefits may effectively be frozen, which can cause hardship. It is important to consider what

38 AWI(S)A 2000, s 6(2).

39 AWI(S)A 2000, s 3.

40 Social Security (Claims and Payments) Regulations 1987 (SI 1987/1968), reg 33, Housing Benefit (General) Regulations 1987 (SI 1987/1971), reg 71(3), Council Tax Benefit (General) Regulations 1992 (SI 1992/1814), reg 61(3).

41 Social Security (Claims and Payments) Regulations 1987 (SI 1987/1968), reg 33.

alternative arrangements are going to be put in place so that the adult has enough for day-to-day expenses. It can take several months for a financial guardian to be appointed and so, in the interim, the local authority or a care provider may need to step in and act as a corporate appointee.

Appointment or removal of withdrawer

7.21 Where an adult lacks capacity to manage their own money, an organisation or individual can apply to open or access a bank account on their behalf.[42] There is more information about how this works in Chapter 10. The application process is not as onerous as for financial guardianship and the decision on appointment is made by the Public Guardian rather than a court. The applicant is required to provide a medical certificate confirming the adult's incapacity and a certificate from an independent person confirming suitability to act. There is less scope for financial abuse due to strict limits on what they can do. For example, the applicant must specify the amount they will use on each item of expenditure. It only confers financial decision making powers and most adults who lack capacity will also need welfare decisions made on their behalf. The restrictions make the scheme less flexible when compared with other options. These limitations are reflected in the low number of applications under the Access to Funds provisions.[43] Any expenditure not anticipated at the outset needs to be approved by the Public Guardian and the person managing money has little or no discretion. The Scottish Government has recognised that there is a need for more flexibility in the scheme and at the time of writing is consulting on ways to achieve this.[44]

7.22 If there are concerns about the actions of a withdrawer, the Public Guardian should be notified immediately. The withdrawer's authority can be suspended while further investigations take place, or it can be terminated permanently.[45]

42 AWI(S)A 2000, s 25.

43 In the year 2023–24 there were 193 access to funds applications registered compared to 3,235 guardianships and 550 intervention orders.

44 The Adults with Incapacity Amendment Act Consultation (July 2024) (www.gov.scot), p 31.

45 AWI(S)A 2000, s 31(3).

Criminal offences

7.23 Sometimes people who experience financial harm and abuse are described in terms such as being 'taken advantage of'. This minimises what they are experiencing which is often a criminal offence. Using direct language, such as theft, extortion or embezzlement emphasises the seriousness of an individual's actions.

The following criminal offences are of relevance:

- A deliberate deception that causes someone to do something they would not otherwise have done may constitute fraud. This includes misleading a person into handing over money or property or otherwise acting to their disadvantage. The false pretence must have a causal link to the practical result. However, there is no minimum requirement of loss for the crime to be committed and there is no requirement that the perpetrator has gained as a consequence.
- Misusing a person's benefit money or taking money from a person who is not able to understand, may constitute theft.
- Using or attempting to use a counterfeit or forged document with the intent to defraud, may constitute the common law crime of 'uttering'.
- A person who misuses property they originally received legally, for example as an appointee or financial adviser, may be guilty of the crimes of breach of trust or embezzlement. These crimes are generally considered more serious than theft due to the abuse of trust.
- Threatening a person in order to force them to hand over money, or to comply with any other demand, is extortion or assault and robbery.[46]
- The Adults with Incapacity (Scotland) Act 2000, s 83 created an offence of ill-treatment and wilful neglect. It states that 'it shall be an offence for any person exercising powers under this Act relating to the personal welfare of an adult to ill-treat or wilfully neglect that adult'.[47]

[46] For more information see Sheriff Andrew Cubie, *Scots Criminal Law* (5th edn, Bloomsbury Professional, 2022).

[47] At the time of writing the Scottish Government are consulting on the creation of a similar offence for financial abuse: see the Adults with Incapacity Amendment Act Consultation (July 2024) (www.gov.scot), p 74.

There can be difficulties in taking forward prosecutions and obtaining convictions for these financial offences. In some cases, the adult's capacity might have an impact on their ability to give evidence in court. The adult may have voluntarily disclosed bank details and authorised access making it difficult to prove a crime has happened. The consequences for the adult in going through a criminal investigation must also be considered. This can cause significant stress, particularly where the accused is a close family member, and may have serious repercussions for relationships the adult views as important. That said, the Crown Office and Procurator Fiscal Service issued guidance in relation to older victims of crime in June 2023. This states that 'where there is sufficient evidence and the crime was perpetrated because of the perceived or actual vulnerability based on their age or perceived age, there is a strong presumption in favour of prosecution'.[48] There are measures available to support adults in the criminal justice system and these are discussed in Chapter 12. Financial crimes are serious and decisions on prosecution should be based on all the facts of the case. A decision may be made to move forward with a prosecution even where the adult does not want this to happen.

Banning order

7.24 In some cases, it may be appropriate to consider a banning order to deal with cases involving financial harm and abuse. The Adult Support and Protection (Scotland) Act 2007 gives a Sheriff the power to ban a person from a specified place for up to six months.[49] The local authority must apply for the order if it is satisfied that the grounds for making an order apply.[50] The procedures for applying for a banning order, and the criteria for granting, are covered at para **12.31**.

7.25 This can be a useful remedy where the harm is being caused by someone in the adult's home, or some other public place. However, there can be obstacles to an order's effectiveness where the harm is caused by a close family member or friend. Banning orders are difficult to monitor and enforce, especially where the adult is not willing or able to report breaches of their terms. If the adult wants to continue a relationship with the person subject to the banning order, it can be challenging to prevent this happening.

48 COPFS 'Older Persons Policy' (June 2023), published on www.copfs.gov.uk

49 ASP(S)A 2007, s 19.

50 ASP(S)A 2007, s 22(2).

Another issue is that the criteria for granting an order involve establishing 'serious harm'. Where financial abuse is on a significant scale this is easier to prove. However, where it involves regular appropriation of smaller amounts, the criteria are more difficult to satisfy. That said, even being deprived of a small amount each week might have an impact on the adult's ability to pay bills, heat their house or buy food. This could amount to 'serious harm' justifying consideration of a formal order. Anyone applying for an order needs to set out clearly that the test of 'serious harm' is met.[51]

Banning orders are based on the concept of banning individuals from a particular place or places although they could have other conditions added secondary to this. For example, there could be a prohibition on contacting the adult by any means and arranging to meet elsewhere. Where an individual has remote access to finances or it is not certain who the perpetrator is, then a banning order may be of limited use.

Residents' finances in care homes

7.26 Some adults' finances can be managed by the hospital or care home in which they live.[52] It was expected this would happen where there is no one else able to act and the amount involved does not justify the appointment of a financial guardian. The hospital or care home can become a corporate DWP appointee. There is also provision for them to manage finances, other than benefits, provided they are an 'authorised establishment'. This means a care home service registered with the Care Inspectorate or an NHS or private hospital.[53] The Care Inspectorate, Healthcare Improvement Scotland and health boards are the 'supervisory bodies' and must carry out inquiries from time to time about the operation of the scheme.[54] This scheme has not been a success. Most care homes do not want the responsibility of becoming a benefits appointee or of managing large sums of money. There is no requirement that authorised establishments have to offer this option. As part of a review of the Act, the Scottish Government wrote to all health boards in Scotland to find out more about how often this service was used. They received no information to suggest it was used at all. The Care Inspectorate advised there were no

51 Paragraph **12.22** considers the definition of 'serious harm' further.

52 Under Part 4 of the AWI(S)A 2000.

53 AWI(S)A 2000, s 35 and Adults with Incapacity (Management of Residents' Finances) (Scotland) Regulations 2005 (SSI 2005/610).

54 AWI(S)A 2000, s 40(2).

users of Part 4 in the care home sector. As a result, at the time of writing the Scottish Government are consulting on scrapping this option.[55] There is more information about this scheme at para **10.18**.

7.27 Anyone concerned about how an adult's finances are managed by a care home or a hospital can make a complaint to the appropriate supervisory body. Both can cancel an establishment's authority to manage a specific resident's, or all residents', finances.[56] This can happen where the establishment has failed to carry out its duties properly or if for any other reason it is no longer appropriate for it to manage funds. There can be recourse to an appeal to the Sheriff against this decision.[57] There are codes of practice for both the role of those managing residents' finances and supervisory bodies.

Misuse of direct payments

7.28 Some adults receive direct payments, rather than services, from their local authority to allow them to arrange and pay for their own care. There are controls over the use and management of direct payments. The Self-directed Support Regulations 2014[58] make it clear that there is no requirement to give the option of direct payments to an adult where there are concerns that such a payment may put the adult's safety at risk.[59] There are also provisions that allow payments to be made to a third party, provided the adult retains total control over the way the money is spent.[60] This allows individuals to contract with organisations to manage their direct payments on their behalf.

Where concerns arise after direct payments have commenced the local authority may consider termination. This can apply where payments are used for purposes other than the support or care for which they were intended. There is nothing in the regulations requiring the misuse to be deliberate on the part of the adult. Theft or misuse of funds by a third party, including a care provider, would allow the payments to be terminated.

55 The Adults with Incapacity Amendment Act Consultation (July 2024) (www.gov.scot), p 39.

56 AWI(S)A 2000, s 45(1).

57 AWI(S)A 2000, s 45(6).

58 Self-directed Support (Direct Payments) (Scotland) Regulations 2014 (SDS(DP)(S) Regulations 2014) (SSI 2014/25).

59 SDS(DP)(S) Regulations 2014, reg 11(2)(b).

60 SDS(DP)(S) Regulations 2014, reg 5.

7.29 The use of direct payments to employ family members is strictly regulated. The term 'family member' covers spouses, civil partners, cohabitees, parents, children, aunts, uncles, nieces, nephews, grandparents and children.[61] A family member can only provide support using a direct payment where the service user and local authority agree to this and the person is capable of providing support.[62] In addition, at least one of the following factors must apply:

- There is a limited choice of service providers who could provide the support.
- The direct payment user has specific communication needs which mean it will be difficult for another provider to provide the support.
- The support is required at times at which the family member is able to provide it and where other providers would not reasonably be available.
- The intimate nature of the support required by the direct payment user makes it preferable to them that support is provided by a family member.
- The direct payment user has religious or cultural beliefs which make the provision of support by a family member preferable to them.
- The direct payment user requires palliative care.
- The direct payment user has an emergency or short-term necessity for care.
- There are other factors in place which make it appropriate, in the opinion of the local authority, for that family member to provide the support.[63]

7.30 A further safeguard is that guardians or attorneys who have powers to make decisions regarding support are prohibited from being paid for support by a direct payment.[64] There has been some controversy about this prohibition, as often a close family member is the most obvious person to be guardian and to provide care and support. However, this clearly results in a significant concentration of power, and it was felt safer to exclude the possibility rather than allowing it in exceptional circumstances. Families

[61] SDS(DP)(S) Regulations 2014, reg 8(4).
[62] SDS(DP)(S) Regulations 2014, reg 8(2).
[63] SDS(DP)(S) Regulations 2014, reg 8(3).
[64] SDS(DP)(S) Regulations 2014, reg 9(b).

will need to take this into account when considering who should apply to be a guardian.

Recovery of funds

7.31 Where an adult has suffered financial harm or abuse, consideration should be given to the following options to recover some, or all, of the money or property lost:

- An attorney, withdrawer, guardian, intervener or manager of residents' finances who misuses the adult's funds, or acts outside their authority, can be required to repay the adult with interest.[65] The person who has misused funds should be approached in the first instance and asked to return funds. If this does not happen it may be necessary to apply to the sheriff court for an order requiring repayment. Where the individual has spent misappropriated money, there may be limited prospects of recovery.
- Financial guardians and interveners are normally required to obtain a form of insurance before any formal appointment is issued. This is called 'caution'.[66] A claim can be made on this insurance for any loss.[67] The guardian can be asked for information about which company provides the insurance. Alternatively, the Public Guardian receives copies of the insurance documents prior to issuing the certificate of appointment and so can provide this information. Anyone acting under a bond of caution should be aware that, unlike most insurance, if a claim is successful the provider of caution may pursue them for the amount paid out following a claim.
- Where the perpetrator is convicted of a criminal offence the court can be asked to make a community payback order, including a requirement that compensation is paid to the victim.[68] Of course, where the person convicted has no resources this may be very difficult to enforce. The Procurator Fiscal dealing with the case, or Victim Information and Advice will be able to provide more information about such an order in a particular case.[69]

65 AWI(S)A 2000, s 81.

66 This is pronounced to rhyme with 'nation'.

67 AWI(S)A 2000, ss 58(6) and 53(7).

68 Criminal Procedure (Scotland) Act 1995, ss 227A and 227H (inserted by the Criminal Justice and Licensing (Scotland) Act 2010, s 14).

69 There is more information about the role of the Procurator Fiscal in Chapters 4 and 12.

- The adult could take civil court action for recovery of the money against the person or organisation involved. Again, this may have limited success where the perpetrator has no resources. Court action could also be considered where a company, local authority or other organisation has caused the financial loss. In most cases, it is advisable to contact the person or organisation to request funds are repaid. If this approach is not successful it may be necessary to consult a solicitor or local advice centre. If the loss has been caused by failures on the part of the local authority or another public body, pursuit of an official complaint through their complaints procedure may lead to compensation being paid. If that is unsuccessful, an application to the Scottish Public Services Ombudsman may be appropriate. The Ombudsman can recommend that compensation be paid. Such recommendations are not binding, but are usually followed.[70]
- If a bank or other financial institution has failed in duties to the customer and a loss has occurred, a complaint may be made to the Financial Services Ombudsman, who can order compensation.[71]
- Where the abuse involves a change to formal legal documents then it may be possible to restore the original position. For example, where someone has unduly pressured an adult to change their will. If the adult has capacity, a new will can be instructed. If the adult lacks capacity, then a guardian or intervener may be granted a specific power to sign a will on the adult's behalf. This will be appropriate where there was a previous will and a new one can be executed in the same terms. It may also be possible to sign a will where the adult has left clear instructions from a time they had capacity. Otherwise, the option will be to revoke the will and leave the adult's estate to be dealt with under the rules on intestacy. These options will require a specific power to be included in the guardianship order or power of attorney.

Where an adult lacks capacity to take any action to recover funds it may be necessary for a guardian to be appointed with powers to do this on their behalf.

70 Information about the procedures is available from www.scotcourts.gov.uk
71 www.financial-ombudsman.org.uk

CONCLUSION

7.32 Financial abuse of adults is common and takes many forms. It can be particularly difficult to tackle when the perpetrator is a close family member. The consequences to the adult of taking legal action or starting criminal proceedings can be significant and the potential impact needs careful consideration before any action is taken. The project report which followed the identification of financial harm as a National Adult Support Priority suggests extending initiatives between the public and private sector. For example, the increased involvement of financial institutions might help identify potential harm earlier, deter abusers and minimise loss.

Chapter 8

LOCAL AUTHORITIES' DUTY TO INVESTIGATE HARM

8.1 This chapter looks at the duties and powers of local authorities where formal measures are necessary in relation to the investigation of harm. These powers and duties arise under various pieces of legislation, each of which has a different emphasis, although inevitably some of the provisions overlap. The role of other organisations is explored in Chapter 4.

The local authority will generally be the first point of contact where there is suspicion of harm or abuse. It should consider seriously any report that an adult may be at risk of harm, even when it is from an anonymous source.[1] The social work department should carry out the inquiry in accordance with local adult protection procedures and may work with other agencies as necessary.[2]

In many cases, initial investigations will be relatively informal and will not involve applications for court orders. It is hoped that the adult will often be prepared to accept assistance.[3] However, there will be situations in which the adult refuses to cooperate, despite the fact that they are suffering, or are likely to suffer, harm. In other cases, a third party might deliberately obstruct an investigation by insisting that an adult is unavailable, continually refusing to answer the door or failing to attend appointments. This will mean the local authority needs to consider the use of statutory powers.

A decision about such a course of action will be influenced by a number of factors, including the specific circumstances of the case, the relevant legal powers, the adult's capacity and the benefit an intervention could produce.

1 *Adult Support and Protection (Scotland) Act 2007 Code of Practice* (ASP(S)A 2007 Code of Practice) (July 2022), p 45.
2 ASP(S)A 2007 Code of Practice, p 47.
3 Although this might not be possible in emergencies. See Chapter 9 for further details.

POWERS AND DUTIES UNDER ADULT SUPPORT AND PROTECTION (SCOTLAND) ACT 2007

Duty to investigate

8.2 Local authorities have a key role in adult protection under this Act, with wide-ranging duties to make inquiries. The legislation makes it clear that the primary responsibility for investigating any risk to adults is with the local authority.

A local authority must make inquiries wherever it considers an adult protected by the legislation is at risk of harm[4] and that action may be necessary to protect their well-being, property or finances.[5] This duty extends to all people who are, for the time being, within the area of the local authority in question: and thus includes those living in their own homes, in residential care and in hospital and health care settings, and those who are only in the area on a temporary basis.[6]

The Act also provides the local authority with powers of compulsion in circumstances where the adult or a third party is obstructive or refuses to cooperate with the investigation. The local authority can apply for an order to remove the adult to a place where they can be interviewed or examined.

However, these powers will normally only be used when other methods have failed. The previous code of practice recognised that the system should be 'flexible and professional in its approach' and that interventions must be 'person centred and based on an individual's personal circumstances'.[7] While these points are not explicitly reiterated in the revised code of practice, it is suggested they remain relevant expressions of good practice.

Other organisations are obliged to cooperate in any investigations[8] and the police should also be involved at the earliest possible point where it appears a crime has occurred.

4 See Chapter 2 for a discussion of who is protected by the Act.

5 ASP(S)A 2007, s 4.

6 ASP(S)A 2007, s 53(1).

7 ASP(S)A 2007 Code of Practice 2008, Ch 6, para 6.

8 For further information see Chapters 4 and 13.

PRINCIPLES AND PRACTICE

The general principles, as outlined in Chapter 5, must be applied whenever the legislation is considered or used. Any intervention must be the least restrictive alternative, must offer a benefit to the individual and should maximise the participation of the adult in the decision making process.

In line with this last principle, the Code of Practice states the local authority should keep the adult informed at every stage of the process and record any reason why this is not done.[9] One reason for not doing so might be if this would risk prejudicing investigations. There may be situations where the local authority will have to weigh up the need to involve the adult against the ultimate benefit a successful investigation might produce.

In line with the principle of participation, if, after making inquiries, the local authority considers it needs to intervene, it should consider whether the adult should be referred to an independent advocacy organisation or provided with other appropriate services.[10]

Visits

8.3 The Adult Support and Protection (Scotland) Act 2007 gives a council officer the formal power to enter any place if this is considered necessary as part of an inquiry to establish whether an adult in the premises is an adult at risk and whether the local authority needs to take any action (under the Adult Support and Protection (Scotland) Act 2007 or otherwise) to protect them from harm.[11]

A visit must be at a reasonable time and the officer must state the objective of the visit and produce evidence of their authority to visit.[12] Good practice will be to provide notice of a visit where possible, although it is recognised that in some cases an unannounced visit might maximise the chances of getting access to the adult.[13]

9 ASP(S)A 2007 Code of Practice, p 47.

10 ASP(S)A 2007, s 6.

11 ASP(S)A 2007, s 7(1). This includes a right to enter any adjacent place for the same purpose. ASP(S)A 2007, s 7(2). See para **4.3** for the definition of council officer.

12 ASP(S)A 2007, s 36(1) and (2).

13 ASP(S)A 2007 Code of Practice, p 54.

Another person can accompany a council officer on the visit.[14] Some examples of circumstances in which this might be helpful are listed in the Code of Practice:

- **To facilitate joint investigation of concerns.** For example, allowing the council officer to investigate concerns jointly with a key worker, a police officer, health professional or a representative from the Care Commission or Office of the Public Guardian.
- **To help assess the risk to the adult.** A general practitioner, community nurse, key worker or other person already known to the adult and any other members of the household might be involved.
- **To assist with record taking and to witness anything that occurs**.
- **To assist with communication.** For example, where an interpreter is required.[15]

If there is concern that the council officer might face violence or threats at the premises, consideration should be given to how the visit will take place, including involving the police, if necessary.[16]

If the council officer is refused entry, they may not use force to gain entry,[17] but the local authority may apply for a warrant for entry.

Warrant for entry

8.4 Where a council officer has been refused entry, the local authority should consider whether a different approach might be more successful.[18] However, it has the option of applying to the sheriff court for a warrant for entry to carry out a visit.[19]

The Sheriff may grant a warrant for entry if satisfied that a council officer has been (or reasonably expects to be) refused entry or is unable to enter the premises or that any attempt by a council officer to visit the place without a warrant would defeat the object of the visit.[20]

The warrant for entry authorises a council officer to be accompanied by a police constable. The police constable can use reasonable force to gain

14 ASP(S)A 2007, s 36(3).
15 ASP(S)A 2007 Code of Practice, p 53.
16 ASP(S)A 2007 Code of Practice, p 53.
17 ASP(S)A 2007, s 36(4).
18 ASP(S)A 2007 Code of Practice, p 55
19 ASP(S)A 2007, s 37(1)(a).
20 ASP(S)A 2007, s 38(2).

entry.[21] The Code of Practice emphasises that force is '...an absolute last resort, to be used in very exceptional circumstances, and only when all other options have been exhausted'.[22]

The warrant must be used within 72 hours of being granted.[23] In urgent cases, the local authority can apply to a justice of the peace for a warrant.[24]

Interviews

8.5 During the course of a formal visit the council officer may interview anyone over the age of 16 who is in the premises.[25] This includes the adult who may be at risk and any carers, relatives or friends or other service users.

The legislation states that the interview must be held in private,[26] but this does not necessarily mean that only the adult and the council officer may be present. The Code of Practice is clear that the officer undertaking the interview should ask the adult whether they wish another person to be present, such as a family member, carer or independent advocate.[27] Nonetheless, it is equally clear that individuals may be excluded from the interview by the council officer, where to do so would advance the objectives of the investigation.[28] It is suggested that 'private' in this context therefore means 'giving due respect to the adult's privacy, while allowing appropriate support to be given.' Any decision to exclude an individual should, of course, be made in reference to the general principles of the legislation.

The council officer should consider how to maximise the adult's participation in the interview and whether any communication assistance would facilitate the interview.[29]

No one is required to answer any questions during an interview and interviewees must be informed of that fact before the interview begins.[30] If an adult at risk (or any other adult in the place being interviewed)

21 ASP(S)A 2007, s 37(1)(b).
22 ASP(S)A 2007 Code of Practice, p 55.
23 ASP(S)A 2007, s 37(2).
24 ASP(S)A 2007, s 40(1). See Chapter 9 for additional information about dealing with emergencies.
25 ASP(S)A 2007, s 8(1).
26 ASP(S)A 2007, s 8.
27 ASP(S)A 2007 Code of Practice, p 59.
28 ASP(S)A 2007 Code of Practice, p 59.
29 ASP(S)A 2007 Code of Practice, p 57.
30 ASP(S)A 2007, s 8(2).

refuses to answer questions, the local authority has no power to override the refusal and compel participation.[31] The concept of undue pressure (explained in Chapter 12) cannot be used in these circumstances (although consideration should be given to the appropriateness of an assessment order (see below) where such pressure is suspected[32]).

Medical examinations

8.6 In some cases, it will be desirable for a medical examination to take place, in particular, where the adult has suffered injuries that need to be treated. An examination might also provide evidence of harm that will help an application for a banning order or criminal prosecution.

The Adult Support and Protection (Scotland) Act 2007 provides that a health professional[33] visiting an adult with a council officer may examine anyone in the place who is believed to be an adult at risk.[34] The examination must be held in private. Although the Code of Practice is silent on the matter, it is suggested that similar considerations as to what may be considered 'private' apply to medical examinations as do to interviews (see above): with the exception that, of the persons carrying out the visit, it would appear that only the health professional carrying out the examination may be present. Of course, depending on its purpose, an examination may be more intrusive to the adult's privacy, and this fact must be taken into account in considering the appropriateness of any proposed supporter being present.

The adult has the right to refuse to consent to a medical examination and they must be informed of this before any medical examination takes place.[35]

The Code of Practice suggests that if an adult is not able to give informed consent to the medical examination, the local authority should establish whether there is a welfare attorney or guardian with relevant powers who may be able to consent on their behalf. If not, it suggests that consideration should be given to the use of the Adults with Incapacity (Scotland) Act 2000 or the Mental Health (Care and Treatment) (Scotland) Act 2003.[36] Further

31 ASP(S)A 2007, s 35(6).
32 ASP(S)A 2007 Code of Practice, p 59; and see further paras **8.7–8.12**.
33 This means a doctor, nurse or midwife. ASP(S)A 2007, s 52(2).
34 ASP(S)A 2007, s 9.
35 ASP(S)A 2007, s 9(2).
36 ASP(S)A 2007 Code of Practice, p 59.

discussion of the issues surrounding medical examination and treatment of individuals without capacity to consent is contained in Chapter 9.

Assessment orders

8.7 If it is not possible to interview or examine an adult at risk during a visit, the local authority can apply to the sheriff court for an assessment order. This authorises moving the adult to a specified place so that the interview or medical examination can take place.[37]

An assessment order may be appropriate if the local authority needs to establish if the person is an adult at risk and whether or not the local authority needs to take action (under the Adult Support and Protection (Scotland) Act 2007 or otherwise) to protect them from harm.[38]

Grounds for order

8.8 The Adult Support and Protection (Scotland) Act 2007, s 12 provides that a Sheriff may only grant an assessment order if satisfied that:

- there are reasonable grounds to suspect that the person is an adult at risk who is being, or is likely to be, seriously harmed;
- the order is necessary to establish this; and
- the place to which the adult will be moved is suitable and available. (This place could, for example, be a friend or relative's house or a care home, hospital or GP surgery. In light of the minimum necessary intervention principle, the place chosen should be that which is least disruptive for the adult, while still able to facilitate the interview or medical examination.)

In addition, the Sheriff must not grant the order if they know that the adult has refused to consent to it, unless they reasonably believe that the refusal is due to undue pressure being brought to bear on the adult.[39] The general requirement to ensure that any intervention is of benefit and the least restrictive option will mean that a Sheriff will also have to be satisfied that it is not possible to undertake the interview or examination envisaged without moving the adult to the place proposed.

[37] ASP(S)A 2007, s 11(1).
[38] ASP(S)A 2007, s 11(2).
[39] ASP(S)A 2007, s 35. The issues surrounding consent and undue pressure are considered in detail at para **12.20**.

It should be noted that the Sheriff must be satisfied that there are reasonable grounds to suspect a risk of 'serious harm' rather than 'harm'. This is required because the granting of a protection order is considered a serious intervention in an adult's life. There is no definition of 'serious harm' in the legislation, so an assessment will need to be made in individual cases. What constitutes serious harm may be different for different people.[40]

It is also noteworthy that the purposes of an assessment order stated in the Act (to establish if the person is an adult at risk and whether or not the local authority needs to take action) do not correspond exactly to the second criterion upon which a Sheriff must base the decision to grant an order (that the order is necessary to establish that the person is an adult at risk who is suffering, or is likely to suffer, serious harm).

The phrase 'necessary to establish' is important here and potentially rather limits the practical use of the order. It would appear that an assessment order may not be used solely to assess whether the local authority is required to take action (and what action it may take), but that there must remain some doubt that the adult has suffered or is likely to suffer serious harm, notwithstanding there being a reasonable belief that that is the case.

This problem may be illustrated by an example:

Example 8.1

An elderly adult is known to services as suffering from general physical frailty. He is cared for at home by his daughter, who owns the home. There are concerns that he may be losing capacity, but no formal diagnosis has been completed. Any attempt to assess the adult's capacity is frustrated by the daughter, who will not allow a psychiatrist to enter the home. A home support worker reports that the adult has stated that his daughter is taking money from him against his wishes and that it is making him upset and depressed. A visit under the Adult Support and Protection (Scotland) Act 2007 is carried out. The adult refuses to take part in an interview or undergo a medical examination which would establish whether or not he has capacity, stating he does not want to cause problems for his daughter, since she is the only family he has. The council officer leading the investigation feels that a capacity assessment is essential to any long-term protection plan, since guardianship may be necessary to protect and support the adult.

[40] For more on 'serious harm' see para **12.22**.

In this case, the issue of whether or not the adult has capacity is central to consideration of whether the local authority should take action under the Adults with Incapacity (Scotland) Act 2000. It might be suggested that, if the adult were taken to a safe place away from his daughter in terms of an assessment order, he would consent to being examined. He appears to be under undue pressure, so his lack of consent does not prevent the Sheriff granting the order.

Nonetheless, it is suggested that an assessment order would not be available. There are clearly reasonable grounds to suspect that the adult is an adult at risk who is likely to be seriously harmed. But in satisfying that criterion, it becomes impossible to show that the order is necessary to establish this. The capacity assessment is not relevant to the question of whether the adult is an adult at risk, since his physical frailty is sufficient in itself to bring him within that description.

Further, the distinction between *a reasonable belief* that an adult is *likely* to suffer serious harm and *it being established* that an adult is *likely* to suffer serious harm is not immediately apparent, due to the inherent uncertainty implied by the word *likely*. There is surely an argument that a reasonable belief that something is likely is the same as establishing that it is likely and the first and second criteria for the granting of an order therefore become mutually exclusive in such circumstances. This may prevent orders being granted in situations where matters have not yet reached the point where serious harm has actually been inflicted.

On the other hand, it is clear that the council does not have to have previously tried and failed to examine the person during the course of a visit. There may be circumstances, perhaps where an adult or carers are known to services, where the council officer will be aware that they will not be able to obtain access to the adult during the course of a visit. In such circumstances it might be pointless for the council officer to attempt to visit without an order.

Making the application

8.9 The local authority's legal department will generally make the application. The application follows the summary applications procedure. For court procedure, see Chapter 12.

Limits to powers

8.10 The adult cannot be compelled to participate in an interview or a medical examination even if they are thought to be under undue pressure (explained further at para **12.22**). Therefore, if it is known that the adult will refuse to participate, an assessment order might be of limited use (and therefore of questionable benefit to the adult) and the local authority should consider other formal and informal approaches. Where the adult lacks capacity, or requires treatment for a mental disorder, it may be possible to use other legislation.

An assessment order does not carry the power to detain the adult, who can choose to leave at any time.[41]

Impact of order

8.11 An assessment order is valid from the date specified in the order and must be used within seven days, after which it lapses.[42] The date specified does not count as one of the seven days and the seven-day limit therefore starts at midnight at the end of that date. The local authority continues to have a duty of care and so must provide reasonable assistance to allow the adult to return to the place from where they were removed, or another suitable place.

The adult must only be taken to the place specified on the order, but may agree to go to some other place (provided they have capacity to do so). The assessment should be carried out in the shortest time practicable, so as to minimise any possible distress or confusion to the adult.[43]

An anomaly in the legislation relates to the protection of the adult's property. When an adult is moved under a removal order, the local authority is under a duty to protect their property.[44] However, there is no corresponding legal obligation made explicit where the move is authorised by an assessment order. It is clearly good practice that steps be taken to protect property, nonetheless.

Where the Sheriff grants an assessment order, a warrant for entry is automatically attached to the order.[45]

Appeals

8.12 There is no appeal against the granting of, or the Sheriff's refusal to grant, an assessment order.[46]

41 ASP(S)A 2007 Code of Practice, p 77.
42 ASP(S)A 2007, s 11(3).
43 ASP(S)A 2007 Code of Practice, p 79.
44 ASP(S)A 2007, s 18.
45 ASP(S)A 2007, s 38(1).
46 ASP(S)A 2007, s 51(1).

Access to records

8.13 A council officer may require anyone holding health, financial or other records relating to someone whom they believe to be an adult at risk to make the records (or copies of them) available to them.[47]

The legislation does not prescribe the form a request should take, although if it is not made in the context of a visit, it must be in writing.[48] E-mail requests are permissible.[49]

The council officer should be able to demonstrate they are authorised to access records, and each local authority should have agreed procedures in place for obtaining and verifying authorisation.[50] This could involve specifying post holders at certain grades have authority to make requests (although, note that only a person that is a 'council officer' may validly make the request[51]).

Any other person the council officer considers appropriate can also inspect the records.[52]

Health records can only be inspected by a health professional.[53] They are defined as records relating to an individual's physical or mental health made by or on behalf of a health professional in connection with the care of the individual.[54] Records made, for example, by a psychologist or occupational therapist do not, at present, come within these rules, as such professions are not currently regarded as health professions for the purposes of the Adult Support and Protection (Scotland) Act 2007. They could be inspected, but it would not be necessary for a health professional to do this.

It is an offence to refuse or otherwise fail to comply with a request to make records available without reasonable excuse.[55] This is punishable by a fine not exceeding level 3 on the standard scale and/or three months' imprisonment. It is unlikely that criminal law would be used other than in highly exceptional circumstances. A reasonable belief that the person did not have appropriate authority is likely to be a legitimate defence. The Code of Practice anticipates that compulsion will be a last resort and states

47 ASP(S)A 2007, s 10.

48 ASP(S)A 2007, s 10(2), (3).

49 ASP(S)A 2007, s 10(6).

50 ASP(S)A 2007 Code of Practice, p 72.

51 ASP(S)A 2007, s 10(1). See the definition of 'council officer' at para **4.3**.

52 ASP(S)A 2007, s 10(4).

53 This means a doctor, nurse or midwife. ASP(S)A 2007, s 52(2).

54 ASP(S)A 2007, s 10(7).

55 ASP(S)A 2007, s 49(2).

that '[c]ouncils should make reasonable efforts to resolve disagreements when record holders refuse to disclose them. Informal or independent conciliation might be considered, depending on the circumstances and reasons given for refusal'.[56]

It is good practice for agreements to be reached with the record holder about the length of time records should be kept and how they are returned or destroyed. Local information sharing protocols, possibly with input or oversight from adult protection committees, may inform decisions around such matters.[57]

Chapter 13 discusses the confidentiality issues these provisions raise.

Outcome of inquiries

8.14 In some cases, the local authority's inquiries may suggest further action is needed. In other cases, no further action will be needed. In all cases proper recording is essential, because an accumulation of events may indicate that a concerning situation is worsening, or reveal the true nature of the risk to the adult in a way that a one-off investigation may not. If no further action is required, the local authority should place a note on the adult's case file on the circumstances giving rise to the initial inquiries, the action taken and why no further action was required.[58]

ADULTS WITH INCAPACITY (SCOTLAND) ACT 2000: INVESTIGATORY DUTIES

8.15 The Adults with Incapacity (Scotland) Act 2000 will be of relevance in cases where an adult is incapable of making some or all decisions about their welfare, medical matters, property or finances.[59] It imposes duties on the local authority to investigate and provides a regime for authorising such decisions. These remedies are discussed in Chapters 10 and 12.

Despite imposing a duty to investigate, there are no formal powers granted to the local authority to apply for warrants to take entry to premises, make records forthcoming, or require an adult believed to lack

56 ASP(S)A 2007 Code of Practice, p 73.

57 ASP(S)A 2007 Code of Practice, p 72. The same page of the Code of Practice indicates that a Protocol for Requesting Information under Section 10 was published by Social Work Scotland in 2020, to inform such local procedures.

58 ASP(S)A 2007 Code of Practice, p 50.

59 Adults with Incapacity (Scotland) Act 2000 (AWI(S)A 2000), s 1(6).

capacity to submit to a medical examination. Where actions of this type are considered necessary, the various options contained in other legislation (and described elsewhere in this chapter) will have to be explored.

Duty to investigate

8.16 The local authority has a general duty to investigate any circumstances where it appears to them that the personal welfare of an adult with incapacity is at risk.[60]

It must also investigate complaints about welfare attorneys, welfare guardians and people with welfare powers under intervention orders.[61] (Concerns about risk to the person's property and finances should be passed to the Public Guardian, see Chapter 7.)

The local authority should consult with the Public Guardian and/or the Mental Welfare Commission if they have an interest in the case.[62] These bodies are legally obliged to cooperate with the local authority.[63]

The *Adults with Incapacity (Scotland) Act 2000 Code of Practice* gives guidance on good practice.[64] The local authority should generally arrange to visit the adult, and must consider the principles of the Act when carrying out its investigations. Following its investigations, the local authority will consider whether it is necessary to make an application to the Sheriff to safeguard the property, financial affairs or personal welfare of the adult.[65] It should copy its investigation report to the Mental Welfare Commission.[66]

POWERS AND DUTIES UNDER MENTAL HEALTH (CARE AND TREATMENT) (SCOTLAND) ACT 2003

8.17 The Mental Health (Care and Treatment) (Scotland) Act 2003 can be relevant in adult protection, particularly in cases involving individuals with a mental disorder who are at risk of self-harm, abuse or neglect.

60 AWI(S)A 2000, s 10(1)(d).
61 AWI(S)A 2000, s 10(1)(c).
62 AWI(S)A 2000, s 10(1)(b).
63 AWI(S)A 2000, s 12(2).
64 *Code of practice for local authorities exercising functions under the Act* (Scottish Executive, 2008) (*Local Authority Code*), Ch 9.
65 AWI(S)A 2000, s 12(1).
66 *Local Authority Code*, para 9.26.

As well as giving local authorities clear powers and duties to investigate where someone with a mental disorder in their area may be at risk, the Act provides that, if necessary, a local authority can obtain a warrant to enter premises, to authorise a medical examination or to gain access to medical records. It can apply to move someone to hospital or a care home for assessment and medical examination.

Where an adult at risk has a mental disorder and may need medical treatment for the disorder, further intervention can be sought under the Mental Health (Care and Treatment) (Scotland) Act 2003 to provide care and treatment to them[67] (see Chapter 12). The Act also includes the possibility of criminal charges where a local authority is obstructed in an investigation.

Duty to inquire

8.18 The Act places a local authority under a clear duty to investigate where it believes that a person aged 16 or over has a mental disorder and may be at risk. The risk might be:

- ill-treatment, neglect or inadequate care (other than care in hospital), either currently or in the past;
- where someone appearing to be living alone or without care seems unable to look after themselves or their property or finances;
- to other people because of the person's mental disorder (unless they are already in hospital);
- loss or damage to the person's property because of their mental disorder.[68]

The local authority should bear in mind the principles of the Mental Health (Care and Treatment) (Scotland) Act 2003. It should not seek formal powers if a less restrictive alternative is available. It should try to involve the person at risk and any carers as far as possible when carrying out investigations and bear in mind the wishes of the person at risk.

The Act's Code of Practice gives further advice on how these powers should operate in practice.[69]

[67] Under Mental Health (Care and Treatment) (Scotland) Act 2003 (MH(CT)(S)A 2003), ss 36, 44 or 63.

[68] MH(CT)(S)A 2003, s 33.

[69] *Mental Health (Care and Treatment) (Scotland) Act 2003 Code of Practice* (MH(CT)(S)A 2003 Code of Practice), vol 1, Ch 15.

Cooperation with local authority

8.19 A wide range of bodies should cooperate with a local authority carrying out a Mental Health (Care and Treatment) (Scotland) Act 2003 investigation. These include the Mental Welfare Commission, the Public Guardian, the Care Inspectorate, Healthcare Improvement Scotland and any relevant health board.[70] These bodies must cooperate, except where the organisation believes that this would prejudice their other duties.[71]

Warrants for entry

8.20 If the local authority is unable to, or has reasons for believing it will be unable to, gain access to the adult, it can apply to a Sheriff or justice of the peace for a warrant to enter any premises for the purpose of its investigation.[72] The mental health officer generally makes the application.

A warrant authorises the mental health officer and anyone named in the warrant to enter the premises within eight days (the first day being the day of the granting of the warrant), and authorises a police constable accompanying the mental health officer to force entry.[73] Before granting such a warrant, the Sheriff or justice of the peace must have evidence on oath that the mental health officer is likely to be denied access.

If forced entry is used, the mental health officer must take steps to protect the person's premises and belongings.[74] The Code of Practice contains guidance to minimise the impact on the person.[75]

Medical examinations and access to records

8.21 The Mental Health (Care and Treatment) (Scotland) Act 2003 provides that a mental health officer can apply to a Sheriff or justice of the peace for a warrant to allow a medical practitioner to carry out a medical examination of an adult with a mental disorder who is believed to be at risk. The mental health officer must demonstrate that such an examination is necessary and that the adult involved will not consent.[76] This could be

[70] MH(CT)(S)A 2003, s 34.
[71] MH(CT)(S)A 2003, s 34(4).
[72] MH(CT)(S)A 2003, s 35.
[73] MH(CT)(S)A 2003, s 35(2).
[74] MH(CT)(S)A 2003 Code of Practice, vol 1, para 15.24.
[75] MH(CT)(S)A 2003 Code of Practice, vol 1, para 15.25.
[76] MH(CT)(S)A 2003, s 35(4).

either because the mental health officer has been unable to speak to the person or because the person has refused consent.

The application is to the Sheriff or justice for the area where the person is at the time the application is made.[77]

If the order is granted, it allows the adult to be detained for up to three hours so that a medical examination can take place. The three hours runs from the time of the detention, not the time of the warrant. The procedure should be in accordance with the local psychiatric emergency plan.[78] This examination can happen without the adult's consent.

Access to records

8.22 The mental health officer may apply for a warrant to allow access to someone's medical records.[79] The application is to the Sheriff or justice for the area where the person is living.

The mental health officer must satisfy the court that it is necessary for a doctor to see the records and the mental health officer cannot obtain the person's consent.[80]

If the court grants the warrant, any person who has the medical records must allow the doctor named in the warrant to inspect them.[81]

Making the application

8.23 A mental health officer may apply for all or any of the warrants.

For a warrant to enter premises, a mental health officer employed by the local authority where the premises are situated should make the application. For other warrants, the mental health officer must be an employee of the local authority conducting the inquiries.[82]

The mental health officer will be required to attend the hearing and to give evidence on oath.[83]

There are prescribed forms for the application and warrant.[84] These are available on the Scottish Government's mental health law website.

[77] MH(CT)(S)A 2003, s 35(6).
[78] MH(CT)(S)A 2003 Code of Practice, vol 1, para 15.28.
[79] MH(CT)(S)A 2003, s 35(7).
[80] MH(CT)(S)A 2003, s 35(7).
[81] MH(CT)(S)A 2003, s 35(8).
[82] MH(CT)(S)A 2003, s 35(12).
[83] MH(CT)(S)A 2003, s 35(1).
[84] Mental Health (Form of Documents) (Scotland) Regulations 2006 (SSI 2006/12).

As soon as possible after the hearing, the mental health officer must notify the Mental Welfare Commission of the outcome.[85]

It is not possible to appeal against the decision of the Sheriff or justice to grant or refuse a warrant.[86]

CHOICE OF PROCEDURES

8.24 There may be cases where it is not clear to a local authority whether to take action to investigate an adult's situation under adult protection, adults with incapacity or mental health legislation. The requirement to investigate under one legislative provision may become apparent only during an investigation conducted under another.

As with any situation where duties under various pieces of legislation overlap, it is important to ensure that legal duties imposed are complied with across the board: but that any duplication of efforts is avoided, wherever possible. This is particularly the case in regard to the interview or examination of adults at the centre of investigations, which should ideally only be required on one occasion.

On the other hand, the different Acts described provide a range of powers, some of which may be used interchangeably. It may be that the investigatory and other powers available under the Adult Support and Protection (Scotland) Act 2007 could be appropriately used in a particular case despite the adult's apparent incapacity or mental health issues and even though further long-term measures might be sought under other legislation. For example, the formal visiting powers in s 7 of the Act may provide sufficient authority to enable a council officer to gain access to the adult and others living with them. Under the principle of the least restrictive alternative, this would be preferable to seeking a warrant under the Mental Health (Care and Treatment) (Scotland) Act 2003. Conversely, the limitations in the use of assessment orders under the 2007 Act may be superseded by the use of powers under the 2003 Act, in appropriate circumstances.

It is suggested that all decisions about the appropriate use of legislation should be made on a case-by-case basis, bearing the principles of the various Acts in mind and using such powers as are appropriate to ensure all relevant information is obtained.

85 MH(CT)(S)A 2003, s 35(10).

86 MH(CT)(S)A 2003, s 35(11).

Table **8.1** contrasts the duties of the local authority to investigate the various types of risk an adult might experience and Table **8.2** summarises their investigatory powers.

Table 8.1 – Risk to be investigated

Act	Person at risk	Nature of risk
ASP(S)A	Person unable to safeguard interests At risk of harm Vulnerable because of disability, illness etc	Any form of harm (see Chapter 6)
AWI(S)A	Person with mental disorder (or person unable to communicate) unable to protect welfare/finances/property	Personal welfare Complaints about welfare attorney/guardian/person acting under intervention order Financial Harm (Referral to OPG)
MH(CT)(S)A	Person with mental disorder	Ill treatment/neglect/risk to property/finances Person living alone unable to protect welfare/property/ finances

Table 8.2 – Powers to investigate

Act	Powers given	Can adult refuse?
ASP(S)A	Visit Warrant for visit Medical examination Access to records Assessment order + warrant	Yes No Yes No Yes unless undue pressure
MH(CT)(S)A	Warrant for entry Warrant for medical examination Warrant for assessment Removal order	No No No No

CONCLUSION

8.25 The local authority has a number of statutory powers to investigate abuse or harm with, or without, the adult's consent. In some cases, a single piece of legislation will be used, while in others more than one will be necessary to achieve a positive result. It is important, where possible, to consider carefully the merits of using each piece of legislation. This will depend on issues such as the nature of the harm, the adult's ability and the desired outcome.

Chapter 9

EMERGENCIES

9.1 Ideally, any intervention where an adult is at risk would follow careful consideration of all the options and comprehensive discussion between the professionals involved. The adult and other interested parties would be fully consulted and have their opinions taken into account.

However, the reality is that detailed planning is not always possible and situations inevitably arise that need immediate action. This chapter examines the range of options available to deal with urgent situations.

ADULT SUPPORT AND PROTECTION (SCOTLAND) ACT 2007

9.2 The Adult Support and Protection (Scotland) Act 2007 anticipates that urgent action will sometimes be required to remove an adult at risk from a situation of harm or abuse.[1] Provision is made for emergency applications for either a warrant for entry to carry out a visit or a removal order.[2]

Where the local authority considers an order is needed within a short timescale, it can make an application to the sheriff court. This can normally be done within a matter of days. However, if the situation is very urgent, the local authority can apply to a justice of the peace at any time during the day or night.

Application to justice of the peace

9.3 Where the local authority makes an application to a justice of the peace for an emergency warrant for entry to carry out a visit or a removal order it must be able to demonstrate that:

1 The term 'adult at risk' is defined in the Adult Support and Protection (Scotland) Act 2007 (ASP(S)A 2007), s 3: see further Chapter 2.

2 Under the ASP(S)A 2007, s 40. Removal orders and warrants for entry are discussed in Chapter 12.

- it is not practical to apply to a Sheriff;
- the adult at risk is likely to be harmed if there is any delay in granting the order or warrant;[3] and
- the usual criteria for an order or warrant are, on the evidence available, met.[4]

A strict time limit of 12 hours is set within which an emergency order, or warrant for entry to carry out a visit, must be used.[5] This is to reflect the intent that they be used for urgent situations.

Involving the adult

9.4 Where an order is needed within a short timescale there may be less, or indeed no, opportunity to find out the adult's views and, in particular, whether or not they consent to the order. In some circumstances, the adult's views might be known because there have been previous investigations. However, this will not always be the case, and if the local authority does not know the adult's views, it should be prepared to explain to the justice of the peace the reasons why these cannot be obtained.

Where emergency orders are granted, there might still be a difficulty if the adult refuses to comply. This is because the requirement to respect the adult's wishes applies to both the granting, and the exercise, of the order. Therefore, any council officer acting under an order must respect the adult's refusal unless they believe there has been undue pressure. This might be difficult to determine in urgent situations.

Another reason for careful consideration of an order where an adult is not likely to accept help is that the orders give no right of detention, even where undue pressure can be established. This means they are of limited use where the adult is likely to be resistant and unwilling to accept any help. However, where there is a reason to believe the adult would accept help if removed from a specific situation, an order might still be appropriate.

3 ASP(S)A 2007, s 40(2).

4 ASP(S)A 2007, s 15(1) (removal order) and s 38(2) (warrant for entry).

5 ASP(S)A 2007, s 40(7) and (8).

Temporary banning order

9.5 Another option available in an emergency is an application for a temporary banning order. This means a temporary order can be put in place while the application for a full banning order is considered.[6]

The purpose of any banning order is to ban the person believed to be causing harm from a specific place or places to prevent future harm. Banning orders can also include specific conditions and are discussed further at para **12.31**. Temporary orders may include any provision which could be included in a banning order.[7]

Banning orders, and, by extension, temporary banning orders, are different to the other orders available under the Act, as applications are not restricted to local authorities. An adult at risk, as well as anyone living in the place to which an application relates, may apply.[8]

Using the emergency measures

9.6 The emergency procedures of the Adult Support and Protection (Scotland) Act 2007 are most likely to be used where an adult is believed to be at risk of harm if immediate action is not taken and:

- there are reasonable grounds to believe that access will be obstructed by a third party;
- the adult is believed to be under undue pressure and it is thought they may cooperate if moved from the harmful situation; or
- there are reasonable grounds to believe the adult is at risk of harm and lacks capacity to take decisions about their welfare. In such cases, access to the adult might be needed to allow the position to be determined.

ADULTS WITH INCAPACITY (SCOTLAND) ACT 2000

9.7 The Adults with Incapacity (Scotland) Act 2000 is generally less useful than other legislation in emergencies. This is because the procedures are more complicated and preparation for an order takes time. However, in some cases, interim guardianship might be a useful option.

6 ASP(S)A 2007, s 21.
7 ASP(S)A 2007, s 21.
8 ASP(S)A 2007, s 22.

Interim guardianship

9.8 When an application is made to the sheriff court for the appointment of a guardian, it can include a request for the appointment of an interim guardian.[9] An interim (or temporary) appointment lasts until a permanent guardian is appointed, or until such period as is specified in the order has passed, whichever happens first.[10] The Sheriff may specify an effective period of up to six months. If no period is specified, the order will last for up to three months.[11]

The application still needs to be submitted with two medical certificates, as well as a report from a mental health officer. Where the powers sought are solely financial, a report from someone with financial expertise replaces the mental health officer's report.[12]

An interim guardian can be appointed with some, or all, of the powers requested in the full application. For example, the interim guardian could be given the power to decide where an adult lives pending consideration of the full application. This could allow the adult to be moved from a situation of harm in the short term.

An important advantage of using an interim guardianship order is that the guardian has a continuing power to make decisions about the adult's welfare and life. This can be useful where an adult lacks capacity and refuses to consent to any intervention. It allows the guardian to consent on their behalf, provided the power to do so has been granted. However, the guardian would obviously need to have regard to the general principles,[13] including taking account of the adult's views, as well as respecting the adult's human rights.[14]

The Act can also be used to authorise medical treatment using the procedure set out in Part 5 of the Act. This is discussed further below.

This Act is not appropriate in all adult protection cases. It can be used only when dealing with adults who, because of mental disorder (or, rarely, communication difficulties) lack the capacity to make some or all of their own decisions[15] or to safeguard or promote their interests (or where there are reasonable grounds to believe that this is the case).

9 Adults with Incapacity (Scotland) Act 2000 (AWI(S)A 2000), s 57.

10 AWI(S)A 2000, s 57(6).

11 AWI(S)A 2000, s 57(6A).

12 AWI(S)A 2000, s 57(3).

13 See Chapter 5 for details of the general principles.

14 Powers of guardians to detain or restrain are considered in the human rights context in Chapter 14.

15 As defined in the AWI(S)A 2000, s 1(6).

The need to obtain reports means that guardianship and intervention orders inevitably take time, so are not of use in very urgent situations. The Adults with Incapacity (Scotland) Act 2000 is most likely to be relevant where:

- the situation involves an adult with incapacity and requires action within days or weeks rather than hours; and
- the adult lacks capacity and is not likely to agree voluntarily to leave a harmful situation. In such a case, guardianship or an intervention order can be sought instead of, or following, a removal order; or
- an incapable adult requires immediate medical treatment (see below). However, the Act cannot authorise the adult's admission to a psychiatric hospital against their will.[16]

At the time of writing the Scottish Government is consulting on changes to the Act, including new provisions for interim guardianship. One proposal is that an application for interim guardianship could be made independently from an application for a full order. This might involve abbreviated reports and prescribed timescales for decisions.[17]

MENTAL HEALTH (CARE AND TREATMENT) (SCOTLAND) ACT 2003

9.9 The Mental Health (Care and Treatment) (Scotland) Act 2003 provides a framework for the care and treatment of people with a mental disorder. It can be used to authorise urgent investigations or action and may be relevant in some adult protection cases where the adult involved has a mental disorder and falls within its terms.

The Mental Health (Care and Treatment) (Scotland) Act 2003 gives the local authority a duty to investigate possible harm and abuse to a person with a mental disorder.[18] If it is refused entry, or has reasonable grounds to believe this may happen, a Sheriff or justice of the peace can grant a warrant for entry.[19] This allows a council officer to attend with the police, who can use reasonable force to gain entry. A warrant in these terms can

16 AWI(S)A 2000, s 47(7).

17 The Adults with Incapacity Amendment Act Consultation (July 2024) (www.gov.scot), p 50.

18 Mental Health (Care and Treatment) (Scotland) Act 2003 (MH(CT)(S)A 2003), s 33. This is discussed further in Chapter 8.

19 MH(CT)(S)A 2003, s 35. See Chapter 8.

be obtained at very short notice and so this can be useful in emergencies to assess situations of harm or abuse.

Removal orders

9.10 Removal orders available under the Mental Health (Care and Treatment) (Scotland) Act 2003[20] are somewhat different from those available under the Adult Support and Protection (Scotland) Act 2007. A removal order under the Mental Health (Care and Treatment) (Scotland) Act 2003 allows a mental health officer to attend with the police and remove the adult to a place of safety.[21] A removal order does not authorise the giving of medical treatment to the person.

Making the application

9.11 The application is to the sheriff court for the place from which the person at risk is to be removed.[22] In an emergency, a justice of the peace may grant an order.[23] The mental health officer making the application should be an employee of the local authority for the place from which the person at risk is to be removed.[24] A statutory form is used to make the application[25] and is available on the Scottish Government's mental health law website.[26]

The mental health officer must satisfy the Sheriff that the person is aged over 16 and has a mental disorder, that they are likely to suffer significant harm if they do not go to a place of safety, and that at least one of the following applies:

- they are subject or exposed to ill-treatment, neglect or inadequate care;
- their property is suffering loss or damage, or is at risk of suffering loss or damage, because of their mental disorder; or

20 Under MH(CT)(S)A 2003, s 293.

21 MH(CT)(S)A 2003, s 293(3)(c).

22 MH(CT)(S)A 2003, s 293(4).

23 MH(CT)(S)A 2003, s 294.

24 MH(CT)(S)A 2003, s 293(8).

25 Under the Mental Health (Form of Documents) (Scotland) Regulations 2006 (SSI 2006/12).

26 www.gov.scot/publications/mental-health-law-forms/

- they are living alone or without care and unable to look after themselves or their property or finances.[27]

The Sheriff may dispense with a hearing if they consider this would cause delay likely to prejudice the interests of the person at risk.[28]

Effect of order

9.12 A removal order authorises the mental health officer and anyone named in the order to enter the place specified within 72 hours of the making of the order. A police officer may accompany them and may use reasonable force to gain access. The person can be taken to a place of safety (see below) within 72 hours of the order.

Unlike an Adult Support and Protection (Scotland) Act 2007 order, a person subject to a Mental Health (Care and Treatment) (Scotland) Act 2003 removal order can be detained under this order. The detention can last for up to seven days, as specified in the order.[29] In line with the principles of the Act, if less than seven days is sufficient, the mental health officer should apply for a shorter period.

Appeal

9.13 There is no appeal against the Sheriff or justice's decision to make or refuse to make a removal order,[30] but the person subject to the order and anyone with an interest may apply for a variation or recall.

The mental health officer should notify all relevant parties of the outcome of the application and advise them of their rights to apply for variation or recall. The mental health officer should also notify the Mental Welfare Commission of the making of the order, or if the application is refused.[31]

Place of safety

9.14 The removal order will specify the address of the place of safety to which the person is to be taken. The place of safety should be a hospital, a

27 MH(CT)(S)A 2003, s 293(1), (2).
28 MH(CT)(S)A 2003, s 293(7).
29 MH(CT)(S)A 2003, s 293(3).
30 MH(CT)(S)A 2003, s 296.
31 MH(CT)(S)A 2003, s 295A.

care home service[32] or any other suitable place.[33] A police station may not be used as a place of safety.

An accident and emergency department is not a suitable place, unless the person has significant physical health problems, perhaps because of self-harm. A place of safety should have qualified mental health staff. It should generally be a specialist assessment unit linked to, or with access to, a psychiatric hospital or clinic.[34] Unlike the removals under the Adult Support and Protection (Scotland) Act 2007, the Mental Health (Care and Treatment) (Scotland) Act 2003 does not envisage the use of private homes for removal orders, and this would not be suitable where someone is to be detained under the order.

Cancellation or variation of removal order

9.15 A person subject to a removal order and any person with an interest in their welfare may apply to a Sheriff (not a justice of the peace) to set the order aside or to move the person to a different place.[35]

As with the original application, the correct statutory form should be used and is accessible on the Scottish Government's website.[36] It should be submitted to the sheriff court for the area from which the person was moved.[37]

The Sheriff must give the relevant people a chance to make representations and to lead or produce evidence. These people are the person subject to the removal order, the mental health officer who applied for the order, the nearest relative of the person, any guardian or welfare attorney of the person and the person's primary carer.[38] The Sheriff cannot dispense with this requirement on grounds of urgency.[39]

If the Sheriff cancels the order, they may order the local authority to return the person to the place from where they were removed or to another suitable place chosen by the person.[40]

32 As defined in Public Services Reform (Scotland) Act 2010, Sch 12 para 2.

33 MH(CT)(S)A 2003, s 300.

34 *Mental Health (Care and Treatment) (Scotland) Act 2003 Code of Practice*, vol 1, para 15.86.

35 MH(CT)(S)A 2003, s 295.

36 www.gov.scot/publications/mental-health-law-forms/

37 MH(CT)(S)A 2003, s 295(3).

38 Mental Health (Recall or Variation of Removal Order) (Scotland) Regulations 2006 (SSI 2006/11).

39 MH(CT)(S)A 2003, s 295(4)–(5).

40 MH(CT)(S)A 2003, s 295(6).

It is not possible to appeal against a Sheriff's decision to cancel or vary a removal order or to refuse to do so.[41] As with the original grant of a removal order, the mental health officer should notify the Mental Welfare Commission of any decision in relation to recall or variation (including refusal).[42]

POLICE POWER TO REMOVE AND DETAIN

9.16 The police also have a power to remove a person with a mental disorder from a public place to a place of safety, where they appear to be in immediate need of care or treatment, provided they think this is in that person's interests or necessary for the protection of another person.[43] The person can be detained for up to 24 hours to allow a medical examination to be carried out, or for other arrangements for their care or treatment to be made.

Emergency detention

9.17 Even in an emergency, it may be possible to arrange for a psychiatrist and mental health officer to see a patient and arrange their short-term detention in hospital. This is often the preferred route because of the safeguards for patients.

However, there may be situations where a doctor believes that using these provisions will cause undue delay and that emergency detention is necessary. A registered medical practitioner can sign an emergency detention certificate if, after carrying out a medical examination, they believe that a person's ability to make decisions about medical treatment is significantly impaired because of a mental disorder.[44] This authorises the removal of the individual to a specified hospital, if they are not already in a hospital, and for their detention there for up to 72 hours.[45]

Before signing a certificate the medical practitioner must be satisfied that:

- there is an urgent need to detain the person in hospital to assess the medical treatment they need;

41 MH(CT)(S)A 2003, s 296.
42 MH(CT)(S)A 2003, s 295A.
43 MH(CT)(S)A 2003, s 297.
44 MH(CT)(S)A 2003, s 36(3)(b).
45 MH(CT)(S)A 2003, s 36(8).

- if the person was not detained, there would be a significant risk to their health, safety or welfare, or the safety of any other person; and
- any delay caused by starting the short-term detention procedure is undesirable.[46]

However, an emergency detention certificate does not authorise any medical treatment. If any treatment is needed the short-term detention procedure must be used. The other options for detention are discussed further in Chapter 12.[47]

MEDICAL TREATMENT

9.18 In some cases, an adult may require immediate medical attention. For example, they might have significant physical injuries or need treatment following an overdose.

If the adult has capacity, medical treatment cannot be carried out without their express consent. The concept of undue pressure under the Adult Support and Protection (Scotland) Act 2007 does not apply to a refusal to consent to medical treatment.[48]

However, there will be some situations where it is not possible to obtain consent because the adult is unconscious or otherwise lacks capacity to make such decisions. In such circumstances, a medical practitioner may treat the patient under the general authority in the Adults with Incapacity (Scotland) Act 2000.[49] A doctor relying on the general authority to treat must issue a certificate in the prescribed form.[50] Other health professionals, including dentists, opticians and registered nurses, may sign certificates for treatment within their area of expertise, provided they have undergone prescribed training on assessing capacity.[51]

The certificate can cover a specific treatment, such as an operation, or a range of treatments, as set out in a treatment plan. A treatment plan avoids

46 MH(CT)(S)A 2003, s 36(3)(c).

47 For a comprehensive guide to detention under the MH(CT)(S)A 2003 see Hilary Patrick and Jill Stavert, *Mental Health, Incapacity and the Law in Scotland* (2nd edn, Bloomsbury Professional, 2016, new edn forthcoming 2025).

48 ASP(S)A 2007, s 35. A medical examination or treatment without consent may constitute an assault.

49 AWI(S)A 2000, s 47(1).

50 The form is on the Scottish Government's website: www.gov.scot/publications/section-47-certificate.

51 AWI(S)A 2000, s 47(1A).

the need for excessive certification for an adult with various predictable health care needs.[52]

The general authority does not allow the use of force or detention, other than in an emergency[53] or the admission of an adult to hospital for psychiatric treatment against their will.[54] Treatment for a mental disorder may be authorised by the Mental Health (Care and Treatment) (Scotland) Act 2003.[55]

Where a guardian or attorney has been appointed, they should be asked for consent, where practicable. However, the statutory certificate must still be completed, as it is the completed certificate that provides the authority to treat rather than the consent of another person. Where a guardian or attorney disagrees with proposals for medical treatment, the decision can be referred to an independent medical practitioner and, ultimately, to the Court of Session. The Mental Welfare Commission can provide additional information about this procedure.

If there is no time to complete a certificate due to an imminent threat to the adult of death or significant injury, medical treatment may still be carried out in terms of the common law doctrine of necessity. The treatment provided must be restricted to that which is necessary to avert the serious risk envisaged. It must also be reasonably likely that consent would be granted to the procedure by a reasonable person, and by the adult themselves, insofar as their wishes may be known or inferred. In this regard, any formal advance statement made by the adult may be relevant. Chapter 10 gives further consideration to such statements. Should it become possible during the course of a procedure to complete a certificate (for example, during a point where the patient is being prepared for surgery) this should be done.[56]

There is no specific authority to convey a person to hospital where they lack the capacity to make that decision. It is generally considered that the common law principle of necessity would allow this to happen. In addition, section 47 gives the medical practitioner 'authority to do what is reasonable in the circumstances, in relation to the medical treatment in question, to safeguard or promote the physical or mental health of the adult'. At the time of writing, the Scottish Government is consulting

52 See *Adults with Incapacity (Scotland) Act 2000 Part 5 Code of Practice* (AWI(S)A 2000 Part 5 Code of Practice) (Scottish Executive, 2002), paras 2.17–2.25.

53 AWI(S)A 2000, s 47(7)(a).

54 AWI(S)A 2000, s 47(7)(c).

55 See Chapter 12 further on compulsory treatment.

56 AWI(S)A 2000 Part 5 Code of Practice, para 2.41.

on changes to section 47 to explicitly allow the medical practitioner to authorise the person to be conveyed to hospital.[57]

CONCLUSION

9.19 The law provides a range of options allowing for interventions in urgent or emergency situations. In many cases, it will be clear which is the most appropriate provision to use. For example, if an adult needs urgent medical treatment for a mental disorder and refuses consent, use of the Mental Health (Care and Treatment) (Scotland) Act 2003 may be appropriate.

In other cases, a combination of measures might be used. A temporary banning order in terms of the Adult Support and Protection (Scotland) Act 2007 may provide a stable enough home situation to allow medical and other assessments in relation to a potential application for guardianship to be completed.

Clearly where urgent action is taken there is often less opportunity to explore the options with the adult and seek consent. However, it is vital that the adult is as fully involved in decisions as possible and that they are given the opportunity to contribute to ongoing decisions about their personal or financial welfare.

57 The Adults with Incapacity Amendment Act Consultation (July 2024) (www.gov.scot), p 43.

Chapter 10

SUPPORTING THE ADULT

10.1 Where an adult is experiencing abuse or harm, it is important to consider how best to provide support at the same time as, or instead of, using court powers. Some of these supports are specifically provided for by legislation.

This chapter provides an introduction to the ways in which adults can be supported. This is a crucial part of making sure the adult's views are known and considered. It may also improve the likelihood of the adult avoiding situations of harm and abuse in the longer term. The Code of Practice states that 'the adult's views and wishes are central to adult support and protection, and every effort should be made at each stage of the process to ensure that barriers to the adult's participation are minimised'.[1] Over recent years there has been a move towards using supported decision making processes rather than the more traditional substitute decision making models. There is no legal definition of 'supported decision making' but the central concept is that people should always be supported to make their own decisions. Any action, or decision not to act, should genuinely reflect the person's choices.[2]

The provisions of the Vulnerable Witnesses (Scotland) Act 2004 include specific support to give evidence in court. These are explained at para **12.53**.

INDEPENDENT ADVOCACY

10.2 Independent advocates help those who have difficulty understanding situations, or telling others what they think. The advocacy worker finds out an individual's views and makes sure these are properly expressed and taken into account.

1 *Adult Support and Protection (Scotland) Act 2007 Code of Practice* (ASP(S)A 2007 Code of Practice) (July 2022), p 39.

2 *Support decision making: Good Practice Guide* (Mental Welfare Commission, 2021).

An individual might struggle to participate in decisions about their life for a number of reasons. They may lack the confidence or ability to express their views or find it difficult to ask for the information they need about the options available. This can particularly be the case for individuals who are not used to being asked what they think or having their opinions taken seriously.

An individual may also feel inhibited or pressured by other people to provide specific responses. This can happen even when the person they are dealing with is trying to help. An independent advocate will make sure the adult's views are heard and that the adult has the information they need to make an informed choice.

The consequences of not involving and consulting adults in decisions can include frustration for all involved, as well as creating a lack of confidence in the system. This may in turn, reduce the prospects of achieving a satisfactory outcome. Therefore, the role of the independent advocate can be vital. The Code of Practice is clear that there should be an assumption that adults are involved in meetings about them. It further suggests that where adults are not present then the reasons for this should be clearly recorded in the minutes.[3]

Some advocacy is provided by people who know the adult or by volunteers. This is often referred to as citizen or peer advocacy. Professional advocacy involves the use of paid and trained advocacy workers. Group advocacy refers to situations where people with similar issues get together to support each other to express their views, often with the help of a facilitator. Self-advocacy involves building the capacity of individuals to speak for themselves. In some cases, the adult might lack capacity to convey their views or feelings to an advocate. However, the advocate can still seek to ensure rights are upheld and decisions are taken with full consideration of the adult's preferences and perspectives. This is often referred to as 'non-instructed advocacy'.

In September 2022, the *Scottish Mental Health Review Final Report* was published. The Scottish Government issued a response identifying seven high level priorities for action in 2023–26 including 'identifying and addressing gaps in the provision of independent advocacy'.[4]

3 ASP(S)A 2007 Code of Practice, p 43.

4 *Scottish Mental Health Review: Our Response* (Scottish Government, June 2023). The *Scottish Mental Health Review* was published in September 2022.

Legal right to advocacy

10.3 The Mental Health (Care and Treatment) (Scotland) Act 2003 states that 'every person with a mental disorder shall have a right of access to independent advocacy'.[5] Health boards and local authorities have a duty to work together to secure the provision of independent advocacy. There is also a duty to take appropriate steps to make sure individuals have the opportunity to use such services.

Advocacy services are defined as being 'services of support and representation made available for the purpose of enabling the person to whom they are available to have as much control of, or capacity to influence their care and welfare, as is, in the circumstances, appropriate'.[6] An advocacy service is considered to be independent where it is not involved with the welfare, care or provision of other services to the person for whom it provides advocacy. It should also be provided by an organisation whose sole role is independent advocacy or whose other tasks either complement, or do not conflict with, the provision of independent advocacy.[7] This would not include informal arrangements where a friend or family member provides support to express views.

The Mental Health (Scotland) Act 2015 updated the legislation to include a duty on local authorities and health boards to provide information to the Mental Welfare Commission on how they have exercised their duties in relation to the provision of advocacy as well as how they intend to exercise these duties in future.[8]

The right to access advocacy services, and the corresponding duty to provide these services, is not restricted to individuals subject to compulsory measures under the Act. In a sense, the right and duty are freestanding. Everyone with a mental disorder (mental illness, learning disability or personality disorder) is entitled to access independent advocacy, regardless of which piece of legislation is being considered, and indeed, when no legislative intervention is being considered at all.

A local authority should be able to provide information about the services available in its area. The Scottish Independent Advocacy Alliance also produces useful information about advocacy.[9]

5 Mental Health (Care and Treatment) (Scotland) Act 2003 (MH(CT)(S)A 2003), s 259(1).

6 MH(CT)(S)A 2003, s 259(4).

7 MH(CT)(S)A 2003, s 259(5) and *Mental Health (Scotland) Act Code of Practice*, paras 108–110.

8 MH(CT)(S)A 2003, s 276A (inserted by the Mental Health (Scotland) Act 2015).

9 See www.siaa.org.uk

Adult Support and Protection (Scotland) Act 2007

10.4 Under the Adult Support and Protection (Scotland) Act 2007, local authorities are required to 'have regard to the importance of the provision of appropriate services (including, in particular, independent advocacy services)' to the adult concerned.[10] The Code of Practice advises that the adult should be asked if they know about and would like advocacy. Where the adult declines advocacy or it is not considered appropriate the reasons for this should be clearly recorded. The decision should also be revisited at formal reviews.[11]

The extent of the obligation 'to consider' the provision of advocacy has not been tested and it is doubtful if this creates an enforceable legal right. However, if an adult has a mental disorder, they have an automatic right to access advocacy services under the Mental Health (Care and Treatment) (Scotland) Act 2003. This means that in cases involving adults with a mental disorder the duty on local authorities goes beyond simply having regard to the importance of advocacy services. That said, the meaning of having a 'right to access' is not entirely clear. For example, it might be argued that being referred or placed on a waiting list would satisfy this right, even if the service has not actually been delivered.

Advocacy and the principles

10.5 The general principles of all the adult protection legislation include a duty to consult the adult and take account of their wishes.[12] The provision of independent advocacy can have an important role in this process.

There may also be a duty to provide access to advocacy where someone whose views must be considered has a mental disorder. This could be a friend, family member or other person with an interest in the affairs of the adult involved.

10 Adult Support and Protection (Scotland) Act 2007 (ASP(S)A 2007), s 6(2).

11 ASP(S)A 2007 Code of Practice, p 42.

12 Adults with Incapacity (Scotland) Act 2000, s 1(4)(a), MH(CT)(S)A 2003, s 1(3)(a) and ASP(S)A 2007, s 2(b). See Chapter 3.

COMMUNITY CARE SERVICES

10.6 Each local authority has duties to provide community and residential care services for those living within its area. The law relating to such services is lengthy and largely outside the scope of this book.

However, it is relevant, as a local authority may have a duty to carry out a community care assessment and provide services as well as, or in place of, an adult protection intervention.

In some instances the local authority will charge for the provision of community care services on the basis that the recipient can afford to pay.[13] The Scottish Government have produced national guidance on charging for residential accommodation.[14] However, the position varies and a copy of the charging policy should be requested from the relevant local authority in individual cases.

Community care assessments

10.7 The Social Work (Scotland) Act 1968 creates a duty on each local authority to assess the needs of any person living within its area who appears to require community care services.[15] In many instances, individuals subject to adult protection investigations or measures will have a need for such services.

In the first instance, the local authority must carry out a formal community care assessment identifying the person's needs. The local authority then records how it intends to meet that need.

A community care assessment should take place along with any adult protection measures. In some cases, the provision of such services may reduce or prevent harm or abuse. For example, services to assist an individual diagnosed with dementia to remain safely at home may remove the need for them to be moved.

The Social Care (Self-directed Support) (Scotland) Act 2013 gives individuals a wider range of choice about how services are to be provided, and those needing services should be fully advised of the options. There is more information about this in Chapter 2.

13 Guidance for charging for community care can be found on the COSLA website (www.cosla.gov.uk/) under 'Social Care Charging Information'.

14 CCD1/2014 – *Revised Guidance on Charging for Residential Accommodation* (www.scot.nhs.uk).

15 Social Work (Scotland) Act 1968, s 12A.

Carers (Scotland) Act 2016

10.8 Unpaid carers have a right to have their own support needs identified under the Carers (Scotland) Act 2016. A 'carer' is defined as an 'individual who provides, or intends to provide, care for another individual'.[16] There is no requirement for care provided, or to be provided, to be regular or substantial. The inclusion of people who are anticipating providing care recognises the need for a preventative and anticipatory approach. For example, in situations where the adult has new, or increased, care needs following a change in their physical or intellectual capacity. Adult carers are entitled to an Adult Carer Support Plan (ACSP) and those under 18 are entitled to a Young Carer Statement. These assessments can be requested at any time and can be carried out independently of any community care assessment.[17]

There are no national eligibility criteria for services with each local authority responsible for setting their own, after consulting interested parties.[18] The plan includes information about identified needs. The local authority must then look at those needs and come to a decision on eligibility. Local authorities are also required to develop local carer strategies.[19]

Charges cannot be made for support provided for carers.[20] However, if following the assessment, the support is actually provided to the cared for person then charges can be made in terms of the local authority's charging policy.

In terms of adult protection, a carer's assessment will be relevant where harm is the result of the carer struggling, physically, mentally or emotionally, to cope with caring responsibilities. An assessment of needs and subsequent provision of services may help the carer to cope and allow the relationship to continue, for example, with provision of breaks from caring responsibilities. It may also help where someone is considering whether they can take on more caring duties to support an adult to stay at home. As part of the ACSP or Young Carer Statement the local authority must assess if the carer is able and willing to provide care.[21]

16 Carers (Scotland) Act 2016, s 1(1).

17 Carers (Scotland) Act 2016, ss 6(2) and 12(2). A young carer is a carer under the age of 18 (or over the age of 18 but still at school).

18 Carers (Scotland) Act 2016, s 21.

19 Carers (Scotland) Act 2016, s 31.

20 Carers (Waiving of Charges for Support) (Scotland) Regulations 2014 (SSI 2014/65).

21 Carers (Scotland) Act 2016, ss 9(1)(b) and 15(1)(b).

Services under Chronically Sick and Disabled Persons Act 1970

10.9 Under this Act, a local authority must arrange to provide specific services if it assesses a disabled person in its area as needing them.[22] The services include practical help at home, meals, telephone equipment, home adaptations and help with transport to services.

When an intervention is made in an adult protection case and the adult falls within the terms of this Act, a formal assessment may be required. Where an individual is being assessed under other legislation, such as the Social Work (Scotland) Act 1968, and it becomes apparent they fall within the terms of the 1970 Act, a disabled person's assessment should be carried out.

Mental Health (Care and Treatment) (Scotland) Act 2003

10.10 This Act places a duty on local authorities to provide care and support services for individuals with a mental disorder living in their area.[23] These are services to minimise the effect of the mental disorder and to allow the person to lead a life that is as normal as possible.[24]

There is a further duty on local authorities to provide services that promote the well-being and social development of those with a mental disorder residing in their area. These services include social, cultural and recreational activities, as well as training and assistance in obtaining employment for those over school age.[25]

Where adult protection measures are being considered in relation to an adult with a mental disorder, it may be necessary for the local authority to consider providing services under this Act.

22 Chronically Sick and Disabled Persons Act 1970, s 2(1), as amended by the Chronically Sick and Disabled Persons (Scotland) Act 1972 and the Disabled Persons (Services, Consultation and Representation) Act 1986.

23 MH(CT)(S)A 2003, s 25. Under s 25(3), this includes residential accommodation and personal care and support services (as defined by the Social Work (Scotland) Act 1968, s 59(1)).

24 MH(CT)(S)A 2003, s 25(2).

25 MH(CT)(S)A 2003, s 26. See Chapter 11 for the definition of 'school age'.

Free personal and nursing care

10.11 In 2002, free personal care was introduced for everyone in Scotland over the age of 65 assessed as needing such care. On 1 April 2019, this right was extended to everyone in Scotland regardless of age. In addition, free nursing care is available to individuals of any age, regardless of income or capital.[26] The rules apply to people living in their own homes and to those in residential care or nursing homes. Local authorities can still charge for care that does not fall within the definition of personal care.

Personal care includes care that relates to the day-to-day physical needs of the person. It also covers care in relation to the mental processes related to those needs and tasks.[27] Eating and washing are examples of physical tasks, while remembering to eat is an example of a mental process. This test could also cover a person with short-term memory loss who is at risk when using a cooker or someone with depression who lacks the motivation to cook.

The provision of free personal or nursing care may be of relevance in adult protection cases, where an individual is unable to care for themselves in appropriate ways. The provision of support following an assessment may often be the most appropriate intervention. Where an adult is moving into residential care an application for free personal and/or nursing care is normally made.

Provision of suitable housing

10.12 The Housing (Scotland) Act 1987 places local authorities under a duty to provide housing. They have particular duties to those who may be considered homeless in terms of the legislation.[28] In some cases, an adult will be suffering harm or abuse in their home. This might mean that they are unable to return home, particularly when the individual causing the harm continues to reside there.

In some cases, there will be a need to find the adult alternative accommodation in the short term. In addition, where there are no

[26] Community Care and Health (Scotland) Act 2002, s 1(1), as amended by the Community Care (Personal Care and Nursing Care) (Scotland) Amendment (No 2) Regulations 2018 (SSI 2018/200).

[27] Public Services Reform (Scotland) Act 2010, Sch 12, para 20. Types of social care that should not be charged for are listed in the Community Care and Health (Scotland) Act 2022, Sch 1.

[28] Housing (Scotland) Act 1987, ss 31 and 32.

reasonable prospects of the adult returning home, they might need permanent re-housing. In these circumstances, the individual could be considered to be homeless, and this creates a legal duty on the local authority to provide housing.

FINANCIAL SUPPORT AND ADVICE

10.13 An adult might need financial advice or support for many reasons. They may have suffered financial abuse or be leaving a relationship in which finances were dealt with jointly. Any change in living arrangements may have consequences for welfare benefits. In such cases, assistance from a welfare rights officer,[29] the Citizens Advice Bureau[30] or other money advice agency might be needed. Some of the ways to provide financial support are set out below. Formal court applications for guardianship orders are looked at in Chapter 12. Dealing with financial harm and abuse is dealt with in detail in Chapter 7.

Appointees

10.14 Where a person is unable to manage their welfare benefits, the Department for Work and Pensions (DWP) can appoint someone to manage them for them.[31] The person who is appointed is normally referred to as an 'appointee'.

Before the appointee system is used, it is necessary to have evidence that the person cannot manage their own affairs.[32] In order to assess this, a representative of the DWP will visit the claimant and proposed appointee. The representative may request further medical evidence where there are any doubts about the adult's capacity, or this is considered necessary for another reason. The appointee receives the benefits and manages these for the adult. This can include welfare benefits, housing and council tax benefits, as well as tax and pension credits. If the DWP has accepted someone as an appointee, the local authority and HM Revenue & Customs

29 Local authorities can provide information about services in their area or visit www.rascot.co.uk/local-advice

30 www.cas.org.uk

31 For more details, see 'Become an appointee for someone claiming benefits' at www.gov.uk

32 Social Security (Claims and Payments) Regulations 1987 (SI 1987/1968), reg 33, Housing Benefit (General) Regulations 1987 (SI 1987/1971), reg 71(3), Council Tax Benefit (General) Regulations 1992 (SI 1992/1814), reg 61(3).

normally recognise the appointment. The appointee is responsible for reporting any changes in the adult's financial, or other, circumstances.

Where the sole source of an adult's income is welfare benefits, the appointee system may avoid the need for more cumbersome procedures, such as financial guardianship. The appointee would not be able to access the adult's bank account and can only deal with benefits payable from the date of appointment (including any backdated benefits withheld pending an appointment).

Access to funds

10.15 The access to funds scheme is intended to be a simple way to manage the financial affairs of a person who is unable to do this themselves.[33] The scheme is also sometimes referred to as 'the withdrawers' scheme' or 'intromission with funds'. It allows the Public Guardian to authorise an individual or organisation to access an adult's bank or building society account to pay bills and meet regular expenses. One-off payments can also be made, for example, for a holiday or item of furniture. The access to funds scheme is useful where an adult's finances are uncomplicated and generally predictable, but do not only consist of benefits income. It can avoid the need for an application for financial guardianship. However, access to funds is not available if a guardian or attorney with relevant powers has already been appointed.[34]

It is also possible to receive authority from the Public Guardian to obtain information about any existing bank accounts of the adult,[35] where the information is necessary to allow an application for access to funds to be made.

10.16 The application is made on a standard form on which the applicant sets out the adult's income and projected expenditure. These details can be amended at a later date if the adult's circumstances change. The form includes a certificate of incapacity for completion by a medical practitioner. If the Public Guardian is satisfied that the applicant is a suitable person to be authorised, it will issue a certificate. This provides the authority to open, or access, a bank account in the adult's name. The certificate lasts

33 Set out in Part 3 of the AWI(S)A 2000, as amended by the ASP(S)A 2007.

34 AWI(S)A 2000, s 24B.

35 AWI(S)A 2000, s 24C (as amended).

for three years, but a request can be made to the Public Guardian for this to be reduced or extended.[36]

Organisations can apply to use the access to funds scheme in relation to people they support. The organisation must first demonstrate to the Public Guardian that it is fit and proper to do so. This is done by a formal 'fitness to access funds' application process.[37] Once approved the organisation must make a separate application for each individual for whom it is proposing to act. Where an individual is making the application, the form must be countersigned by another party who has known the applicant for at least one year and can verify that they are suitable for appointment.[38] A joint or reserve withdrawer can be appointed.[39]

10.17 As with any other appointment under the Adults with Incapacity (Scotland) Act 2000, the withdrawer must apply the general principles. Anyone acting in a professional capacity must exercise the level of care and skill normally associated with their profession. The withdrawer should keep receipts and records and comply with any request from the Public Guardian for a report on their actions.[40]

There has been a relatively low take up of this scheme. In the year 2023–24 there were 193 access to funds applications registered compared to 3,235 guardianships and 550 intervention orders. The scheme is relatively inflexible compared with financial guardianship. The applicant needs to set out in detail how much they propose to spend and on which items or services. If there is any other expenditure, then they need to make an application to amend the order. This means it can be time consuming and difficult to plan for circumstances or one-off expenditure. At the time of writing, the Scottish Government is consulting on changes to the scheme to make it more useful and flexible.[41]

Management of funds in residential homes and hospitals

10.18 Provisions exist allowing for a care home or hospital to manage the financial affairs of an adult who is unable to do this themselves.

36 AWI(S)A 2000, s 31.

37 The forms and guidance can be found on the OPG Scotland website. Forms and publications (publicguardian-scotland.gov.uk)

38 AWI(S)A 2000, s 26(1).

39 AWI(S)A 2000, ss 26B-E.

40 AWI(S)A 2000, s 30(2).

41 The Adults with Incapacity Act Amendment Consultation (July 2024) (www.gov.scot), p 35.

The intention was that this would be used in preference to financial guardianship where:

- an adult needs support with managing finances; or
- there has been financial abuse; and
- the adult is living in, or moving to, residential accommodation.

However, there are financial limits on the amount that can be managed. The limit, at the time of writing, is £10,000.[42] In addition, the scheme cannot be used if a guardian or attorney has been appointed with relevant financial decision making powers.[43]

10.19 The hospital or care home seeking to manage finances must be an 'authorised establishment'. This means a care home registered with the Care Inspectorate or an NHS or private hospital.[44] A service which is not a registered care home can seek limited registration for the sole purpose of managing finances.[45] On the other hand, no service is obliged to offer this service and can opt out by giving notice to the Care Inspectorate or relevant health board.[46]

10.20 A certificate of authority to manage residents' finances lasts for three years[47] and managers must apply the general principles of the Adults with Incapacity (Scotland) Act 2000 to all decisions. There are a number of specific duties on managers including:

- to deal with and make claims for all pensions to which the resident is entitled;
- to place any resident's money exceeding £500 in an interest bearing account;
- to keep records and give a copy of these to the resident, their nearest relative or the supervisory body on request;

[42] The Adults with Incapacity (Management of Residents' Finances) (No. 2) (Scotland) Regulations 2003 (SSI 2003/266).
[43] AWI(S)A 2000, s 46.
[44] AWI(S)A 2000, s 35 and the Adults with Incapacity (Management of Residents Finances) (Scotland) Regulations 2005 (SSI 2005/610).
[45] Regulation of Care (Scotland) Act 2001, s 8.
[46] AWI(S)A 2000, s 35(2).
[47] AWI(S)A 2000, s 37(7).

- not to spend the money on items or services that are provided as part of the establishment's normal service.[48]

There is no obligation on a care home to offer this service and most do not and prefer only to hold smaller amounts for personal spending. There is no provision for remuneration for operating access to funds. The additional risk, along with extra staff time and resources, means it is not an attractive service. In many cases, the adult will need other finances managed and their former home sold and cleared. This tends to mean financial guardianship is more appropriate. The Scottish Government asked for information about the take up of the scheme in advance of a review of the Act. The Care Inspectorate advised there were no users of Part 4 in the care home sector. There was also no evidence from health boards that the scheme was being accessed. At the time of writing the Scottish Government is considering repealing these sections and effectively replacing them with an improved Access to Funds Scheme.[49]

PLANNING FOR THE FUTURE

10.21 A key principle of adult protection legislation is respect for the past and present wishes of the adult. There are three main ways in which an adult can make their views clear in the event of future incapacity. These are of particular relevance to those who have been subject to compulsory measures or who have a progressive illness:

- a person can speak to those providing them with health and social care to explain their wishes. These should be noted in their records;
- they can make a formal advance statement or living will;
- they can appoint an attorney to take decisions during any future incapacity.

Advance directives

10.22 An advance directive sets out a person's wishes about future health care should they become incapable of taking treatment decisions in the future. Where these deal with end-of-life situations they are often called living wills.

48 AWI(S)A 2000, s 41 and the Adults with Incapacity (Management of Residents' Finances) (No. 2) (Scotland) Regulations 2003 (SSI 2003/266), reg 5.

49 The Adults with Incapacity Act Amendment Consultation (July 2024) (www.gov.scot), p 39.

An advance directive is most commonly used to refuse certain treatments, in particular at the end of life. For example, if someone is in the final stages of a terminal illness, they may decide to refuse treatment for infections such as influenza, knowing this is likely to lead to their death. They might also state they do not want to be kept alive with a drip or feeding tube if there are no longer any treatment options. It might include a request for specific medication or a wish that any treatment is given that might prolong life. Ultimately, the decision about providing a specific treatment will be a clinical one but a professional would be expected to consider explicit wishes.

Despite the recommendation of the Scottish Law Commission,[50] the Adults with Incapacity (Scotland) Act 2000 did not give advance directives legal force. This means their legal status in Scotland is unclear. The law in England and Wales now recognises advance decisions to refuse treatments (ADRT).[51]

However, it is likely that health professionals and Scottish courts would regard a valid advance directive as binding under the common law providing certain conditions were met:

- the person had capacity at the time the advance directive was made;
- the instructions are up to date. For this reason, it is important that an advance directive is reviewed regularly and this is recorded eg by dating and signing on the date of the review;
- the instructions are relevant to the person's current circumstances or treatment options. Many charities who support adults with particular conditions can provide style advance directives relevant to the likely progression and treatment available.

At the very least the Adults with Incapacity (Scotland) Act 2000 principles would regard an advance directive, or living will, as an expression of the adult's past wishes. This would need to be considered by welfare guardians, attorneys and health professionals.

Advance statements in psychiatry

10.23 An advance statement about psychiatric treatment has a special status where a patient is subject to compulsory measures under the Mental

50 *Report on Incapable Adults*, Scot Law Comm No 151 (1995), recommendation 68.

51 Mental Capacity Act 2005, s 24.

Health (Care and Treatment) (Scotland) Act 2003. Such a statement must be made in accordance with the prescribed procedure.[52]

Anyone intervening under the Act must have regard to any valid advance statement the person has made. This means there is no guarantee the statement will be followed but there is a guarantee it will be considered. A person acting in conflict with the terms of an advance statement must report this to the Mental Welfare Commission.[53]

There is a duty on health boards to make sure that there is a copy of any advance statement held with medical records and the Mental Welfare Commission must be advised. The Commission are also under a duty to keep a register of advance statements that can be inspected by the adult or someone acting on their behalf or anyone making decisions about care or treatment.[54]

In order to be valid, the individual must have capacity at the time they make the statement, and the statement must be in writing, witnessed and signed. The witness must be a clinical psychologist, medical practitioner, occupational therapist, registered nurse, social worker, solicitor or person employed in the provision of (or in managing the provision of) a care service.[55] This is because the witness also has the role of certifying that the individual understood the content of the statement.

The Mental Welfare Commission have produced detailed guidance on advance statements.[56]

Statement of wishes and feelings

10.24 A statement of wishes, feelings and values can be an alternative to an advance statement or directive. This can help inform decision making. It sets out in general terms the person's attitudes to such matters as life-prolonging treatments and future care. It might include details of what is important to the adult including religious and spiritual beliefs. Although it would not bind doctors or other health care professionals, the principles

52 MH(CT)(S)A 2003, s 275.

53 MH(CT)(S)A 2003, s 276.

54 MH(CT)(S)A 2003, ss 276A and 276B (inserted by Mental Health (Scotland) Act 2015, s 26).

55 The Mental Health (Advance Statements) (Prescribed Class of Persons) (Scotland) Regulations 2004 (SSI 2004/387).

56 See 'Advance Statements' on the Mental Welfare Commission for Scotland website (www.mwcscot.org.uk).

of the Adults with Incapacity (Scotland) Act 2000 would require it to be considered.

There is no prescribed form for such a statement.[57]

Appointing an attorney

10.25 A power of attorney is useful for an adult who has someone they trust to act on their behalf. In basic terms, it is a legal document used by an individual to authorise another person to take financial, medical and/or welfare decisions on their behalf. Where an individual is diagnosed with a progressive or degenerative condition it is particularly important to discuss the options for future decision making. Thinking about a power of attorney should be part of that process.

Financial powers can come into effect straight away while the person making the appointment retains capacity, but perhaps needs some help managing their finances. Provided the requirements of the Adults with Incapacity (Scotland) Act 2000 are met, the appointment continues after capacity is lost.[58] For this reason, financial attorneys are referred to as 'continuing attorneys'.[59] Welfare powers can only ever come into force when capacity is lost.

Only individuals who have capacity to understand the powers being granted can grant powers of attorney. They are normally used to provide for the possibility of capacity being lost on a permanent or temporary basis, at some point in the future, because of illness or injury. If an individual does not understand the legal documents needed to appoint an attorney, they will not be able to make an appointment.[60] In such cases other mechanisms, including guardianship, are available and may be appropriate.

Many people in Scotland now grant powers of attorney. In the year 2023/24, The Public Guardian registered a total of 77,226 powers of attorney.[61]

57 For an example, see Ward, *Adult Incapacity*, Appendix 5, Part 5.

58 AWI(S)A 2000, s 15.

59 At the time of writing, the Scottish Government is consulting on changing wording from 'continuing attorney' to 'financial attorney': see the Adults with Incapacity Act Amendment Consultation (July 2024) (www.gov.scot), p 14.

60 This does not mean that the person has to be able fully to manage their own affairs. The test is whether they understand the nature of the power of attorney document *Re K, Re F* [1988] Ch 310.

61 Of these 20,156 were postal submissions and 57,290 were electronic submissions.

10.26 It is not necessary to use a solicitor to draw up a power of attorney, although many people now grant powers of attorney at the same time as drawing up a will. However, a solicitor, doctor or member of the Faculty of Advocates must certify both the person's capacity to sign and that there was no undue influence. However, it is worth considering asking a lawyer to help and legal aid may be available. Practice changes and if a necessary power is not specifically included, for example to amend a will to take into account tax changes, then it may be necessary to go to court at a later date and seek a financial guardianship or intervention order. The Law Society of Scotland has produced guidance on drafting powers of attorney for vulnerable adults (see para **7.6** for further details).

Named person

10.27 A person may wish to appoint a named person to act in connection with any compulsory measures under the Mental Health (Care and Treatment) (Scotland) Act 2003.[62] The named person is consulted by professionals, can make appeals on the patient's behalf and can appear at the tribunal. The role of named persons is discussed generally at para **4.35**.

COUNSELLING AND MEDIATION

10.28 An adult who has experienced harm or abuse might need some practical or emotional support, and it will be important to consider counselling services. These will often be accessed through the adult's general practitioner. Where the harm or abuse is also a criminal offence, specific services might be available.[63]

Where a criminal investigation is ongoing, counselling, and mediation must be carefully considered and managed.

Counselling may also be appropriate where a banning order sets out the circumstances in which contact is allowed between the adult and the subject of the order. In addition, supervised contact or mediation might be used to maintain the relationship, if this is in the adult's best interests.

[62] MH(CT)(S)A 2003, s 250.

[63] See 'Victim Information and Advice' on the COPFS website (www.copfs.gov.uk/).

CRIMINAL INJURIES COMPENSATION

10.29 A person injured because of a crime may be entitled to criminal injuries compensation. Full details of the scheme are available from the Criminal Injuries Compensation Authority.[64] A person can apply for criminal injuries compensation even where there has been no prosecution or conviction, as applications are decided on the civil standard of proof. Some solicitors and law centres will assist with applications.

CONCLUSION

10.30 There are a number of formal and informal ways to offer support to an adult at risk. It is unlikely that an adult protection case will have a successful outcome unless the adult's wider needs are taken into account and they are supported and included to the maximum degree possible in all aspects of the decision making process. It is important the adult is able to maintain existing family and social contacts if they wish to do this. The Code of Practice also recognises that every effort should be made to ensure that action taken under the Act does not have an adverse effect on the adult's relationships.[65]

[64] For more details see the Criminal Injuries Compensation Authority at www.gov.uk/government/organisations/criminal-injuries-compensation-authority

[65] ASP(S)A 2007 Code of Practice, p 14.

Chapter 11

TRANSITION FROM CHILD TO ADULT PROTECTION

11.1 The Adults with Incapacity (Scotland) Act 2000 and the Adult (Support and Protection) (Scotland) Act 2007 both define an 'adult' as a person aged 16 and over.[1] However, there is no consistent definition of the term 'child' in Scots law, and the various statutes regarding what may loosely be termed the support and protection of children cover differing age ranges. In many cases, this will include individuals who would not generally be referred to as 'children' in normal usage. As a result, there is a significant overlap between those measures directed at children, in this wider sense, and adults: and a consequent potential for confusion with regard to the various duties and powers available to the public bodies (principally the local authority) dealing with such cases.

This chapter will give an overview of the primary powers and duties of public bodies of relevance to supporting individuals negotiating the transition from childhood to adulthood. The focus will necessarily be on the local authority, as it is local authorities which have the clearest duties in terms of child protection and support and which also act as education authority for their area.

11.2 Many of the provisions outlined below are considered in greater detail elsewhere in this book. The support of looked after children and children requiring additional support at school are both complex areas subject to extensive regulation, and it is not within the ambit of this book to deal with them in detail. Rather, a description of the general duties and powers available will be given, with the hope that this will enable those engaged principally in adult protection work to give full consideration to

1 Adults with Incapacity (Scotland) Act 2000 (AWI(S)A 2000), s 1(6), Adult (Support and Protection) (Scotland) Act 2007 (ASP(S)A 2007), s 53(1).

where colleagues in children's services or education can, and should, be asked to contribute to providing support.[2]

PARENTAL RESPONSIBILITY

11.3 Before examining the duties and powers of public bodies in relation to young people, it is worth considering the position of their parents as they move towards adulthood. In general terms, a child's parents cease to have both rights and responsibilities towards them in a legal sense when the child reaches the age of 16.[3] This cut-off applies even in situations where, on turning 16, a person has additional support needs, lacks capacity or is at risk in terms of the 2007 Act. After the person's 16th birthday, they become an adult and their parents do not have either a legal responsibility or right to make decisions about their care or act as their legal representative purely as a result of their status as parent.

11.4 There are two exceptions to this general position, which may be of relevance in an adult support and protection context (notably, both in regard to continuing obligations, not rights):

- the responsibility to provide guidance to the child, which subsists until the child turns 18;[4]
- the responsibility to aliment the child, which subsists until the child turns 18; unless the child is 'reasonably and appropriately undergoing instruction at an educational establishment, or training for employment or for a trade, profession or vocation', in which case the responsibility continues until such instruction or training is complete, or the child reaches the age of 25.[5] 'To aliment' means to provide such reasonable support as is required by the child, with reference to their whole circumstances and, in particular, their needs, resources and earning capacity, and those of their parents.[6]

[2] A more detailed consideration of the practice considerations and policy background to these different areas of practice can be found in H. Martin, *Understanding Age in Child Protection Guidance and Adult Support and Protection Legislation, Iriss* (Scottish Government, 2024).

[3] Children (Scotland) Act 1995 (C(S)A 1995), ss 1 and 2.

[4] C(S)A 1995, s 1(2)(b).

[5] Family Law (Scotland) Act 1985 (FL(S)A 1985), s 1(5).

[6] FL(S)A 1985, ss 1(2) and 4.

11.5 While the responsibility to provide guidance may theoretically be enforced by application to the court by the young adult themselves, embarking on such an action is unlikely to be of any practical benefit. However, in situations where an adult requires financial support and a duty of aliment is owed, an action for payment might be considered. Such an action would have to be pursued by the young adult themselves; although they are likely to need support to do this, as well as independent legal advice and representation.

DUTIES AND POWERS OF PUBLIC BODIES

11.6 There are a wide range of provisions placing responsibility on various public bodies for the support and protection of those aged between 16 and 25. Some of these provisions apply without particular limitation as to age; some are provisions intended to support adults (defined as persons over 16); and some are provisions primarily intended to support children who are 'in need,' which extend beyond the age of 16. Within this last band, there are many provisions which apply to specified sub-groups of ages, principally in relation to children who have been looked after by a local authority.

General powers and responsibilities of public bodies applying to children and adults

11.7 Most of the powers and responsibilities of public bodies, in particular in terms of provision of support to and protection of individuals, are not limited to a specific age-group. For example, the basic duties of the police contained in the Police and Fire Reform (Scotland) Act 2012, s 20 apply with regard to the public as a whole.

Although social work services tend to have separate teams dealing with child protection and family support on one hand, and adult protection and community care on the other, there are also powers and duties applicable to social work which are not age-specific. The foundation of the local authority's duty towards individuals as a social work service is the general duty to promote social welfare in its area found in the Social Work (Scotland) Act 1968, s 12. This is to be done, 'by making available advice, guidance and assistance on such a scale as may be appropriate for their area' and applies to persons of any age (although, the specific power in terms of s 12 to provide assistance in kind or in cash may only be exercised in respect of those over the age of 18).

11.8 The general duty is supplemented by various duties laid out in the following sections of the Social Work (Scotland) Act 1968, which equally apply to persons of any age. The most relevant of these in terms of support through transition from child to adult support are:

- s 12A: which provides a duty to complete a community care assessment where a person is in need of a community care service;
- s 13A: which requires local authorities to provide suitable nursing home provision for those who require it 'by reason of infirmity, age, illness or mental disorder, dependency on drugs or alcohol or being substantially handicapped by any deformity or disability';
- s 14: which contains a duty to provide home help and laundry facilities in certain circumstances (usually referred to now as 'home support');
- s 27: which requires the local authority to supervise and provide advice, guidance and assistance to persons of any age at various stages of incarceration and release/probation (this duty also specifically extends to persons aged 16 and 17 who are subject to a compulsory supervision order by reason of their having committed an offence).

11.9 In addition, the majority of the provisions in the Mental Health (Care and Treatment) (Scotland) Act 2003 apply without limitation as to age. These provisions include, in particular:

- health board duties to provide support to enable mothers or adoptive mothers of a child less than one year old to care for said child in hospital while the mother is treated for post-natal depression, or another mental disorder;[7]
- local authority duties to provide care and support services, services to promote well-being and social development, and assistance with travel (with some minor exceptions regarding provision of training and support in employment, which do not apply to those of school age);[8]
- all of the various orders available in terms of the Act to deal with detention and treatment (with the exception of a removal order,

7 Mental Health (Care and Treatment) (Scotland) Act 2003 (MH(CT)(S)A 2003), s 24.

8 MH(CT)(S)A 2003, ss 25–27. For the definition of 'school age,' see further below.

which may not be granted in regard to an individual below the age of 16) and the police power to remove an individual from a public place.

It should be noted, that this general applicability across age ranges should not be taken to mean that the provision of mental health services is to be made with no regard to the age of the person receiving the service. The legal principles to be borne in mind while exercising functions are slightly different in the case of persons above or below 18, with a specific emphasis on securing the welfare of those in the latter category.[9] In addition, health boards are specifically required to provide accommodation sufficient for the particular needs of those under the age of 18 detained in hospital or otherwise receiving treatment for a mental disorder.[10]

General powers and responsibilities of public bodies applying to those aged over 16

11.10 The duties incumbent on the various public bodies identified in the 2000 Act and the 2007 Act, as well as the various powers conferred, apply almost exclusively in regard to adults, defined as individuals over the age of 16.[11] The minor exception to this is that an application for a guardianship order may be made and granted within the three months preceding a child's 16th birthday: with the proviso that any such order granted will not become effective until the child actually turns 16.[12] In practical terms, where a guardianship order is considered necessary from 16, it is advisable to start the process around six months before the 16th birthday.

As noted above, a removal order in terms of the Mental Health (Care and Treatment (Scotland) Act 2003 may only be granted in regard to individuals over the age of 16.

'Adult carers' and 'young carers'

11.11 The Carers (Scotland) Act 2016 created a right for persons meeting the definition of 'carer' in the Act to be offered, or to request, either an 'adult carer support plan' or 'young carer statement'. Where an offer is

9 MH(CT)(S)A 2003, ss 1 and 2.
10 MH(CT)(S)A 2003, s 23.
11 AWI(S)A 2000, s 1(6); ASP(S)A 2007, s 53(1).
12 AWI(S)A 2000, s 79A.

accepted or a request made, the plan or statement must be made up, in accordance with the statutory requirements.[13]

A 'carer' is a person who provides or intends to provide care to another person, other than in terms of a contract, or on the basis of the person's age (thus excluding the ordinary care provided for children, simply because they are children, for example by their parents).[14] The 'young carer statement' is appropriate where the carer in question is under the age of 18 or continues to attend school, having been there since that age.[15] Otherwise, the right is to an 'adult carer support plan'.[16]

There is some differentiation on the basis of age in the operation of the right; but this is generally more notable in the differing 'eligibility criteria' applied by local authorities to the two categories of carer. These criteria set out the support that will be made available by the authority to meet needs assessed under either the adult carer support plan or the young carer statement. Where the needs are eligible under the criteria, support must be provided to meet them.[17] Eligibility criteria are largely more generous to young carers than they are to adult carers. Where an adult at risk aged 16 to 18 has caring responsibilities, these provisions may therefore be able to provide some means of support, even for needs that might not be eligible for support for older persons.

'Children in need' and looked after/accommodated children

11.12 Local authorities have a general duty to safeguard and promote the welfare of children in their area who are in need, and to promote the upbringing of such children by their families by providing a range and

13 Carers (Scotland) Act 2016 (C(S)A 2016), ss 6 and 12. Sections 9 and 15 set out the required content of the plan or statement, respectively.

14 C(S)A 2016, s 1.

15 C(S)A 2016, ss 2 and 12. Basic responsibility to prepare the plan is incumbent on the local authority where the child resides. If the child attends a public school, however, the responsibility lies with the authority where the school is, unless they were placed there by the authority of residence. Where a child attends a grant-aided school or an independent school, the directing authority of that school is responsible, subject to approval by the local authority (ss 12(6), 19 and 20).

16 C(S)A 2016, ss 3 and 6.

17 C(S)A 2016, s 24. There is a discretionary power granted in the same section to meet other identified needs.

level of services appropriate to the children's needs.[18] 'Children' in this context means anyone under the age of 18,[19] so there is scope for this duty to overlap duties in terms of the 2000 and 2007 Acts. A child is 'in need' if:

- they are unlikely to achieve or maintain, or to have the opportunity of achieving or maintaining, a reasonable standard of health or development unless services are provided for them by a local authority;
- their health or development is likely to be significantly impaired, or further impaired, unless such services are provided;
- they are disabled; or
- they are affected adversely by the disability of any other person in their family.[20]

11.13 Taking this general duty further, the local authority has a duty in terms of the Children (Scotland) Act 1995, s 25 to provide accommodation for a person under 18 where no-one has parental responsibility for them, they are lost or abandoned, or the person who has been caring for them is prevented from providing them with suitable accommodation or care. They also have discretion to provide accommodation to a young person between 18 and 21, where they are satisfied that their welfare requires it.[21]

11.14 Beyond these general duties, local authorities have more precise duties in relation to children looked after by them. A child is 'looked after by a local authority' if they are a child (ie person aged under 18):

- for whom a local authority is providing accommodation under the Children (Scotland) Act 1995, s 25;
- who is subject to a compulsory supervision order or an interim compulsory supervision order;
- who is subject to an analogous order made outside of Scotland, as specified in regulations; or
- in respect of whom a permanence order has been made in terms of the Adoption and Children (Scotland) Act 2007 which has not ceased to have effect.[22]

18 C(S)A 1995, s 22.
19 C(S)A 1995, s 93(2).
20 C(S)A 1995, s 93(4).
21 C(S)A 1995, s 25.
22 C(S)A 1995, s 17(6). A permanence order is an order removing rights and responsibilities from a child's parents and vesting them in the local authority and, on occasion, other individuals.

11.15 If a child fits this definition, the local authority has duties towards them that extend until they become 18 (or until they cease to be looked after, if before that age). These are:

- to safeguard and promote the child's welfare (which is the paramount concern). This duty specifically includes providing advice and assistance with a view to preparing the child for the time when they are no longer looked after by a local authority;
- to make such use of services available for children cared for by their own parents as appears to the authority to be reasonable in the child's case;
- to take such steps to promote, on a regular basis, personal relations and direct contact between the child and any person with parental responsibilities in relation to them as appear to be both practicable and appropriate; and
- to promote personal relations and direct contact with a sibling of the child, and any other person the child has lived with, and with whom they have an ongoing sibling-like relationship, as practicable and appropriate.[23]

Leaving care, continuing care and after-care

11.16 The local authority continues to have powers and duties to support individuals who have been looked after beyond the time they cease to be of that status.

If a person ceases to be looked after by the local authority at any point while aged between 16 and 21, the authority must continue to provide whatever accommodation and support it was providing while they were looked after (known as 'continuing care'). This duty does not apply if the person was accommodated in secure accommodation, a care placement which the carer is no longer able or willing to provide, or where their welfare would be significantly adversely affected by continuing in the accommodation. The duty comes to an end when the person turns 21, or sooner, if they leave the accommodation of their own volition, the accommodation ceases to be available, or where their welfare would be significantly adversely affected by continuing to be there.[24]

[23] C(S)A 1995, s 17(1) and (1A).

[24] C(S)A 1995, s 26A, Continuing Care (Scotland) Order 2015 (SSI 2015/158), arts 2 and 3.

11.17 In addition, the local authority has an obligation to advise, guide and assist any person in their area aged over 16 but not yet 19 who, at age 16 or at any subsequent time was, but who is no longer, looked after by a local authority.[25] Where a young person is between 19 and 26, but otherwise falls within this definition, they may apply to the authority for advice, guidance and assistance. The authority must complete an assessment of their needs and must provide such advice, guidance or assistance as is required in terms of that assessment to meet what are termed their 'eligible needs'.[26] Eligible needs are defined as:

- financial support to meet essential accommodation and maintenance costs;
- support, in the form of information or advice, to assist them to access education, training, employment, leisure and skills-related opportunities; and
- any other support, in the form of information or advice, relating to their well-being.[27]

Such other advice, guidance and assistance may also be provided as the local authority considers appropriate, having regard to the person's welfare. The local authority has discretion to continue to provide such support after the person receiving it turns 26.[28] These obligations are collectively termed, 'after-care' and do not apply where continuing care is being provided.[29]

11.18 Finally, the local authority may at its discretion make grants to anyone between 16 and 25 inclusive, who was looked after either when they turned 16 or at any subsequent time. These grants must be to enable the young person to meet expenses connected with receiving education or training or be contributions to accommodation and maintenance near where they may be employed, seeking employment, or receiving education or training.[30]

25 C(S)A 1995, s 29(1).
26 C(S)A 1995, s 29(5) and (5A).
27 Aftercare (Eligible Needs) (Scotland) Order 2015 (SSI 2015/156), art 2.
28 C(S)A 1995, s 29(5B).
29 C(S)A 1995, s 29(2A).
30 C(S)A 1995, s 30.

LOCAL AUTHORITY DUTIES AS EDUCATION AUTHORITY

11.19 Schools may provide an important source of support for many individuals between 16 and 18. Local authorities, as Education Authority for their area, have specific duties regarding the support of school pupils. It is important that school staff are aware of the possibility that pupils at 16 and over may present as adults at risk and that there is a duty upon them to refer such cases to their colleagues in social work. Similarly, any investigation into such a referral is likely to require input from education professionals, who may already be working with the pupil in question.

School age

11.20 The scale of the potential for school pupils to fit into the category of adults at risk can be appreciated by looking at the definition of 'school age' in ss 31–33 of the Education (Scotland) Act 1980. This sets the ages at which children must begin attending school and when they may leave. In an adult protection context, the important issue is when school age comes to an end. If a child turns 16 on or after 1 March and before 1 October, they will cease to be of school age as of the last day of the May falling between those two dates. If the child's birthday falls on or after 1 October and before 1 March, they will cease to be of school age as of the first day of the Christmas holidays falling between those two dates. If the pupil is not actually attending school, this last date is taken to be 21 December.[31] It follows that some individuals will spend some time over school age but under 16, while others will spend some time over 16 but still be of school age. There is therefore a significant portion of the population who have the potential to present as adults at risk, even though they are not yet old enough to leave full-time schooling.

11.21 In the context of education law, a 'young person' is defined as an individual over school age but under 18. The word 'child' refers to anyone

[31] For example, if they are home-schooled. Education (Scotland) Act 1980, ss 31 and 33.

of school age, but as noted above, this will include some individuals who are over 16 and who therefore fall within the ambit of the 2007 Act.[32]

Once a child is over school age, the requirement to attend school no longer applies. However, young people have a right to remain at the school they already attend, and may request a place at a different school. If in attendance at school, young people largely have the same rights as other pupils. The school may not exclude a young person without going through the usual procedure and the local authority will have the same duties towards them as they do towards any child in terms of the Education (Additional Support for Learning) (Scotland) Act 2004 ('the 2004 Act'), as described below.

Additional support and coordinated support plans

11.22 Under the 2004 Act, a child or young person has 'additional support needs' where they are, or are likely to be, unable to benefit from school education without the provision of additional support. 'Additional support' means provision which is additional to, or otherwise different from, the educational provision made generally for children/young people of the same age in schools (other than special schools) that are under the management of the education authority.[33] Children or young people who are looked after by the local authority are presumed to have additional support needs; but if, following consideration of their case, the local authority is satisfied that they do not require additional support, that presumption will cease to apply.[34]

11.23 Local authorities, in their role as education authority, must:

- make adequate and efficient provision for the additional support required for each child or young person with additional support needs for whose school education they are responsible;
- make arrangements to identify additional support needs;

[32] Education (Scotland) Act 1980, s 135(1). The definition of 'young person' for the purposes of the Education (Additional Support for Learning) (Scotland) Act 2004 (E(ASL)(S)A 2004) is someone who is 16 or over and has attended school since turning 16: E(ASL)(S)A 2004, s 29(1). There is therefore no upper age limit in relation to that Act.

[33] E(ASL)(S)A 2004, s 1.

[34] E(ASL)(S)A 2004, s 1(1A) and (1B).

- keep under consideration additional support needs identified and the adequacy of support provided to meet the needs of each child or young person;
- provide those children or young people who need it with a coordinated support plan and keep this under regular review.[35]

11.24 A Coordinated Support Plan (CSP) must be provided to children or young people who have additional support needs arising from one or more complex factors, or multiple factors, if those needs are likely to continue for more than a year and require significant additional support to be provided by education and other services (whether provided by the local authority, or another specified body).[36] Social work input would be an example of support being provided by another service.

Complex factors are factors which have a significant adverse effect on the school education of the child or young person. Multiple factors are factors which are not complex of themselves, but which taken together will have the same adverse effect. Factors falling under either category could be disabilities (within the meaning of the 2007 Act) or any other factors, for example, the fact that the child/young person is looked after by the local authority or has been 'at risk,' in terms of the 2007 Act. If a child or young person is looked after, consideration *must* be given to whether a CSP is required.[37]

11.25 A CSP is likely to be a key part of a whole range of statutory and non-statutory plans that may apply to a child or young person at this transitional stage. The Scottish Government has produced a statutory Code of Practice for the 2004 Act,[38] which provides instruction on how to integrate various plans with a CSP. It states:

> 'There is a range of plans, which a child or young person may have. Education authorities and other agencies should seek to ensure that assessment for, and production of, learning plans takes account of any other planning processes within the local authority and across agencies. The ultimate aim is to have one plan in line with *Getting It Right for Every Child*. Educational objectives should be shared across plans. In particular,

[35] E(ASL)(S)A 2004, ss 4 and 9.

[36] E(ASL)(S)A 2004, s 9.

[37] E(ASL)(S)A 2004, s 6(1A). This duty does not apply if the child or young person has already been assessed as not having additional support needs.

[38] *Supporting Children's Learning: Code of Practice* (revised edn).

education plans should link with any health or social care plan. This will help prevent duplication and facilitate the co-ordination and implementation of support for children and young people. Nevertheless … co-ordinated support plans are statutory plans and where a child or young person fulfils the requirements for having one then it must be prepared. Other plans cannot substitute for a coordinated support plan.

Particular issues may arise with statutory care plans. There is a statutory duty on the local authority as 'corporate parent' to review children and young people looked after by them. Although the emphasis of the care plan will quite properly focus on the child or young person in placement, and contact arrangements with the family, it must also reflect fully the child's or young person's learning needs. Effective planning is important to ensure that children and young people receive the services they need'.[39]

11.26 No specific mention is made in the Code of Practice of adult support and protection, however, it can be seen that the considerations it mentions may be equally applicable to planning that form of support.

INCORPORATION OF THE UNITED NATIONS CONVENTION ON THE RIGHTS OF THE CHILD

11.27 The United Nations Convention on the Rights of the Child (Incorporation) (Scotland) Act 2024 requires public authorities to act in manner that is compatible with the United Nations Convention on the Rights of the Child (UNCRC) when they are discharging certain of their functions. The UNCRC is an international treaty that sets out various fundamental rights for children, who, for the purposes of incorporation of their rights into Scots law, are defined as being persons under the age of 18.[40]

The functions in question are defined as functions:

'(a) it is within the legislative competence of the Scottish Parliament to confer on the authority, and

[39] *Supporting Children's Learning: Code of Practice* (revised edn). Ch 3, paras 85 and 86.

[40] United Nations Convention on the Rights of the Child (Incorporation) (Scotland) Act 2024 (UNCRC(I)(S)A 2024), Sch 1, para 1.

(b) is conferred by—

(i) an Act of the Scottish Parliament,

(ii) a Scottish statutory instrument originally made wholly under a relevant enabling power,

(iii) a provision in a Scottish statutory instrument originally made partly under a relevant enabling power, provided that the provision itself was either—

(A) originally made under the relevant enabling power, or

(B) inserted into the instrument by an Act of the Scottish Parliament or subordinate legislation made under a relevant enabling power, or

(iv) a rule of law not created by an enactment.'[41]

A 'relevant enabling power' means a power to make subordinate legislation conferred by a provision emanating from the Scottish Parliament.[42]

It can be a complicated question whether the various functions of public bodies described above and elsewhere in this book constitute 'relevant functions' for the purposes of the United Nations Convention on the Rights of the Child (Incorporation) (Scotland) Act 2024, in their application to persons between the ages of 16 and 18. Public bodies will have to take care to identify the precise source of any power they exercise and check whether it comes from a Scottish provision, or one emanating from Westminster. It is important to note that this will not correspond to provisions primarily aimed at children, on one side, and adults, on the other. For example, functions contained in the Adults with Incapacity (Scotland) Act 2000, the Mental Health (Care and Treatment) (Scotland) Act 2003, and the Adult Support and Protection (Scotland) Act 2007 are relevant functions, insofar as they are applied to persons under the age of 18, these being Acts of the Scottish Parliament. On the other hand, perhaps counter-intuitively, functions exercised under the Children (Scotland) Act 1995, or the Education (Scotland) Act 1980 are not, since these are Acts of the UK Parliament.

Where a function is a relevant function, the Act makes it unlawful for the public authority, in exercising it, to act or refrain from acting in a way

[41] UNCRC(I)(S)A 2024, s 6(2).

[42] UNCRC(I)(S)A 2024, s 6(3).

that is incompatible with the UNCRC requirements, as these are set out in Schedule 1 to the Act. [43] There is an exception to this rule, where the authority is required or entitled to act or refrain from acting by a provision that does not emanate from the Scottish Parliament.[44] Interpreting this exception adds a further complication to the question of when the duty will apply to a public authority's actions, particularly where very general powers exist in UK legislation, that might allow similar action to be taken as is set out in detail in subsequent, Scottish Acts. It might, for example, be said that the provision of a coordinated support plan is something an education authority is entitled to do in terms of the Education (Scotland) Act 1980, s 1, albeit very few would have done precisely this until a specific duty to do so was set out in Education (Additional Support for Learning) (Scotland) Act 2004.

It is not possible to give a full consideration here of the various UNCRC rights set out in the United Nations Convention on the Rights of the Child (Incorporation) (Scotland) Act 2024. Many of them are similar to rights set out in the European Convention on Human Rights;[45] and many of them relate to outlawing activity that is already illegal in Scotland, such as child prostitution or using children as soldiers. There are several that might be of direct relevance to adult protection situations.[46] The Scottish Government has produced guidance on how to implement what it terms as a 'children's human rights approach', including in relation to the rights set out in the UNCRC.[47]

Where a person considers a public authority to have failed in its duty to act compatibly with their rights, they may raise proceedings against the authority in a civil court or tribunal which has jurisdiction to grant the remedy sought.[48] This would most likely be an application to the Court of Session for judicial review of the decision to act or refrain from acting. A party may also seek damages, although these are only to be granted on the basis of 'just satisfaction'. There is authority to suggest that this is a

43 UNCRC(I)(S)A 2024, ss 6(1), 1(2).

44 UNCRC(I)(S)A 2024, s 6(4).

45 See Chapter 14 for further information on human rights.

46 See, for example, UNCRC(I)(S)A 2024, Sch 1, paras 12, 19, 23 and 39.

47 *Guidance on taking a children's human rights approach* (Scottish Government, January 2024). This is available at: www.gov.scot/publications/guidance-taking-childrens-human-rights-approach/documents/

48 UNCRC(I)(S)A 2024, s 7(1)(a).

more limited award than might be made in other types of action, such as those relating to personal injury.[49]

A person may also rely on the UNCRC requirements in any legal proceedings that have already been instituted.[50] They might, for example, make an argument that the granting of a protection order in relation to a person under 18 would not be in accordance with that person's UNCRC rights.

CONCLUSION

11.28 Support and protection of individuals in transition from childhood to adulthood is a complicated area in which there are many overlapping legislative duties. This is particularly the case for children who are looked after by the local authority. It is therefore incumbent on public agencies dealing with such cases to consider the full range of powers available to them, including those that are not age-specific, to ensure that all duties are complied with and that a coherent and comprehensive package of support is maintained. This may involve working alongside colleagues in teams specialising in areas other than adult protection and community care. Where the individual in question is still at school, a coordinated support plan may provide a means of bringing the different strands of support together into one overall package. In employing these powers, public authorities must consider carefully whether they are subject to the requirements of the United Nations Convention on the Rights of the Child (Incorporation) (Scotland) Act 2024 and, if they are, take care to ensure they are acting in accordance with the UNCRC.

49 UNCRC(I)(S)A 2024, s 8. On 'just satisfaction', see, for example, *R (Greenfield)* v *Secretary of State for the Home Department* [2005] UKHL 14.

50 UNCRC(I)(S)A 2024, s 7(1)(b).

Chapter 12

COURT MEASURES OF PROTECTION

12.1 This chapter looks at legal remedies which may be appropriate where informal support does not provide a solution that appropriately balances the risk to an adult and respect for their autonomy. Many of these remedies are in the form of orders made by sheriffs placing restrictions on an abuser. Sheriffs are also responsible for hearing applications for guardianship and intervention orders relating to adults with incapacity. Accordingly, this chapter will mainly deal with matters concerning the sheriff court. Nonetheless, there are also a number of provisions regarding adults with mental disorders which are the preserve of the Mental Health Tribunal. It is therefore appropriate to begin with a brief overview of the tribunal and some of the orders subject to its supervision.

MENTAL HEALTH TRIBUNALS

12.2 The Mental Health Tribunal for Scotland was set up under the Mental Health (Care and Treatment) (Scotland) Act 2003[1] and deals with applications and appeals under that Act.[2] A legally qualified convener chairs each tribunal. They sit with a medical member (usually a consultant psychiatrist) and a general member with specific experience of providing or using mental health services (including experience gained as a user of services and/or as a carer).

Tribunals are held in various locations throughout the country, including both hospital and community settings. The proceedings are less formal than a court setting, but still relatively formal, in view of the importance of the matters under discussion. Hearings take place in private.[3]

1 Mental Health (Care and Treatment) (Scotland) Act 2003 (MH(CT)(S)A 2003), s 21.

2 For more details, see Hilary Patrick and Jill Stavert, *Mental Health, Incapacity and the Law in Scotland* (2nd edn, Bloomsbury Professional, 2016, new edn forthcoming 2025), Part 4.

3 Mental Health Tribunal for Scotland (Practice and Procedure) (No. 2) Tribunal Rules 2005 (SSI 2005/519) ('Tribunal Rules'), rule 66(1).

All parties receive notice of the hearing, together with the papers. The tribunal can withhold information from any party, including the patient, if the tribunal is satisfied that disclosure could cause serious harm to the patient or any other person.[4]

The patient and their named person are entitled to attend the hearing, and the patient should be encouraged to do so where appropriate. The patient's primary carer, and any welfare guardian or attorney, are also entitled to make representations to the tribunal.[5] The tribunal can appoint a curator *ad litem* if the person is unable to instruct a solicitor. The curator is a solicitor who acts on the adult's behalf in the proceedings, in accordance with the general principles. If a party is unable to attend, the convener or other members of the tribunal should offer that party a chance to meet to explain why they cannot attend and whether they wish to proceed.[6]

As well as a legal representative, the patient can have an independent advocate for support at the hearing.[7]

There is a right of appeal against a tribunal's decision only where a party alleges that the tribunal has made a legal mistake or that there were irregularities in the hearing.[8]

MENTAL HEALTH (CARE AND TREATMENT) (SCOTLAND) ACT 2003 MEASURES

12.3 The Mental Health (Care and Treatment) (Scotland) Act 2003 provides for both compulsory detention in hospital and community-based treatment orders.[9] The usual means of admission to hospital is via a short-term detention certificate[10] but the Act also provides for longer-term orders, either in hospital or in the community.[11] All orders authorising detention or compulsory treatment of an adult are subject to the oversight of the tribunal, with the exception of emergency detention certificates and removal orders.[12]

4 Tribunal Rules, rule 47(1).
5 MH(CT)(S)A 2003, s 64(3).
6 Tribunal Rules, rule 70(3).
7 Tribunal Rules, rule 66(6).
8 MH(CT)(S)A 2003, s 324(2).
9 MH(CT)(S)A 2003, Parts 5–7.
10 MH(CT)(S)A 2003, s 44.
11 See MH(CT)(S)A 2003, Part 7.
12 MH(CT)(S)A 2003, ss 36 and 293. See Chapter 8.

This topic is discussed in detail in *Mental Health, Incapacity and the Law in Scotland*.[13] Briefly, a person could be subject to compulsory measures under the Act where:

- the person has a mental disorder (mental illness, learning disability or personality disorder);
- there is a significant risk to the person's health, safety or welfare or to the safety of any other person. (What is a significant risk is a question of judgement for the health and social care professionals. The tribunal will test this assessment during an appeal or on an application for a compulsory treatment order.);
- treatment is available which should prevent the patient's condition from deteriorating or relieve its symptoms or effects;[14]
- compulsory admission is necessary, because the person will not agree to admission and/or treatment; and
- the person's ability to make decisions about the provision of medical treatment is significantly impaired because of a mental disorder.[15] (This means that a person with a diagnosis of mental illness or other mental disorder cannot be subject to compulsory measures unless the disorder has in some way distorted their ability to take decisions about treatment for the disorder. A person who fully understands the issues involved and takes an informed and balanced decision to refuse treatment cannot be subject to compulsory measures.)

The Mental Welfare Commission can advise in complex cases.

THE SHERIFF COURT

12.4 The sheriff courts deal with a wide variety of cases, including family matters and some criminal matters. There are six sheriffdoms in Scotland, with a Sheriff Principal appointed to each. Each sheriffdom is divided into districts, a sheriff court sitting in each district. Cases are heard by sheriffs or summary sheriffs. Only certain decisions may be appealed. Such appeal is heard by the sheriff appeal court, which consists of appeal sheriffs. Sheriffs principal automatically hold office as appeal sheriffs, and

[13] Patrick and Stavert, *Mental Health, Incapacity and the Law in Scotland* (2016).

[14] The test for emergency and short-term detention is slightly different. MH(CT)(S)A 2003, see ss 36(4) and 44(4).

[15] See, for example, MH(CT)(S)A 2003, s 44(4).

sheriffs may also be appointed to that office.[16] A further appeal may be allowed in some cases to the Court of Session.

The majority of formal adult protection measures require an application to the sheriff court and will continue to be heard by sheriffs.[17] Different sheriffdoms employ different practice rules and there is some discretion granted to individual sheriffs as to how cases should proceed. They are required to ensure that cases are dealt with as efficiently as possible, but at all times in a manner that respects the rights of all parties involved and allows an opportunity for a fair hearing of the relevant matters. These factors lead to a certain variation in procedure across Scotland and even within the same district.

There follows a consideration of the most important sheriff court orders available for the support and protection of adults. Where appropriate, observations will be made on points of procedure or practice. Unless otherwise noted, the application is heard by a sheriff. Assessment orders under the Adult Support and Protection (Scotland) Act 2007 are dealt with in Chapter 8.

GUARDIANSHIP AND INTERVENTION ORDERS

12.5 Where mental disorder (or, more rarely, physical disability) means that a person lacks capacity to manage their welfare, property or finances, formal measures to protect the person's interests may be appropriate. This lack of capacity may not be global, and the law recognises that a person may have capacity in respect to some decisions, but not others.[18] The Adults with Incapacity (Scotland) Act 2000 provides for intervention orders and guardianship orders, tailored to the specific needs of the individual.

The local authority is under an obligation to apply for a guardianship or intervention order where it appears an order is necessary for the protection of the property, financial affairs or personal welfare of an adult and no other suitable person has applied, or is likely to apply, for an order.[19]

16 Courts Reform (Scotland) Act 2014, ss 46, 49, 50, 109 and 110.

17 Certain complex medical decisions go directly to the Court of Session (see eg Adults with Incapacity (Scotland) Act 2000 (AWI(S)A 2000), s 50(6)).

18 See Chapter 2 for the legal definition of capacity.

19 AWI(S)A 2000, s 53(3) contains the duty to apply for an intervention order while s 57(2) contains the duty to apply for a guardianship order.

Intervention order

12.6 An intervention order can authorise a specific one-off procedure or transaction, such as a discharge of legal rights or termination of a tenancy agreement.[20] An intervention order is generally not appropriate where continuing management of an adult's welfare or finances is required. For example, it is not a good way to authorise moving an adult to residential care, since this requires some ongoing supervision of the adult.[21] It may not be appropriate to seek an intervention order to authorise the signing of a contract for care, where there are doubts about the adult's capacity to comply with ongoing contract terms such as payment of care fees. In such cases, guardianship will be the preferred option.

The exception to this may be where the adult's welfare or finances are capable of ongoing management by some other means. For example, an intervention order may be used to end a tenancy following a move into care where the adult's finances can thereafter be managed by a benefits appointee. Similarly, if a welfare attorney has been appointed, but lacks authority to make a specific one-off decision, an intervention order may be the best way to permit this.

Guardianship

12.7 A guardianship order contains specific powers, which should be directly related to the circumstances and needs of the adult. There are many situations where guardianship can help protect an adult at risk who does not have capacity. In general terms, guardianship allows potentially harmful aspects of such an adult's life to be managed on their behalf in the medium to long term. Some examples might be:

- moving an adult from an unsuitable living situation, to protect them from abuse or neglect (including self-neglect), and maintaining them there;
- preventing an adult from consorting with certain harmful individuals, including supporting an adult to keep such individuals away from the adult's home;

[20] AWI(S)A 2000, s 53.

[21] *Adults with Incapacity (Scotland) Act 2000 Code of Practice for Local Authorities* (Scottish Executive, 2008), Ch 5, para 5.2.

- authorising community care arrangements for an adult's protection, even where the adult or relatives resist such care. This is of particular relevance in cases of self-neglect and may be less restrictive than an unwelcome move to residential care;
- where an adult with incapacity is engaging in problematic alcohol or other substance misuse, allowing the local authority (or another individual) to restrict access to such substances.

Guardianship may also be appropriate where an individual or local authority is already exercising a significant degree of informal control over the adult's life. In such circumstances, it may be appropriate to consider seeking formal powers to give the adult legal protection and ensure that their human rights are respected.[22]

A guardianship order can last for up to three years, or any other period (including indefinitely) if the Sheriff is satisfied there is a case for this.[23]

Complaints about guardian or intervener

12.8 The Public Guardian supervises everyone with financial powers under both guardianship and intervention orders.[24] It has wide powers to apply to the court to protect an adult from financial harm at the hands of a guardian or intervener and can recall a guardian's powers if they are no longer necessary.[25] Further detail as to the various means of dealing with financial abuse on the part of a guardian or intervener may found in Chapter 7.

The local authority supervises welfare guardians. Either the local authority or the Mental Welfare Commission can apply to the court to protect an adult from harm caused by a welfare guardian or intervener and can recall a welfare guardianship order if the order is no longer necessary.[26]

On receipt of an application from the Public Guardian, local authority or Mental Welfare Commission, or any other person claiming an interest in the adult's affairs, the Sheriff has wide powers to manage guardianships or intervention orders, including giving directions to a guardian or

[22] See Chapter 14.

[23] AWI(S)A 2000, s 58(4). See further below at para **12.15** regarding the potential human rights issues raised by indefinite or long-term orders.

[24] AWI(S)A 2000, s 6(2)(a).

[25] AWI(S)A 2000, s 73(1).

[26] AWI(S)A 2000, s 73(3).

intervener.[27] The Sheriff can recall financial and welfare guardianship and can replace a guardian or change the terms of an order.[28]

Court procedure

12.9 Applications under the Adults with Incapacity (Scotland) Act 2000 follow the summary applications procedure.[29] This is a very flexible form of court procedure and the Sheriff has wide powers and considerable discretion in dealing with applications. Nonetheless, the Act itself imposes certain procedural requirements and there are others contained in specific court rules.[30] Both the Sheriff considering an application under the Adults with Incapacity (Scotland) Act 2000 and anyone exercising a power in terms of any order granted must act at all times in accordance with the general principles of the Act.[31]

Making the application

12.10 A new application must be made in the form specified in the rules.[32] Subsequent applications, including applications for renewal and counter-applications, are made by lodging a minute.[33] A new application must be supported by two medical certificates confirming incapacity. Where the application involves welfare powers, a mental health officer also provides a report. Where only financial powers are sought, a report from an individual with expert financial knowledge is needed instead of the mental health officer report.[34]

27 AWI(S)A 2000, s 3(3).
28 AWI(S)A 2000, ss 71, 74.
29 AWI(S)A 2000, s 2(2).
30 Act of Sederunt (Summary Applications, Statutory Applications and Appeals etc. Rules) 1999 (SI 1999/929), Ch 3, Part XVI. Most sheriffdoms also have practice notes which set out requirements for applications being made within that area. These can be accessed at: https://www.scotcourts.gov.uk/rules-and-practice/practice-notes-and-directions/#/
31 See Chapter 5 for further consideration of the principles of the Act.
32 Form 23, SI 1999/929, para 3.16.7. Forms are available at: www.scotcourts.gov.uk/rules-and-practice/forms/sheriff-court-forms/summary-applications-statutory-applications-and-appeals-etc-forms
33 SI 1999/929, para 3.16.8.
34 AWI(S)A 2000, s 57(3).

Notice to adult and other parties

12.11 Despite the possible incapacity of the adult, the rules impose a clear legal duty to give the adult notice of the proceedings. The Sheriff can dispense with notice only if two medical certificates, including one from a Mental Health (Care and Treatment) (Scotland) Act 2003-approved doctor, confirm that giving notice would be likely to pose a serious risk to the health of the adult.[35] Where the adult is in a care home or hospital, the manager of the facility in question must take responsibility for ensuring the application is delivered to them and its contents explained. The manager must then return a certificate confirming that they have done so to the court, before the first hearing.[36]

Notice must also be given to:

- the nearest relative of the adult;
- the primary carer of the adult;
- the named person of the adult;
- any guardian, continuing attorney or welfare attorney of the adult who has any power relating to the application;
- the Public Guardian;
- the Mental Welfare Commission;
- the local authority (where the application is not made by it); and
- any other person directed by the Sheriff.[37]

It is common for sheriffs to require notification of the application to any close relatives and any other interested parties who are mentioned in the reports accompanying it. For example, the latter might include a service provider, school or independent advocate.

The authority to proceed to serve the application on those to be notified comes in the form of a warrant signed by the Sheriff, fixing a date for the case to be heard. Before granting a warrant, the Sheriff will have to be satisfied that the application is formally correct and accompanied by all the necessary reports, in the correct form and fully completed. It is

35 SI 1999/929, para 3.16.5.

36 SI 1999/929, para 3.16.5.

37 SI 1999/929, para 3.16.4. There are also further notification requirements where the application is for renewal of an order granted as part of criminal proceedings.

common for sheriffs to take the opportunity before granting the warrant to ask for further detail relating to any preliminary issues they may have identified in the content of an application and, in some cases, to ask for amendments to the terms of the application, even where an application is formally valid. This practice serves to minimise the number of, and time required for, hearings, as the increase in the number of applications has put increased pressure on court resources.

The hearing

12.12 At the hearing the Sheriff may simply grant the application, if it is unopposed and they are satisfied that it is well-founded. Alternatively, they may make any other order they think necessary regarding further procedure.[38] The hearing usually takes place in a closed court, or other private setting, but may be ordered by the Sheriff to take place anywhere appropriate.[39] There is no specific requirement that the setting be private. The Mental Welfare Commission has expressed concern about hearings taking place in open court, to which the public can have access.[40] It believes that generally hearings should be in private, to protect the adult's privacy. Anyone concerned can formally ask the Sheriff to hear a case in private. Many courts now conduct preliminary hearings through Webex, an online video conferencing application. Some courts also allow a preliminary hearing to be conducted on written submissions alone.

Protecting the adult's interests

12.13 Where an adult is unable to instruct a solicitor, the court may appoint a curator *ad litem*. This will usually be a solicitor with experience in mental health law issues. The curator acts on the adult's behalf in the proceedings, in accordance with the general principles.[41]

In addition, or as an alternative, the Sheriff may consider whether it is necessary to appoint a safeguarder for the adult.[42] The safeguarder protects the interests of the adult (again, with reference to the general principles), and, in particular, tries to establish the adult's views. In some circumstances the Sheriff may even appoint two safeguarders, one

38 SI 1999/929, para 3.16.6.

39 SI 1999/929, para 3.16.3. An example might be a hospital or care home, if an adult had mobility difficulties that would prevent their attendance in court.

40 Mental Welfare Commission, *Annual Report* (2002–3), para 3.3.

41 See Chapter 5 on the general principles applicable.

42 AWI(S)A 2000, s 3(4).

to protect the adult's interests and the other to advise the Sheriff of the adult's views.[43]

Appeals

12.14 There is a right to appeal most decisions of the Sheriff to the Sheriff Appeal Court and, beyond that where leave is granted, to the Court of Session.[44]

Human rights issues

12.15 For some years, there has been concern that, while there is not necessarily an explicit breach of human rights protections, there are aspects of Scots law concerning guardianship that have the scope to be put into practice in ways that do breach these protections. In particular, the possibility for indefinite orders to be granted; the use of long-term orders in circumstances where they give power to authorise deprivation of the adult's liberty (for example, in a care home); and the ability to dispense with notice of an application on the adult, without fully exploring alternative means of their being informed and involved in the process, have all been highlighted as practices which are problematic.[45]

In the past, some sheriffs were persuaded to grant orders for an indefinite or very lengthy period. This was sometimes considered appropriate where the adult was elderly and incapacity was as a result of a progressive condition such as dementia, on the basis that the situation was unlikely to change and the period of the order would be naturally be limited. However, where they are authorising interventions in the adult's affairs that have the potential to infringe their human rights, and especially where the guardian may make a decision to authorise the deprivation of the adult's liberty, guardianship orders must be subject to regular review.[46] Limiting this requirement in a way that is age-discriminatory is likely to

[43] AWI(S)A 2000, s 3(5).

[44] AWI(S)A 2000, s 2(3), as modified by the Courts Reform (Scotland) Act 2014, s 109.

[45] See, for example, the consideration given to these issues by the English Court of Protection in *Aberdeenshire Council* v *SF (No 2)* [2024] EWCOP 10. At the time of writing, the Scottish Government is consulting on various reforms aimed, among other things, at introducing legislation that will require more human rights-compliant practice (Adults with Incapacity Amendment Act Consultation (July 2024)).

[46] Chapter 14 gives more detail on this point.

be a breach of an adult's human rights in itself. It is suggested therefore that all applications should take care to limit the length of any order sought, to allow the court to provide independent review of its continuing appropriateness through the renewal procedure.

Care must also be taken to ensure that adults have been given a full opportunity to participate in the process as far as they are able to do so. This may involve a more proactive role for advocacy services, or specifically asking the court to appoint a curator or safeguarder.[47] At the least, any application to the sheriff to exercise their discretion to dispense with service on the adult must be supported by a full consideration of all of the alternative means of involving the adult that have been considered and information as to why these cannot be used.

Non-compliance with decisions of a welfare guardian

12.16 Where a decision made lawfully by a welfare guardian in exercise of powers granted to them is disregarded by either the adult or a third party, an application may be made for an order to enforce it. An example may be where a specific support is being denied to an adult by a third party, or where a decision that an abuser should refrain from visiting the adult's home is not followed.

Where a decision about the place where the adult is to reside is not complied with by the adult, a warrant may be granted authorising a police officer to enter premises and remove the adult to another place, as directed by the guardian.[48]

Either type of application is made in the form contained in regulations.[49] Once made, the court notifies the adult or the person (to whom the order would apply) of the application. Objections to the granting of the warrant or order must be made within 21 days. After hearing any objections, the Sheriff may grant the order or warrant.[50] Where there is good reason to do so, the Sheriff may dispense with the requirement to give notice or hear objections.[51]

[47] See para **12.13**, above. See also para **12.53** below, regarding support for vulnerable witnesses.

[48] AWI(S)A 2000, s 70(1) and (2).

[49] Adults with Incapacity (Non-compliance with Decisions of Welfare Guardians) (Scotland) Regulations 2002 (SSI 2002/98), reg 2.

[50] AWI(S)A 2000, s 70(3) and (4), SSI 2002/98, reg 3.

[51] AWI(S)A 2000, s 70(4A).

Protection orders under the Adult Support and Protection (Scotland) Act 2007

12.17 The 2007 Act creates three types of court order, collectively known as 'protection orders,' which may be used to advance an investigation and/or protect the adult. These are:

- assessment orders;
- removal orders; and
- banning orders.

Despite being classed as a protection order, the assessment order is primarily an investigative tool and, as such, is described in detail in Chapter 8, dealing with investigations. Nonetheless, questions regarding the adult's consent, undue pressure and the definition of serious harm are relevant to all three types of protection order.

The adult's consent

12.18 All three of the protection orders are considered to be major interventions into an adult's life. For this reason, it is stipulated that the Sheriff must not make an order if they know that the affected adult at risk has refused to consent to the granting of that order.[52] Similarly a person cannot take any action authorised by an order if they know the affected adult at risk has refused to consent to the action.[53] This is in marked distinction to the exercise of most other functions in terms of the Adult Support and Protection (Scotland) Act 2007, where obtaining consent is recommended as best practice, but refusal of consent does not in itself prevent action from being taken (eg initiating an investigation into concerns).

Consent and incapacity

12.19 Making the granting of an order (or carrying out of its terms) contingent on there being no known refusal of consent could be seen as a reversal of the usual principles governing the intervention of public agencies into citizens' lives. Normally, explicit consent must be given to an intervention, or consent is not required and the intervention is submitted

52 Adult Support and Protection (Scotland) Act 2007 (ASP(S)A 2007), s 35(1).
53 ASP(S)A 2007, s 35(2).

to judicial control alone. The reversal might be justified on the basis that, from the point of view of the legislation, the consent issue is the final consideration that a Sheriff will take into account, after the principles of the Act and the criteria for granting the order have been assessed (in that order).[54] The refusal of consent therefore represents a final opportunity for an adult with capacity to refuse support or protection, notwithstanding that such an intervention has been assessed by the court as being of benefit to them and necessary. In other words, it allows the adult to make the 'bad choice' that is often held up as being of the essence of capacity.

The integration of this unusual approach with other aspects of the law raises some issues of both a practical and legal nature. For example, there is a lack of clarity as to what should happen in situations where an adult clearly refuses to consent to an order but is believed not to have the capacity to make that decision. The *Adult Support and Protectiion (Scotland) Act 2007 Code of Practice* suggests that in such circumstances the adult's refusal to consent may simply be disregarded,[55] but it is not at all clear that an inability to consent to something in law necessarily implies an inability to refuse consent. This is particularly the case in relation to interventions on the part of public authorities which impinge on the enjoyment of a citizen's human rights, as all of the protection orders do. For similar reasons, even where an adult is unable to express an opinion or physically resist the exercise of the order, it is potentially problematic simply to interpret inaction as acquiescence.[56] These legal principles may only be reversed by specific legislative provision (if at all), so supersede the guidance in the Code of Practice. Aside from the legal issues, there is the practical question of how to carry an order out if an adult with incapacity refuses to comply.

In light of these issues, it is suggested that, where an adult does not have capacity it may be better practice to take action under other legislation. If the situation is not one of urgency, it may be possible to make an application under the Adults with Incapacity (Scotland) Act 2000 for the appointment of a guardian with the power to take whatever action is necessary to protect or support the adult. Alternatively, if the adult with incapacity has a mental disorder, it may be more appropriate to consider the use of a warrant or order under the Mental Health (Care and Treatment) (Scotland) Act 2003, which can permit an assessment, medical

54 As would appear to be confirmed by the order in which these considerations appear in the Act.

55 *Adult Support and Protection (Scotland) Act 2007 Code of Practice* (2022) (ASP(S)A 2007 Code of Practice), p 74.

56 The issue of human rights is considered in detail in Chapter 14.

examination and, if necessary, the removal of the person at risk to a place of safety without their consent. Emergency situations are considered in more detail in Chapter 9.

Further, it is not clear what role an adult's welfare attorney or guardian should play in the Adult Support and Protection (Scotland) Act 2007 process, where one with relevant powers already exists. The legislation clearly envisages that the adult at risk will be advised of the proposed order or action and asked about consent. For example, there is a requirement to notify the adult of court proceedings.[57] There is no similar requirement to notify an attorney or guardian, and a strict reading of the principles requires such an individual's views to be taken into account only insofar as they are known. This again raises the issue of whether a Sheriff or person acting under an order may competently proceed on the basis that, if there is not any express refusal on the part of an attorney or guardian that they are aware of, they may grant the order or take the necessary action. Where an attorney or guardian actively refuses consent, it may not be straightforward to disregard this, even where they are the suspected abuser (see the consideration of 'undue pressure' below). Again, it may be better in either of these circumstances to consider whether other legislation may provide a clearer solution.

Undue pressure

12.20 There is one major exception to the requirement that the adult must consent to a protection order. The Act specifies that an order can be granted, or used, without consent in situations where either the Sheriff, or the person seeking to enforce the order, reasonably believes that:

- the affected adult at risk has been unduly pressured to refuse consent; and
- there are no steps that could reasonably be taken with the adult's consent which would protect the adult from the harm which the order or action is intended to prevent.[58]

A refusal to participate in an interview or to consent to a medical examination cannot be overridden due to undue pressure.[59]

57 ASP(S)A 2007, s 41(3).
58 ASP(S)A 2007, s 35(3).
59 ASP(S)A 2007, s 35(6).

The Act provides an example of a situation in which 'undue pressure' is present.[60] It states that an adult at risk can be considered to be under undue pressure if:

- the person causing the harm that the order, or action, is intended to prevent is someone in whom the adult at risk has confidence and trust; and
- the adult at risk would consent to the order or action if they did not have confidence and trust in that person.

This is primarily intended to confirm that undue pressure includes situations where an adult refuses to consent to an action either because of an abuse of a relationship of trust which, perhaps, falls short of a threat of force, or some other specific application of pressure. This could be from a family member, partner, spouse, friend or anyone else with a close personal relationship to the adult.

However, the Act is clear that this example is not in itself definitive of undue pressure, so the phrase should otherwise be given its normal meaning.[61] As an example, there will be cases where the adult has been made afraid of the consequences of cooperating because they have been threatened or told that something will happen. Someone might have convinced the adult that they will not be believed, will be blamed or even be removed and held in custody or a hospital, or have benefits cut or other financial penalties imposed.

It should be noted that in this wider sense, undue pressure does not require a relationship of confidence and trust to exist between the third party and the adult. As a result, the concept of undue pressure can, in theory, apply to applications for orders in cases involving self-harm or neglect. However, this would only be the case where a third party is the cause of the undue pressure. Where there is no third party, an adult's refusal to consent to an order cannot be overridden. It should be borne in mind at all times that there is a need to balance the right of the adult to make their own choices with the local authority's obligation to protect those experiencing harm or abuse. Interventions will in any event have more chance of success in the longer term if the adult agrees they should happen.

Undue pressure and attorneys/guardians

12.21 A specific difficulty arises in situations where an adult with incapacity's welfare attorney or guardian (with relevant powers) refuses

[60] ASP(S)A 2007, s 35(4).
[61] ASP(S)A 2007, s 35(5).

consent on their behalf. Many attorneys or guardians are appointed with a specific power to consent or refuse to consent to a protection order. A power to convey the adult to medical appointments, decide where the adult is to reside, or decide with whom the adult is to consort would also empower an attorney or guardian to refuse consent to an assessment, removal or banning order, respectively. Where such refusal is known by the Sheriff considering the application, or the person acting on the order, it must be taken in effect as a refusal made by the adult themselves.

It is difficult to see how such a refusal could be categorised as undue pressure, within the normal sense of the term. There is no pressure being put on the adult as such: merely the exercise of a power granted by the adult or the court. Neither is there pressure on the attorney or guardian actually making the decision. Even if there can be said to be a relationship of confidence or trust (perhaps as formalised in the granting of a power of attorney) it would be difficult to hold that the adult would consent in the absence of that relationship, given that they do not have capacity.

If presented with such a scenario, practitioners should therefore again look beyond the Adult Support and Protection (Scotland) Act 2007 itself. There are steps which may be taken to deal with attorneys or guardians who are not carrying out their duties satisfactorily in terms of the Adults with Incapacity (Scotland) Act 2000, although the court procedures required cannot necessarily be completed quickly. Again, the Mental Health (Care and Treatment) (Scotland) Act 2003 may provide more immediate help in urgent cases.[62]

Serious harm

12.22 In order to grant a protection order of any sort, the Sheriff must be satisfied that there are reasonable grounds to suspect a risk of 'serious harm' to the adult rather than merely 'harm'. There is no specific definition of 'serious harm' in the legislation, so the normal meaning of the phrase, in conjunction with the definition of the word 'harm' contained in the Act, must be applied. It is suggested that this means that serious harm differs from mere harm only in degree and not in substance. In other words, any form of behaviour which may constitute harm may also constitute serious harm, if the impact of it is sufficiently severe.

Further, as with the basic definition of harm, it is the impact on the individual adult at risk that is of relevance. What constitutes serious harm may be different for different people.

[62] See further Chapter 9.

These observations are of particular relevance in regard to financial harm, where it must be borne in mind that even the loss of what may appear relatively small amounts of money may have a serious impact. Adults with fewer means will feel any loss more keenly, but there may also be serious consequences for an adult at risk's self-esteem, confidence in the community and ability to form trusting relationships.

Removal orders

12.23 A removal order under the Adult Support and Protection (Scotland) Act 2007 authorises the local authority to move an adult at risk to a specific place of safety to protect them from harm.[63] It includes the power to enter premises to move the adult.[64] This could be the adult's home or any public, private or commercial premises. A removal order is primarily aimed at protecting the adult, not at assessing their needs or carrying out a medical examination.[65] Despite this similarity in basic purpose, it must be noted that this order is quite different from the order of the same name in terms of the Mental Health (Care and Treatment) (Scotland) Act 2003.[66]

Grounds for order

12.24 The Sheriff may grant a removal order only if satisfied that:

- there is reasonable cause to believe that the person is an adult at risk who is likely to suffer serious harm if not moved to another place; and
- the place to which the adult is to be moved is suitable and available.[67]

As with any protection order, the Sheriff must not grant a removal order if they know that the adult has refused to consent to it, unless they reasonably believe that the refusal is due to undue pressure being brought to bear on the adult.[68] In line with the general principles of the Act, the Sheriff will also have to be satisfied that removal of the adult as proposed will be of benefit to them and represents the least restrictive option.

63 ASP(S)A 2007, s 14(1).
64 ASP(S)A 2007, s 16.
65 ASP(S)A 2007 Code of Practice, p 80.
66 See further Chapter 9 on emergencies.
67 ASP(S)A 2007, s 15.
68 ASP(S)A 2007, s 35.

Impact of order

12.25 The removal order authorises a council officer (or someone nominated by the local authority) to move the adult to the place specified in the order. It also authorises the local authority to take such reasonable steps as it thinks fit to protect the adult from harm.[69]

A removal order must be used within 72 hours of the time it is issued.[70] This means the adult must be moved to the place specified in the order within that time.

While there is no requirement that a removal order itself specify the place from which the adult is to be removed, a warrant for entry must be attached to the order, and the place where such warrant will have effect will, therefore, have to be specified.[71] If the adult moves to a different address before any action is taken under the removal order, and the warrant is required for entry to the premises, the previous warrant will not be valid and a new application for a warrant will be necessary. The removal order will remain valid, unless it also specified the place from where the adult was to be removed.

A removal order must, however, always specify the place to which the adult will be moved. If a decision is made to move the adult somewhere else, following the granting of an order, either a fresh application for a removal order will be necessary, or, if time permits, it may be possible to apply to vary the order.

No detention

12.26 Although a removal order includes no power to detain the adult, the legislation is not explicit about what happens if the adult chooses to leave. However, the local authority will continue to have a duty of care and should make reasonable arrangements to return the adult to the place from where they were removed, or indeed any other appropriate place.

Contact conditions

12.27 The removal order may contain specific provisions allowing certain person(s) to have contact with the adult at risk at certain times during the currency of the order. The order may spell out the conditions attaching to such contact.[72]

69 ASP(S)A 2007, s 14(1).
70 ASP(S)A 2007, s 14(1)(a).
71 ASP(S)A 2007, s 39(1).
72 ASP(S)A 2007, s 15(2).

Before making such a requirement the Sheriff must consider any representations made by the local authority, the adult at risk or any other interested party.[73] (The Sheriff can waive this rule in exceptional cases.[74])

Variation or recall

12.28 The Sheriff can vary or recall an order within the seven-day period it is in force. This can be on the application of the adult at risk, the local authority or any other interested party.[75] Such an application must be made on the basis that there has been a change of circumstances since the granting (or last variation) of the order.

If the Sheriff recalls the removal order, they may direct the council to return the adult to the place from where they were removed or to some other place. The Sheriff should have regard to the adult's wishes before specifying some other place.[76]

Protection of property

12.29 The local authority is under a duty to take reasonable steps to protect and secure the property of an individual moved under a removal order if the adult is unable to deal with it, and no other suitable arrangements have been, or are being, made. A council officer may enter any premises (and any adjacent place) where they know or believe such property is situated.[77] The costs of doing this cannot be recovered from the adult.[78]

Expiry of order

12.30 The legislation specifies that the removal order expires after a period of seven days.[79] The first day is the day commencing at midnight following the adult's arrival at the place specified in the order, and the order continues in force throughout the whole of the seventh day.[80] However, the significance of these seven days is limited, because the legislation does not carry any powers of detention. The adult must be

[73] ASP(S)A 2007, s 15(3).
[74] ASP(S)A 2007, s 41(2).
[75] ASP(S)A 2007, s 17(4).
[76] ASP(S)A 2007, s 17(3).
[77] ASP(S)A 2007, s 18.
[78] ASP(S)A 2007, s 18(5).
[79] ASP(S)A 2007, s 14(2).
[80] ASP(S)A 2007 Code of Practice, p 84.

allowed to leave at any time if they wish to do so, unless they can be detained under the Mental Health (Care and Treatment) (Scotland) Act 2003. This notwithstanding, the removal period should be as short as possible, in line with the general principles of benefit, least restriction and the adult's wishes.[81] A variation cannot be used to extend the order beyond the original seven-day duration.[82] The flip side of these observations is that, once removed, an adult will only remain at the place they have been moved to by consent. If that consent remains, there is of course no issue with the adult remaining where they were brought under the removal order, notwithstanding the order's expiry.

The code of practice says that a further application for a removal order must not be made on the expiry of the order with the intention of extending the order. Since, before granting an order, the Sheriff must be satisfied that the adult is likely to be seriously harmed if not moved to *another* place, it is anyway unlikely such an order could be validly granted in practice. There is no explicit restriction on granting a further order if an adult has been returned to the place from which they were originally removed. Nonetheless, frequent moves under a removal order, particularly if carried out in short succession, are unlikely to be to the adult's benefit, or represent the least restrictive option available.

Banning orders

12.31 There may be circumstances where excluding the person causing risk to an adult is preferable to moving the adult. A banning order bans a person from a specified place for up to six months. This may offer protection for the adult and provide an opportunity to consider their needs for future care and protection.

Grounds for order

12.32 The Sheriff can grant a banning order if satisfied that:

- an adult at risk is being, or is likely to be, seriously harmed by another person;
- the adult's well-being or property would be better safeguarded by banning that other person from the premises in question than it would be by moving the adult at risk; and

[81] ASP(S)A 2007 Code of Practice, p 84.
[82] ASP(S)A 2007, s 17(2).

- either the adult at risk is entitled or permitted to occupy the premises, or neither the adult at risk nor the person to be banned is entitled, or permitted to occupy the premises.[83] (In other words, no order can be made if the adult has no entitlement or permission to occupy and the person to be banned does.)

As with any protection order, the Sheriff must not grant a banning order if they know that the adult has refused to consent to it, unless they reasonably believe that the refusal is due to undue pressure being brought to bear on the adult.[84]

Perpetrator aged under 16

12.33 An adult or a child can be made subject to a banning order. Where the subject is a child, the local authority should consider whether there is a case for referral to the Children's Reporter. If the case is urgent, the local authority should refer the case to the Children's Reporter at the same time as it applies for the order.[85]

Impact of order

12.34 A banning order bans the person subject to the order from being in specified premises for a certain period.[86] Premises could include the adult's home and other places, such as day services, as well as public places, such as a leisure centre or club.[87] The ban may even extend to the area around the premises and can authorise the person's ejection from the area of the ban.[88]

The order can impose additional conditions. These may include an order that the banned person should not remove any items from the premises and a direction that the subject's moveable property left there should be preserved. The banning order can be made subject to conditions (for example allowing the subject to attend the specified place between particular hours, or subject to particular restrictions, to allow contact with the adult at risk). Additional requirements may also be added where the Sheriff is satisfied these are necessary for the proper enforcement of the

[83] ASP(S)A 2007, s 20.
[84] ASP(S)A 2007, s 35.
[85] ASP(S)A 2007 Code of Practice, p 89.
[86] ASP(S)A 2007, s 19(1).
[87] ASP(S)A 2007 Code of Practice, p 89.
[88] ASP(S)A 2007, s 19(2).

order. These may be made of any person and may include a requirement to do something, or refrain from doing something. A common example is a requirement on the subject to refrain from contacting the adult at risk, where there is a reasonable apprehension that they will do so to pressurise the adult into refusing to enforce the order.[89]

In fixing such conditions, the Sheriff must take into account any representations made by the person applying for the order, the adult at risk, anyone with an interest in the adult's well-being or property, and the person to be banned.[90] The Sheriff may waive the need for such representations if they are satisfied that doing so will protect the adult at risk from serious harm or will not prejudice any person affected.[91]

The Sheriff may attach a power of arrest to the order.[92] The police can then arrest the person being banned if they breach the order. The power of arrest becomes effective when the order is served on the person being banned (although, in practice, police will not be able to act on the power until it has also been served on the Chief Constable). It continues for the duration of the order.

There are no specific criteria identified in the legislation for the granting of a power of arrest. The code of practice suggests that the likelihood that the subject will breach the order will be the definitive factor.[93] The risk of immediate harm to the adult in the case of a breach may also be a relevant consideration.

A banning order will specify how long it will last. The maximum period is six months, but it can be for a shorter period.[94]

Where a banning order excludes a spouse from the family home, this does not affect any occupancy rights the adult at risk may have as a non-entitled spouse.[95]

Temporary orders

12.35 In an emergency, an application for a temporary banning order can be made at the same time as the application for a banning order.[96] The

89 ASP(S)A 2007, s 19(2) and (3).
90 ASP(S)A 2007, s 19(4).
91 ASP(S)A 2007, s 41(2).
92 ASP(S)A 2007, s 25.
93 ASP(S)A 2007 Code of Practice, p 90.
94 ASP(S)A 2007, s 19.
95 Under the Matrimonial Homes (Family Protection) (Scotland) Act 1981, s 1(1). ASP(S)A 2007, s 23.
96 ASP(S)A 2007, s 22.

temporary order is intended to protect the adult during the period the banning order application is progressing through court. See para **9.5** for further information.

Where a temporary order is granted, the Sheriff must decide whether to grant a full order within six months of the date the application was lodged.[97] The temporary order expires after those six months or when the Sheriff makes a decision regarding the full banning order, whichever is the earlier. The Sheriff may insert an earlier expiry date.[98]

Variation or recall of order

12.36 The Sheriff may vary or recall (ie cancel) an order or a temporary order, where they are satisfied that a change in circumstances warrants this.[99] For example, it might be varied by attaching a power of arrest.[100] The subject of the order, the person who applied for the order, the adult at risk or anyone with an interest in the adult's well-being or property can apply for a variation or recall.

A banning order cannot be varied to extend beyond six months from the date on which the order was granted, and a temporary order cannot be extended beyond its due date for expiry.[101]

Breach of order without power of arrest

12.37 There is no obligation on the adult at risk to report any breach of an order, but they may wish to do so and seek help from the local authority. Failure to comply with the terms of a banning order or temporary order is a contempt of court and proceedings to find the subject in contempt may be appropriate. Either the person who applied for the order or the adult at risk may commence proceedings, by summary application. It will be necessary to seek confirmation that the procurator fiscal is not initiating criminal proceedings in regard to any of the circumstances surrounding the breach and the application should be docquetted to that effect.[102]

[97] SI 1999/ 929, para 3.35.3.
[98] ASP(S)A 2007, s 21(4).
[99] ASP(S)A 2007, s 24.
[100] ASP(S)A 2007 Code of Practice, p 90.
[101] ASP(S)A 2007, s 24(2).
[102] ASP(S)A 2007 Code of Practice, p 94. A 'docquet' is simply signed confirmation that the procurator fiscal is not pursuing criminal proceedings written on the application itself, once it has been prepared and before submission to the court.

Where the person is found to be in contempt, they may receive up to three months' imprisonment or a fine of level 4 on the standard scale, or both.[103]

If the person breaching the order has committed a criminal offence, such as assault, the procurator fiscal may instead commence criminal proceedings. Bail conditions may provide a further means to protect the adult in such circumstances.

Breach of order with power of arrest attached

12.38 A police officer may arrest a person subject to an order containing a power of arrest if:

- there are reasonable grounds for suspecting the person is in breach of the order or has breached the order in the past; and
- there is a risk they will do so in the future unless arrested.[104]

The police officer does not need a warrant, so can act quickly if there are grounds for concern.

The police officer must take the person arrested to a police station as quickly as reasonably practicable and advise them why they are being arrested.[105] The police should ensure that the person detained receives information about their rights, including their right to notify a solicitor about the arrest.

The person arrested will be kept in custody until they are brought before the Sheriff.[106] The police must issue a report to the procurator fiscal as soon possible.[107]

The police duties towards any person held in custody in terms of a power of arrest granted as part of a banning order are the same as they are towards any person held for any other reason. Worth noting here is that, if the person being detained is a child, the officer must, as soon as reasonably practicable, notify the child's parent(s), or any other guardian or person who has care of them.[108] Where parents cannot be contacted, will not attend, or social work advise they should not be contacted, another

[103] Contempt of Court Act 1981, s 15(2)(a).
[104] ASP(S)A 2007, s 28.
[105] Criminal Justice (Scotland) Act 2016 (CJ(S)A 2016), ss 3 and 4.
[106] ASP(S)A 2007, s 29.
[107] ASP(S)A 2007, s 29(2).
[108] CJ(S)A 2016, s 38. For the purposes of this discussion, 'child' will be taken to mean a person under 16.

appropriate person must be contacted.[109] Anyone so notified has a right to access the child.[110]

Persons over 16 have a right to request that another person is notified of their being held in custody (ie unlike children, the intimation will not be made automatically).[111] If a person appears to be over 16 and unable to understand what is happening or communicate with police due to a mental disorder, an officer must intimate where they are held and what support they require to a person suitable to provide that support.[112] That person will be an 'appropriate adult'.

Provision of appropriate adult support for people with mental disorders who were arrested by the police grew up informally over a period of years, but was set on an explicit legislative footing by the Criminal Justice (Scotland) Act 2016 and the Criminal Justice (Scotland) Act 2016 (Support for Vulnerable Persons) Regulations 2019.[113] Local authorities are now specifically responsible for providing this service and providing training for persons wishing to be appropriate adults.[114] Appropriate adults are there to support the arrested person to understand what is happening to them and communicate with police. They are not legal advisers or advocates.

Any solicitor notified should be advised of the date and time of the court hearing and the person arrested is entitled to a private interview with a solicitor before the hearing.[115] The officer in charge at the police station must keep appropriate records of the person's arrest and detention.[116]

The hearing

12.39 The person must go before the Sheriff or summary sheriff on the next court day practicable.[117] A non-court day may be used if the criminal cases are being heard on that day for any reason.

The procurator fiscal must present the Sheriff or summary sheriff with all relevant information concerning the breach, the circumstances of the

[109] CJ(S)A 2016, s 39.
[110] CJ(S)A 2016, s 40. There are similar rules in relation to persons aged 16 and 17, but allowing more discretion open to the arrestee as to the process.
[111] CJ(S)A 2016, s 38.
[112] CJ(S)A 2016, s 42.
[113] SSI 2019/437.
[114] SSI 2019/437, regs 4 and 6.
[115] CJ(S)A 2016, s 44.
[116] CJ(S)A 2016, s 6.
[117] ASP(S)A 2007, s 32.

granting of the order and anything relevant to the question of whether the person will breach the order again. The Sheriff or summary sheriff must decide whether to extend the detention.[118] The detained person will be able to make representations before a decision is made.

If the Sheriff or summary sheriff is satisfied that the person appears to be in breach of the order and that there is a substantial risk of a further breach, they may order that the person continues to stay in police custody for up to two days more. (Non-court days do not count towards the two days). If the Sheriff does not extend the detention, the person must be released from custody (unless they are also in custody for another offence).[119]

Expiry of order

12.40 There is no procedure allowing renewal of a banning order. Where an adult is still at risk when a banning order expires, it may be appropriate to apply for a new order.

Making an application for a protection order

12.41 Applications for protection orders are subject to the summary applications procedures. As with applications for guardianship or intervention orders, there are some specific procedural rules contained in the legislation itself and others in a separate section of the court rules.[120] Nonetheless, there is even greater freedom afforded to the court to manage the procedure for applications for protection orders. Consequently, there is significant variation around Scotland, and even between individual sheriffs at the same court, as to how an application proceeds. It is advisable to contact the Sheriff clerk's office at the relevant court before making an application, in order to establish what may be required.

The application takes the form of an initial writ, and is made to the sheriff court for the area where the adult is, or, in the case of a banning order, where the premises are situated or where the person to be excluded lives.[121] An application for a banning order must be accompanied by a plan clearly indicating the area from which the subject is to be banned.[122]

[118] ASP(S)A 2007, s 33.
[119] ASP(S)A 2007, s 34.
[120] SI 1999/ 929, Ch 3, Part XXXV.
[121] Civil Jurisdiction and Judgments Act 1982, Sch 8.
[122] SI 1999/929, para 3.35.3.

The person applying for an order must generally give notice to the person to whom the application relates and to the adult at risk. In the case of assessment and removal orders, this will be the same person. Those receiving notice of the application must have a chance to make representations to the Sheriff, either in person or through a solicitor. A friend, relative or other representative (such as an independent advocate) may accompany the adult to the hearing.[123]

There is no requirement that hearings be held in private, but the observations regarding the adult's privacy made in para **12.12** above apply equally in applications for protection orders.

Emergency applications

12.42 In urgent situations, if no Sheriff is available to hear an application, the local authority can ask a justice of the peace to grant an emergency removal order.[124] The time limits for emergency orders are different and are discussed in Chapter 9.

A Sheriff may also disapply the notice requirements described above in any application, where they are satisfied that to do so will protect an adult at a risk of serious harm, or that it will not result in any prejudice to any party.[125] This provision is sometimes used to allow the granting of temporary banning orders at *ex parte* hearings (hearings where the subject of the order has not been made aware of the application and is not present). Such steps should only be taken where there is a real risk that the subject of the proposed order will harm the adult if made aware of the application and no other means of protection of the adult is available. The Sheriff may require written ('affidavit') evidence or wish to hear oral evidence given on oath by professionals involved, to establish that such a hearing is justified.

Protecting the adult's interests

12.43 If the local authority, or anyone else, has concerns that an adult does not understand the process, they should inform the court.[126] Where the adult is unable to instruct a solicitor, the Sheriff may appoint a curator *ad litem* (see para **12.13** above).

[123] ASP(S)A 2007, s 41.
[124] ASP(S)A 2007, s 40.
[125] ASP(S)A 2007, s 41(2).
[126] ASP(S)A 2007 Code of Practice, p 91.

The Sheriff may also appoint a safeguarder.[127] The code of practice suggests that the Sheriff might ask a safeguarder to consider the question of whether the adult consents to the order[128] (and, presumably, also whether the adult is able to consent and/or whether there is undue pressure on the adult).

Protecting the adult

12.44 If an individual suspected of harming the adult wishes to attend court, the code of practice recommends that the local authority advise the Sheriff. The court can consider whether a witness may need special protective measures under the vulnerable witness provisions[129] (see para **12.53** below).

Service of banning orders

12.45 Once a banning order or temporary banning order has been granted it must be served on the adult and the subject of the order before it will become effective. If a power of arrest has been attached, it must also be served on the Chief Constable of Police Scotland, along with proof of service on the adult and subject of the order. The same is true of any variation or recall of the order.[130] Once the required service has been effected, certificates of service should be returned to the court that granted the order, variation or recall.[131]

Appeals

12.46 There is no appeal against the granting of an assessment or removal order, but there is a right to appeal against the making, or the refusal of the Sheriff to make, a banning order.[132] The appeal is to the Sheriff Appeal Court, and from there to the Court of Session. On a successful appeal, the court may cancel or vary an order.[133] The order continues to have effect until the outcome of any appeal is known, however.[134]

127 ASP(S)A 2007, s 41(6).
128 ASP(S)A 2007 Code of Practice, p 91.
129 ASP(S)A 2007 Code of Practice, p 91.
130 ASP(S)A 2007, ss 26 and 27.
131 SI 1999/929, para 3.35.6.
132 ASP(S)A 2007, s 51, as modified by the Courts Reform (Scotland) Act 2014, s 109.
133 Courts Reform (Scotland) Act 2014.
134 ASP(S)A 2007, s 51(4), as modified by the Courts Reform (Scotland) Act 2014, s 109.

An appeal must be submitted within 28 days of the granting of a banning order and seven days of the granting of a temporary order.[135] Appeals against temporary orders require the permission of the Sheriff, or of the Sheriff Appeal Court for an appeal to the Court of Session.[136]

ANTISOCIAL BEHAVIOUR ORDERS

12.47 A local authority may be able to protect an adult at risk by seeking an antisocial behaviour order against an individual.[137] An antisocial behaviour order prohibits such conduct as is described in the order.

'Antisocial behaviour' is speech or conduct that causes or is likely to cause alarm or distress. An order cannot be granted unless there have been at least two incidents of antisocial behaviour. Orders cannot be used to deal with alarm or distress caused by a person in the same household, so are not available in cases of domestic abuse.[138]

A local authority (or a registered social landlord) may apply for an antisocial behaviour order in respect of an adult or a young person over the age of 12. If a young person is involved, the Sheriff must ask a children's hearing to advise whether or not the order is necessary.[139] The Sheriff may also make a parenting order, which directs a parent as to specific actions to take, and may require them to attend counselling or guidance.[140]

The local authority must consult with the police before it applies for an order[141] and a police officer may arrest someone without a warrant if they reasonably believe the person is in breach of an order.[142]

A criminal court may make an antisocial behaviour order at the same time as it sentences a person convicted of an offence.[143] A victim might want to discuss this with the police or procurator fiscal service.

[135] Act of Sederunt (Sheriff Appeal Court Rules) 2021 (SSI 2021/468), rule 6.3(1); SI 1999/929, para 3.35.8.

[136] ASP(S)A 2007, s 51, as modified the Courts Reform (Scotland) Act 2014, s 109.

[137] Under the Antisocial Behaviour etc. (Scotland) Act 2004 (AB(S)A 2004). For more information, see Scottish Executive, *Guidance on Antisocial Behaviour Orders* (2004).

[138] AB(S)A 2004, s 143.

[139] AB(S)A 2004, s 4.

[140] AB(S)A 2004, ss 13 and 103.

[141] AB(S)A 2004, s 4(11).

[142] CJ(S)A 2014, s 1.

[143] Criminal Procedure (Scotland) Act 1995, s 234AA.

An antisocial behaviour order may be for a fixed term or an indefinite period.[144] The Sheriff can make interim orders where appropriate.[145] These can be useful if there is immediate risk.

Applying for an antisocial behaviour order is a civil, not a criminal, matter. This means that the Sheriff has to be satisfied on a balance of probabilities and not on the higher criminal law test of beyond reasonable doubt. It also means that the rules of evidence are less strict. For example, if the adult at risk is not prepared to give evidence, local authority staff could give evidence of what they have said.

Although the proceedings granting the antisocial behaviour order are civil proceedings, breach of an order is a criminal offence. An adult found to be in breach of an order can be fined or imprisoned for up to five years (or both).[146] The court cannot detain a child.[147]

There may be circumstances where an order is appropriate even where someone is unable or unwilling to proceed against the person putting them at risk. An antisocial behaviour order does not need the adult's consent.[148] One advantage for the adult is that the local authority conducts the court case and the victim need not have the stress of raising court proceedings.

FORCED MARRIAGE PROTECTION ORDERS

12.48 Forced marriage protection orders are potentially a very flexible means of protecting an individual who is at risk of being forced into marriage, or civil partnership, or who has been forcibly married or entered into civil partnership.[149] The ceremony constituting a marriage can be either religious or civil in nature and does not have to be legally binding in terms of Scots law or any other jurisdiction. It is immaterial where the ceremony is carried out.[150]

Orders may impose such prohibitions, restrictions, requirements or other terms as the court considers appropriate to protect someone against a forced marriage or civil partnership. These terms may apply

144 AB(S)A 2004, s 4(5).
145 AB(S)A 2004, s 7.
146 AB(S)A 2004, s 9.
147 AB(S)A 2004, s 10.
148 AB(S)A 2004, s 4(11).
149 Forced Marriage etc. (Protection and Jurisdiction) (Scotland) Act 2011 (FM(PJ)(S)A 2011), s 1(1). For a description of what constitutes 'forced marriage', see para **6.21**.
150 FM(PJ)(S)A 2011, s 14.

to conduct within or outwith Scotland and to any person involved, or who may become involved, in any way with the forced marriage or civil partnership.[151] The order may last for a specified period (and may be renewed before expiry) or will last until recalled.[152] Note that, although this type of order has been extended in scope also to address forced civil partnerships, they are still called 'forced marriage protection orders'.

Applications are made by summary application and may be heard by a Sheriff or summary sheriff. They may be made by the person being forced to marry or enter into civil partnership, or by the local authority or the Lord Advocate.[153] Unusually, the order may also be made by any court hearing other civil proceedings without the requirement for an application to be made, where the court considers that an order is necessary. In order for a court to take this step, a person who will be subject to the terms of order, other than the person to be protected by it, must be a party to the proceedings before the court. If a court hearing criminal proceedings regarding such a person feels that an order may be required, a reference is made to the Lord Advocate, who will either make an application or otherwise deal with the matter.[154]

It is an offence to breach an order, punishable by up to two years in prison, a fine, or both.[155]

ORDERS AGAINST AN ABUSER

12.49 Aside from those orders which may be applied for by the local authority, there is a range of orders for which only the adult themselves may apply. So far as circumstances allow, the possibility of supporting an adult to seek one of these orders should be explored fully before any action is taken by the local authority on their behalf. In this way, the principle of least restrictive option and the requirement to maximise the adult's exercise of their own abilities will be most fully respected.

In all such cases, the adult will require independent legal representation, both to advise as to the options available and to make any necessary application to court. Citizens' Advice Bureaux and (where appropriate) Women's Aid may be able to give general advice, but will not usually be able to appear in court on an adult's behalf. The adult must therefore have

[151] FM(PJ)(S)A 2011, s 2.
[152] FM(PJ)(S)A 2011, ss 6–8.
[153] FM(PJ)(S)A 2011, s 3.
[154] FM(PJ)(S)A 2011, s 4.
[155] FM(PJ)(S)A 2011, s 9.

capacity to instruct a solicitor in such matters. A guardian is automatically empowered to instruct legal representation on an adult's behalf, where the subject matter of the application is within the ambit of their powers.[156]

With the exception of interdicts that are not issued under family proceedings, all of these orders may be heard by a Sheriff or summary sheriff.[157]

Interdict

12.50 An interdict is a court order that can be used to prohibit any abusive behaviour, including banning an abuser from entering the home or another place, approaching the adult in public or contacting the adult over the phone or by other media. It may include a power of arrest,[158] which means that a police officer can arrest the person subject to the interdict without warrant if there are reasonable grounds for believing that the person is in breach of the interdict and there is a risk of further breaches.[159]

Interdicts are more flexible in their terms than any of the protection orders available under the Adult Support and Protection (Scotland) Act 2007 and are not necessarily time-limited. For these reasons, they are often a more effective protection for an adult who is able or willing to make an application.

Family proceedings

12.51 It is possible to obtain an interdict to prohibit abusive conduct from a spouse or civil partner and to prevent the abuser from entering the family home or the neighbourhood.[160] Such an order may include a power of arrest and, where an application is made to include this power, the court must grant it.[161]

The court can grant an exclusion order if this appears necessary to protect against conduct likely to damage the physical or mental health of

156 AWI(S)A 2000, s 64(3).

157 Courts Reform (Scotland) Act 2014, Sch 1 (given effect by s 44).

158 Protection from Abuse (Scotland) Act 2001 (PFA(S)A 2001), s 1.

159 PFA(S)A 2001, s 4(1).

160 Matrimonial Homes (Family Protection) (Scotland) Act 1981 (MH(FP)(S)A 1981), s 14. Civil Partnership Act 2004 (CPA 2004), s 113. For more detail see Katy Macfarlane, *Thomson's Family law in Scotland*, (8th edn, Bloomsbury Professional, 2022).

161 PFA(S)A 2001, s 1(1A).

the applicant or of any child in the house.[162] This suspends the excluded partner's right to occupy the home.

(The local authority can also apply for a similar order to protect a child against harm, which may have an ancillary benefit for any adult living at the same address.[163])

Where an interdict is granted against a spouse, civil partner, person living with the adult as a spouse or civil partner, or other individual in an intimate relationship with the adult, an application may be made to have the court determine that it is a domestic abuse interdict.[164] Breach of such an interdict, if a power of arrest has been attached, is a criminal offence.[165]

Non-harassment order

12.52 Scots law offers specific protection to people who are victims of harassment. Harassment can be a particular issue for people with disabilities.[166] 'Harassment' means behaviour causing alarm or distress. This need not include physical violence. A person who has been harassed may apply for a court order requiring the harassment to stop.[167] The court will not make an order unless there is evidence of at least two acts of harassment, unless the conduct amounts to domestic abuse, where only one act need be proven.[168]

Instead of an interdict, the court may make a 'non-harassment order'. Breach of the order is a criminal offence, carrying a prison sentence of up to five years. The criminal courts can also make a non-harassment order where a person is convicted of a crime involving harassment. This can offer some protection for the victim in the future.[169]

162 MH(FP)(S)A 1981, s 4(2), CPA 2004, s 104.

163 Children (Scotland) Act 1995, s 76. *Thomson's Family law in Scotland* (2022), Ch 14, para 6.

164 Domestic Abuse (Scotland) Act 2011 (DA(S)A 2011), s 3.

165 DA(S)A 2011, s 2.

166 See Disability Rights Commission/Capability Scotland, *Hate Crime against Disabled People in Scotland: A survey report* (2004). This research found that one in five disabled Scots had experienced harassment because of their disability. See also Equality and Human Rights Commission report, *Hidden in Plain Sight: an Enquiry into Disability-related Harassment* (2011).

167 Protection from Harassment Act 1997 (PFHA 1997), s 8.

168 PFHA 1997, s 8A.

169 PFHA 1997, s 11.

VULNERABLE WITNESSES

12.53 Witnesses or victims of abuse in adult protection cases may sometimes have a mental illness or a learning disability or be in danger of feeling too intimidated to give evidence in court. The Vulnerable Witnesses (Scotland) Act 2004 allows the court to authorise special measures to assist witnesses to give best evidence. Special measures can be used in both the criminal and the civil courts, although slightly different rules apply in each case. This section will concentrate on the civil provisions.

In order to qualify as a vulnerable witness, a person must be aged under 18, or there must be a significant risk that either a mental disorder or fear or distress about giving evidence at the trial will affect the quality of their evidence.[170]

Where a person is a vulnerable witness because they are younger than 18, the person citing them as a witness must lodge notice with the court stating which special measures should be applied, or that none should be applied. The court must then make an order authorising such special measures as it considers appropriate, or indicating that no special measure will be authorised. Even where no special measure has been indicated in the notice, the court in its order must authorise an appropriate special measure unless it is satisfied that:

- the witness does not wish any measure to be authorised and that that is appropriate; or
- there is a significant risk of prejudice to fairness or to the interests of justice that significantly outweighs any risk of prejudice to the interests of the witness.[171]

In the case of a witness who is vulnerable for any other reason, an application may be made by the party citing the witness for special measures to be authorised. On receipt of the application, the court must decide whether the person is a vulnerable witness, whether special measures are likely to help the witness give better evidence and which measures would be appropriate.[172]

In either case, any of the following special measures may be authorised:

[170] Vulnerable Witnesses (Scotland) Act 2004 (VW(S)A 2004), s 11(1).
[171] VW(S)A 2004, s 12(1)–(4).
[172] VW(S)A 2004, s 12(5)–(7).

- the taking of evidence by a Commissioner on video instead of the witness attending court;[173]
- the giving of evidence using a live television link;[174]
- using a screen so the witness will not see the other parties (although they will be able to see the witness);[175]
- having a supporter in court.[176]

CONCLUSION

12.54 There is a wide range of formal orders available to help protect adults from harm. In cases involving an adult with a mental disorder, these may be granted or overseen by the Mental Health Tribunal. In almost all other cases, the sheriff court will have jurisdiction. Where possible, adults should be supported to pursue court action to protect themselves on their own behalf, by instructing a solicitor or accessing free, independent advice. Nonetheless, there are many measures that may be applied for by the local authority on behalf of adults who are unable or unwilling to do this. At all times during the process, the needs of the adult must be borne in mind and, where appropriate, special measures of support to ensure they can participate in any hearing should be applied.

173 VW(S)A 2004, s 19.
174 VW(S)A 2004, s 20.
175 VW(S)A 2004, s 21.
176 VW(S)A 2004, s 22.

Chapter 13

COOPERATION AND CONFIDENTIALITY

13.1 Specific public bodies are under various duties to cooperate with each other in adult protection cases. This can involve decisions to disclose information with, or without, the adult's consent. This chapter looks at the source and extent of these duties, as well as some of the surrounding issues. The role of other relevant parties such as private care providers, charities, advocacy organisations, friends and family is also examined. Finally, there is a basic introduction to the rules governing data protection and freedom of information.

IMPACT OF THE ADULT SUPPORT AND PROTECTION (SCOTLAND) ACT 2007

Duty to cooperate

13.2 The Adult Support and Protection (Scotland) Act 2007 places a general duty on specific public bodies and office holders to cooperate with any local authority making inquiries under the legislation, as well as with each other.[1]

'Public bodies' currently include all local authorities, the Mental Welfare Commission, the Care Inspectorate, Healthcare Improvement Scotland, the Public Guardian, the chief constable of Police Scotland and health boards.[2] 'Office holders' are not defined and while the Code of Practice refers to them throughout, it does not give guidance about who would be included. The term presumably covers elected officials, board members and senior staff, for example, heads of service in local authorities.

The Scottish Ministers can make an order to include other public bodies in this list but, at the time of writing, no such order has been made.[3]

1 Adult Support and Protection (Scotland) Act 2007 (ASP(S)A 2007), s 5.

2 ASP(S)A 2007, ss 5(1) and (2). Further information about these organisations can be found in Chapter 4.

3 ASP(S)A 2007, s 5(1)(g). No other organisation has been specified at the time of writing – July 2024.

Where the term 'public bodies' is used in relation to the Adult Support and Protection (Scotland) Act 2007 it refers to those bodies listed above. However, it is recognised that a much wider range of organisations can contribute to the protection of adults at risk. The Code of Practice suggests that the fire service, the prison service, independent health professionals, service providers and financial institutions should all be expected to cooperate to assist with inquires.[4]

The general duty to cooperate involves sharing information and working together on specific cases where such cooperation is likely to enable or assist the local authority in making inquiries.

Legal duty to share information

13.3 Many bodies and individuals holding personal information about an adult who may be at risk will be under a general duty to keep that information confidential. Examples would be banks and building societies, the police, voluntary and independent care providers, social workers and health professionals. Normally, professional codes of conduct require that personal information can only be shared with the consent of the adult to whom it relates. Some professionals owe explicit duties of confidentiality to clients. For example, the Law Society of Scotland has strict guidance about the circumstances in which information can be disclosed. This is generally where there is evidence of a crime or illegal activity. In some cases, solicitors may have information helpful to an inquiry. A person may have instructed the solicitor to transfer title to their home or to make changes to a will. Advice should be taken from the Law Society before a decision is made about disclosure of information covered by the duty of confidentiality.[5]

However, the law (and most professional codes of conduct) recognise that where a disclosure is deemed to be in the public interest,[5] or is required by law or a court,[6] information can be shared without consent. Human rights law provides that any such disclosure will only be in the public interest if it is proportionate to the harm it will prevent.[7]

4 *Adult Support and Protection (Scotland) Act 2007 Code of Practice* (ASP(S)A 2007 Code of Practice) (July 2022), pp 29–31.

5 'Guidance to Rule B1.6: Confidentiality Generally' on the Law Society of Scotland website (www.lawscot.org.uk).

5 *A-G v Guardian Newspapers Ltd (No 2)* [1990] 1 AC 109.

6 *W v Edgell* [1990] Ch 359 at para 419.

7 See Chapter 14 for further details.

The Adult Support and Protection (Scotland) Act 2007 requires a public body (as defined above), and its office holders, to advise the relevant local authority where it knows or believes that someone in the local authority's area is an adult at risk and that action needs to be taken, either under the Adult Support and Protection (Scotland) Act 2007 or under other legislation, to protect them from harm.[8] This involves giving all the facts and circumstances of the case to the local authority. The Code of Practice states 'Good Practice would dictate that even if in doubt the referral should be made and should be counted as a referral by the Council'.[9]

Disclosure can, if necessary, be made under this Act without the consent of the adult, as this is 'required by law'.

This strict legal duty applies to all employees and officers of the relevant public bodies and overrides any general duty of confidentiality. Those professions that have a strong emphasis on confidentiality, for example health professionals working for health boards, will need to understand the impact of these rules. The position of other health professionals, and in particular of GPs, is discussed below.

The precise extent of this duty has not been tested, but it is likely to extend to providing any information to the local authority that might indicate an adult is at risk and/or to assist an ongoing investigation.

General practitioners (GPs)

Duty to report harm

13.4 The legal duties to report cases of harm or abuse and to cooperate apply to (among other people) all employees and officers of health boards. This raises an issue about the position of GPs, who are not employed by health boards and so, as the legislation stands, are not under a strict legal duty to cooperate or disclose information. However, GPs clearly have a key role, given they will often be the first professionals to see indications of potential harm.

13.5 Patients are entitled to assume that consultations with their GP will be confidential. This confidentiality survives even after the patient has died.[10] This could lead to potential inconsistencies. If an adult at risk who has capacity presents at an accident and emergency department

8 ASP(S)A 2007, s 5(3).

9 ASP(S)A 2007 Code of Practice, p 27.

10 Access to Health Records Act 1990, s 4(3) and *AB v CD* (1851) 14 D 177.

with injuries indicative of abuse, the treating doctor is under a duty to report this to the relevant social work department, regardless of the patient's wishes. However, if the same patient goes to their GP, with the same injuries, and refuses to allow the information to be passed on, the GP cannot make a disclosure, unless others are at risk. There may be good reasons for this. It would clearly be undesirable that an adult should be reluctant to seek medical attention because they fear this may be reported to the local authority. In some cases, an open and trusting relationship with the GP may increase the prospects of a desirable outcome as, over time, the patient might agree to accept help. However, it is also crucial that situations where an adult is at risk are investigated appropriately.

13.6 The Scottish Government has issued guidance for GPs. This sets out the procedures GPs should follow when considering if a referral is necessary, and provides a useful infographic to assist the decision making process.[11] When GPs are deciding whether to make a referral and what information to share, they should consider what they believe to be relevant and proportionate to the specific concerns they have. There is a useful checklist in the guidance.[12]

GPs should be open and transparent with adults about the information they plan to share and the adult's consent to the disclosure should be sought.[13] In previous guidance, the explicit consent of the adult was viewed as the most appropriate way to justify disclosure. However, the current guidance is clear that consent alone is unlikely to be an appropriate basis to share information on adult protection. This is largely due to increased understanding that adults may not be giving free and informed consent because of the inherent power imbalance between patients and health (or other) professionals.[14] The GP should consider whether another lawful basis also exists, for example 'public task' or 'legal obligation'. There is further information below on identifying whether a lawful basis exists to share information.

Where the adult refuses to consent to disclosure of information, GPs are advised to consider other options, including whether the adult might accept other support. They may also want to make the adult aware of the potential consequences of making a referral or not. There are limited

11 *Guidance for general practice*, p iv.

12 *Guidance for general practice*, pp 13–14.

13 The BMA have produced a useful toolkit in relation to consent: 'Guidance for doctors on patient consent' (www.bma.org.uk).

14 *Guidance for general practice*, p 19.

circumstances where a GP may disclose information about a capable adult without their consent. These include situations where a crime has been committed, a court order requires disclosure, the adult is under undue pressure to refuse consent or where a third party is at risk. For example, there may be evidence that a child or other family member is also suffering harm.

Where an adult lacks capacity and the GP considers they are an adult at risk, the guidance states that a referral should be made to the local authority. If a guardian or attorney has been appointed with powers in relation to medical information, the GP must consult the guardian or attorney, where this is possible.

Duty to provide records

13.7 GPs are under a duty to respond to requests by the local authority for copies of health records (see below). In such cases, the GP is considered under a legal duty to provide these records even if the patient has not consented. The council officer should provide some background information about the risk and why records are being requested. The GP should be satisfied the information they share is relevant and proportionate. For example, if information is required about a specific incident or medication it will be inappropriate to share unconnected medical records.

The right to examine records

13.8 In order for the local authority to decide whether action is needed to protect an adult from harm, the Adult Support and Protection (Scotland) Act 2007 gives a council officer[15] the power to require any person holding health, financial or other records relating to the adult, to grant access to the records, by handing them over, or providing copies.[16] Health records may only be inspected by a health professional (see para **8.13** for the definition of 'health records').

Such records could include those held by voluntary organisations, by health or social care providers, or by banks or building societies, as well as records, such as bank statements or investment valuations, held by private individuals.

[15] The role of a council officer is explained at para **4.3**.
[16] ASP(S)A 2007, s 10.

The holder of information will often be under a duty of confidentiality, so it is important that they know how to verify that the person making the request is properly authorised. This must be made clear at local level, given the possibility of criminal sanctions if the holder of information refuses a proper request.[17]

In accordance with the general principles, the adult's consent should be sought before disclosure wherever this is possible.[18] There is further discussion about the legal basis for sharing information below.

13.9 Although the legislation imposes a clear duty on the holders of records to hand over relevant information, the person holding the records must consider the adult's right to confidentiality in relation to their personal health care information (including medical details, treatment options and wishes) before information is supplied. In particular, the relevant requirements of the regulatory body must be followed.

Human rights concerns mean that similar constraints apply to anyone who is asked to hand over confidential information. The law requires respect for the adult's human rights, and in particular their rights under Article 8 of the Convention.[19] The person holding the information must be satisfied that any such request is lawful and complies with the requirements of the Adult Support and Protection (Scotland) Act 2007. In addition, they need to be satisfied that the request is legitimate, that is, it is for one of the aims set out in Article 8, and that in all the circumstances of the case the request appears to be a necessary and proportionate measure.[20]

Anyone concerned that a request from a council officer for confidential information is not justified may need to discuss this with the local authority and seek further legal and professional advice. The Information Commissioner (see below) may also be able to provide advice.

There are specific regulations allowing employees of Social Security Scotland to share personal data where there is an identification of possible harm.[21]

17 ASP(S)A 2007, s 49.

18 ASP(S)A 2007 Code of Practice, p 71.

19 See Chapter 14.

20 See *Z v Finland* (Application no. 22009/93) (1998) 25 EHRR 371.

21 The Social Security Information-sharing (Scotland) Regulations 2021 (SSI 2021/178) (as amended by the Social Security Information-sharing (Scotland) Regulations 2024 (SSI 2024/8)).

MENTAL HEALTH (CARE AND TREATMENT) (SCOTLAND) ACT 2003 AND CONFIDENTIALITY

Inquiries by local authorities

13.10 The Mental Health (Care and Treatment) (Scotland) Act 2003 gives local authorities powers to request the assistance of certain public bodies in their inquiries.[22] These public bodies are the Mental Welfare Commission, the Public Guardian, the Care Inspectorate, Healthcare Improvement Scotland, and health boards. The public body must comply with such a request, provided it is compatible with, and does not unduly prejudice, the discharge of the public body's functions. As with the Adult Support and Protection (Scotland) Act 2007 duties, this could mean that confidential information is passed to the local authority.

Disclosure of information

13.11 As stated above, a patient is generally entitled to expect that their medical information will not be disclosed without their consent. This applies equally to individuals being treated under the Mental Health (Care and Treatment) (Scotland) Act 2003. Disclosures can only be made without consent where this is required by law or in the public interest.

In some circumstances, it may be necessary to provide information to an agency or a family member to allow proper care to be provided.[23] For example, when a patient is discharged, it might be important the carer knows the possible side effects of medication and other risk factors. This is particularly the case where the patient is unable to manage these matters themselves.

If consent to the provision of information is not forthcoming from a competent adult, the carer has no legal entitlement to receive it. However, if this affects the carer's ability to care, the options for the patient's care might need to be reconsidered. The Mental Welfare Commission has produced useful guidance on carers and confidentiality.[24]

[22] Mental Health (Care and Treatment) (Scotland) Act 2003 (MH(CT)(S)A 2003), s 34.

[23] The general principles recognise the importance of providing information to the carer that they might need. See MH(CT)(S)A 2003, s 1(5).

[24] *Carers, consent, and confidentiality: Good Practice Guide* (April 2024) (www.mwcscot.org.uk).

ADULTS WITH INCAPACITY (SCOTLAND) ACT 2000 IMPLICATIONS

13.12 The Public Guardian, Mental Welfare Commission and local authorities are obliged to cooperate with each other and provide information and assistance necessary to facilitate an investigation where an adult may be at risk.[25] Again, this is likely to involve sharing confidential information.

Health and social care professionals owe a duty of confidentiality even where someone lacks capacity. In such circumstances, it is only appropriate for them to pass on information where there are good reasons to do so. For example, where someone needs to be given medication or treatment by a third party, appropriate instruction may be necessary. The general principles of the Act also require those carrying out functions under it to take into account the views of relevant others.[26]

In some cases a guardian or attorney may have the power to view records and consent to, or refuse medical treatment and social care options. In such circumstances, it is appropriate to disclose information to the guardian or attorney, and reasonable efforts must be made to consult them about treatment.

THE INDEPENDENT AND VOLUNTARY SECTOR

13.13 While the local authority normally pays for services and support, these are usually provided by third parties. In addition, some individuals receive other types of services, such as independent advocacy. This raises issues about the responsibilities of these third-party individuals and organisations in adult protection.

The Adult Support and Protection (Scotland) Act 2007 does not place the independent or voluntary sector under any strict legal duty to report harm or abuse. However, the Code of Practice says they should make referrals, assist enquiries and assist people at risk of harm.[27]

Despite the absence of a direct duty under the Adult Support and Protection (Scotland) Act 2007, most voluntary or independent organisations will now be under an obligation to advise the local authority where there is risk to a person who could be regarded as an adult at risk. This may arise in various ways:

25 Adults with Incapacity (Scotland) Act 2000 (AWI(S)A 2000), s 12(2).

26 AWI(S)A 2000, s 1(4).

27 ASP(S)A 2007 Code of Practice, p 31.

- service level agreements and contracts commissioning services will often specify that the provider must report all suspected incidences of harm or abuse to the local authority. This creates a contractual obligation;
- services and projects registered with the Care Inspectorate are required to have appropriate adult protection policies. Such policies will generally contain a requirement that harm or abuse is reported to the local authority, the police and the Care Inspectorate. Where the local authority which arranged the service is different from the local authority area in which the service is provided, the home authority should also be advised;
- a service or project will be under a general duty of care to both the adult and other service users. This duty could extend to taking steps to ensure that the body with ultimate responsibility for investigating such abuse, the local authority, is informed;
- projects and services will normally be expected to follow their own policies and make sure staff are properly trained. There should be robust procedures in place and staff should know how and when to report concerns.

PRINCIPLES AND PRACTICE

Many staff and volunteers develop a good working relationship with the individuals they support. While this should be supported, it does have the potential to create difficulties about roles and responsibilities.

It is important for staff and volunteers to be clear about the nature, limits and extent of the relationship. Those they support can view them as friends and there have been situations where a client has made a disclosure of abuse but clearly stated they do not want the information to be passed on.

Training and guidance about how to handle these situations is important. In some cases, the person providing the service may need to give the client clear advice that they cannot undertake to keep information private and that they may, indeed, be under a legal duty to pass it on.

PARENTS, INFORMAL CARERS, FAMILY AND FRIENDS

13.14 Those involved in the adult's life in a more informal way, such as parents, family, friends, neighbours and other informal carers, also have a role in adult protection.

In general, the legislation does not place any legal responsibility on such individuals to report harm or abuse, although, of course, if they do report abuse, this should be investigated. However, anyone with a duty of care to the adult may be obliged to report harm or abuse to the appropriate authority. This could include family members and carers, including unpaid carers, as well as those with a formal role in the adult's life, for example, an attorney or guardian, and possibly a person who is the adult's named person.

In all such cases people should have close regard to the relevant codes of practice[28] and should apply the general principles. In cases of difficulty, advice can be sought from the local authority or the Mental Welfare Commission.

DATA PROTECTION

13.15 The Data Protection Act 2018 and the UK General Data Protection Regulation updated the law on holding and sharing personal information.[29] This section provides a brief introduction to the law. There is a wealth of information and advice available from the Information Commissioner's Office which has a Data Sharing Information Hub, including a *Data Sharing Code of Practice*.

Anyone responsible for using personal data must follow strict 'data protection principles'.[30] This means making sure information is:

- used fairly, lawfully and transparently;
- used for specified, explicit purposes;
- used in a way that is adequate, relevant and limited only to what is necessary;
- accurate and, where necessary, kept up to date;

[28] The codes can be found at the www.publicguardian-scotland.gov.uk
[29] www.ico.gov.uk
[30] Data Protection Act 2018, Chapter 2.

- handled in a way that ensures appropriate security, including protection against unlawful or unauthorised processing, access, loss, destruction or damage.

There is stronger legal protection for sensitive information including that which is about race, health, or religious beliefs.[31]

In addition, an individual has rights in relation to any personal information held about them. These include rights to be informed about how data is being used, to be able to access personal data and to have incorrect data corrected. A request for a copy of personal data is usually referred to as a 'subject access request' or 'SAR'. If an individual believes that information is being withheld, they can contact the Information Commissioner's Office for help. Public organisations are under a duty to provide information as soon as possible, and at most within a month of a request. In limited circumstances, they may be allowed more time but are required to explain the reason for this to the person making the request. Information is normally free, but there can be an administration charge where a large amount of information is requested or the request will take a lot of time and effort to process.

Where a public body, local authority or other organisation is under a specific legal duty to share information, the sharing of that information is considered a lawful purpose. However, public authorities are bound by the European Convention on Human Rights. Even when an authority acts under a statutory duty to share information, it must comply with the Convention. Of relevance is the right to respect for family and private life.[32]

Legal basis for disclosure

13.16 There are six lawful bases for processing or sharing information and the most appropriate in a particular case will depend on the circumstances:

- **Consent:** The starting point is that information about a person can be shared if that individual agrees. However, the standard of consent is high and a tick box or signature on a form will not always be sufficient evidence, particularly where adult protection is concerned. The individual must have real control, understanding and choice about the decision. Public authorities, employers and others in a position of power over individuals are encouraged not

[31] Data Protection Act 2018, Sch 1.
[32] Article 8, European Convention on Human Rights.

to rely on consent as a basis to process or share information. Even where there is no intention to pressure someone into a particular decision, the power imbalance can lead individuals to consent where they otherwise may not have done so.[33]

- **Contract:** Information can be lawfully processed where it is provided to enable a contract to be entered into or a contractual service to be provided.
- **Legal Obligation:** This applies where information needs to be processed or shared to comply with a clear legal duty. This will apply where adult protection legislation requires information to be shared. However, the holder must still be satisfied the disclosure is necessary and proportionate.
- **Vital Interests:** This allows information to be processed or shared where it is necessary to protect life. This is given a narrow interpretation to cover genuine emergency situations. For example, if someone falls unconscious and medical staff attending need urgent information to treat.
- **Public Task:** This applies where an organisation or individual needs to process or share information to perform a specific task in the public interest or in the exercise of official authority.
- **Legitimate Interests:** Information can be processed where the organisation or individual is doing so in ways the person would reasonably expect and that have a minimal privacy impact.

FREEDOM OF INFORMATION

13.17 The Freedom of Information (Scotland) Act 2002 gives everyone the right to ask a public authority for information held by it, and to request a copy. This Act does not cover personal information protected by the Data Protection Act 1998, as there must be a balance between the need for transparency in decision making and the privacy of individuals.

The Freedom of Information (Scotland) Act 2002 could be used to obtain information on matters such as adult protection policies or the number of guardianship applications made. It was not intended to be used to obtain

[33] See https://ico.org.uk/for-organisations/uk-gdpr-guidance-and-resources/lawful-basis/a-guide-to-lawful-basis/lawful-basis-for-processing/consent/

information about an individual case, or information that would identify an individual. It also does not apply to information already published.

More information can be obtained from the Scottish Information Commissioner, who is responsible for enforcing and promoting the Freedom of Information (Scotland) Act 2002 in Scotland.[34]

CONCLUSION

13.18 Information indicating an adult is at risk of harm or abuse cannot always be treated as confidential. In some instances, there is a positive duty to report concerns about an adult at risk. For example, certain public bodies are under a duty to cooperate, and must report certain matters. They may also be under a contractual obligation imposed in an agreement to provide services. There is an obligation to provide information following a particular request from an authorised council officer.

It is vital to the protection and support of adults that appropriate information is provided to relevant authorities. In some cases, a lack of information sharing has contributed to continuing harm or abuse. Different agencies often hold pieces of information which do not seem significant in isolation, but which, when added together, indicate further investigation is necessary.

However, it is also essential to respect the rights of individuals to have control over personal information about them as far as this is possible and important that systems are secure and procedures are proportionate to the risks.

[34] See the home page of the Scottish Information Commissioner website (www.foi.scot) for further information.

Chapter 14

ADULT PROTECTION AND HUMAN RIGHTS

14.1 Adult protection cases can involve judgements about significant aspects of an individual's life, including decisions about where a person lives, with whom they live, the medical treatment they receive and the contact they have with family. Many of these decisions have the potential to impact on human rights. Therefore, individuals working in adult protection need to understand the relevance of human rights to their work.

Some human rights are considered so fundamental that a breach is never justified, in any circumstances. An example of such an absolute right is the right not to be subjected to torture or inhuman or degrading treatment or punishment.[1]

However, most human rights can be limited in specific circumstances, where this is proportionate, justified and necessary to protect the individual, others or the interests of the wider community. Generally, any such restriction or interference must:

- be lawful. This means any action must have a legal basis and those involved in a decision should be able to clearly identify the legal authority on which they have relied.;
- be intended to pursue a legitimate purpose. Legitimate purposes are set out in the Article relating to each human right. For example, the rights under Article 8 can only be restricted if necessary, in the interests of national security, public safety or the economic well-being of the country, for the prevention of disorder or crime, for the protection of health or morals, or for the protection of the rights and freedoms of others;
- be necessary in a democratic society. This means the restriction or interference must fulfil a social need and be proportionate to the aim being pursued. Even if a particular policy or action interfering with a convention right is aimed at pursuing a legitimate purpose, the

1 European Convention on Human Rights, Article 3.

interference will not be justified if the means used to achieve the aim are excessive;

- not be discriminatory.

When examining human rights there is often a need to balance rights against each other. This might involve balancing the rights of two individuals or groups. For example, the right to freedom of thought and expression means individuals are free to hold opinions and to receive and impart information and ideas without interference by public authority.[2] However, this does not allow an individual to infringe the rights of other people by making statements to incite hatred.[3] In adult protection, it might involve weighing different rights attached to one person. For example, an individual has the right to make their own decisions about where and with whom they live.[4] However, they also have a right to be protected from harm.

The aim of this chapter is to introduce human rights in the context of adult protection in Scotland and highlight some current issues. Other comprehensive texts are available, providing detailed information and analysis.[5]

HUMAN RIGHTS IN SCOTLAND

14.2 Human rights are a set of basic rights and freedoms that belong to everyone, regardless of any provisions of domestic law. These have been recognised in one form or another in many civilisations, but became more prominent and obtained strong international support after World War II.

In 1948, the United Nations adopted the Universal Declaration of Human Rights.[6] This set out fundamental rights and freedoms, based on widely accepted core principles such as dignity, equality and respect. These principles formed the basis of the European Convention on Human Rights in 1950.[7]

2 European Convention on Human Rights, Article 10.

3 Hate Crime and Public Order (Scotland) Act, s 4(1)(b)

4 European Convention on Human Rights, Article 8.

5 See Hon. Lord Reed and Jim L Murdoch, *A Guide to Human Rights Law in Scotland* (4th edn, Bloomsbury Professional, 2017, new edn forthcoming 2024).

6 For the full text, see www.un.org

7 For the full text, see www.echr.coe.int

The Human Rights Act 1998

14.3 In 1998, the UK Parliament passed the Human Rights Act. Until then, an individual in the UK had to complain directly to the European Court of Human Rights in Strasbourg to pursue a claim that their rights under the European Convention on Human Rights had been breached. The Human Rights Act incorporated most of the rights in the Convention into UK domestic law and allowed UK courts to hear arguments about, and make decisions on the basis of, the Convention.

The Human Rights Act also means that legislation passed by the UK Parliament and Scottish Parliament must be interpreted in a way that complies with the Convention, wherever possible. Domestic courts and tribunals must take account of the decisions of the European Court.

Importantly, bodies carrying out functions of a public nature, including local authorities, are under a duty not to contravene human rights.[8] This means that in adult protection cases those employed by such bodies must always respect human rights when exercising their statutory functions or using legal powers.

The Scotland Act 1998

14.4 The Scotland Act 1998 makes specific reference to the Convention. The effect is that any bill passing through the Scottish Parliament cannot include any provisions incompatible with Convention rights.[9]

Every bill is scrutinised to make sure it complies with the Convention and will be accompanied by a statement to this effect. If a court or tribunal finds a piece of legislation is not compliant, it can declare that part of the law unauthorised or *ultra vires*,[10] with the result that it has no legal effect.[11] This power is only applicable to legislation passed by the Scottish Parliament and cannot be used in respect of UK legislation, although the latter can be declared as being incompatible with the Convention.

The duty to comply with the Convention goes beyond testing legislation at the point that it is passed by the Scottish Parliament. Even if the legislation itself is, in principle, compatible with the Convention, there is a requirement that public authorities (explained below) must not use or

8 Human Rights Act 1998, s 4.

9 Scotland Act 1998 (SA 1998), s 29.

10 A legal concept meaning literally 'beyond powers'.

11 Subordinate legislation and policy are also covered along with primary legislation.

apply the law in a way that infringes Convention rights.[12] This is one of the reasons it is important for those working in adult protection to know about human rights.

Public authorities

14.5 The duty to respect and not do anything to infringe human rights falls on 'public authorities'. In the context of human rights, this term has a wider definition than under adult protection legislation because 'public authorities' are defined by function rather than by reference to a closed list. The Human Rights Act 1998, s 6 defines 'public authority' as including a court or tribunal and 'any person certain of whose functions are of a public nature'.

In this chapter, the term 'public authorities' refers mainly to local authorities, health boards, the courts, the police and the prosecution service. In addition, care homes providing support under the Social Work (Scotland) Act 1968, ss 12 or 13A are specifically included in the definition of public authorities.[13]

In general, private or voluntary sector service providers are not considered public authorities for the purposes of European Convention on Human Rights, and so a public authority will not be liable for alleged breaches of human rights by a private body unless it directly colluded with the breach.[14]

HUMAN RIGHTS ISSUES IN ADULT PROTECTION

Protection of those at risk

14.6 Article 2 of the Convention says that the law shall protect everyone's right to life. Only in very exceptional cases can this right be breached (for

12 SA 1998, s 57(2). For more practical information see the Equality and Human Rights Commission publication, *Human Rights: Human Lives. A Guide to the Human Rights Act for Public Authorities.*

13 Health and Social Care Act 2008, s 145.

14 See *R (on the application of Heather) v Leonard Cheshire Foundation (a charity)* [2002] EWCA Civ 366, [2002] 2 All ER 936. This is the case even when a voluntary or independent organisation is providing a service normally provided by a local authority and *YL (by her litigation friend the Official Solicitor) v Birmingham City Council and others* [2007] UKHL 27. Also, *X and Y v Netherlands* (1986) 8 EHRR 235 at para 23 and *Storck v Germany* (Application no. 61603/00) [2005] ECHR 406, (2005) 43 EHRR 96 at para 89.

example, if someone acts reasonably in self-defence). As well as the duty on the state not to take life unlawfully, the courts have interpreted this Article as imposing a positive duty on the state to preserve the lives of its citizens and to carry out investigations into the deaths of people who die whilst subject to its care and control.

The courts have said that if the authorities know or ought to know of a real and immediate risk to the life or safety of an identified individual, they should take such measures as they can to avoid that risk.[15] For example, the case of *Rabone and another* involved a woman with a recurrent depressive illness who had attempted to end her life on several occasions and had previously been admitted to hospital as a voluntary patient. The hospital granted her two days' home leave, against the wishes of her family, and during that period she killed herself. The Supreme Court held that the NHS Trust had failed in its duty to take reasonable steps to protect her from the real and immediate risk of suicide.[16] In an earlier case, where a vulnerable person died in prison, the European Court of Human Rights said that the UK Government had breached the vulnerable person's right to life because the prison authorities did not offer him suitable treatment for his mental health needs.[17]

Article 3 of the Convention says that no one shall be subjected to torture or inhuman or degrading treatment or punishment. Article 4 says that no one shall be held in slavery or servitude. Again, these articles impose positive obligations on the state to act to protect its citizens from the risk of such treatment.[18] If the authorities know that someone is at risk, they may have to take action. This has clear relevance in adult protection.

Right to liberty

14.7 Under Article 5, everyone has the right to 'liberty and security of person'. This right can only be restricted in specific circumstances laid down by the Convention, including where an individual has been arrested for committing a crime or lawfully convicted by a competent court. If a deprivation of liberty of any individual does not fall within the terms of

[15] *Osman v UK* (Application no. 23452/94) [1999] 1 FLR 193, para 116.

[16] *Rabone and another v Pennine Care NHS Foundation Trust* [2012] UKSC 2.

[17] *Keenan v UK* (Application no. 27229/95) (2001) 33 EHRR 38.

[18] *X and Y v The Netherlands* [1985] ECHR 4, *E and others v the UK* [2002] ECHR 769, para 100 (protection against sexual abuse). *Talpis v Italy* (Application no. 41237/14) [2017] ECHR 224 (protection against domestic violence).

Article 5, it is unlawful and they may have a right to compensation (see para **14.21** below).[19]

The Convention permits detention for the prevention of the spreading of infectious diseases[20] and of 'alcoholics or drug addicts, or vagrants'.[21] Although the Mental Health (Care and Treatment) (Scotland) Act 2003 permits detention of people with mental disorders, Scottish law does not envisage detention of people with certain lifestyles, unless they have committed a criminal offence.

Of more relevance to adult protection, Article 5 permits the lawful deprivation of liberty of persons of 'unsound mind' to protect the public, or the individual subject to detention, or both.[22] This allows detention under the Mental Health (Care and Treatment) (Scotland) Act 2003 provided such detention is in an appropriate place or environment (normally a hospital, clinic or other appropriate institution).[23] However, this can only happen following a lawful process, which must be followed even in cases where there is no objection from the adult involved or their family.

In *Winterwerp v Netherlands*[24] the court said that there were three conditions that must be met before detention of an individual with a mental disorder could be considered justified. These are:

- the presence of a genuine mental disorder;
- the nature of the mental disorder at that particular time must justify detention; and
- the disorder must continue to justify ongoing detention.

There is a significant body of case law about human rights and detention under mental health legislation.[25]

14.8 Some adult protection cases will involve consideration of whether or not an individual is deprived of their liberty. These might happen where someone is being moved into a residential home, restricted to a

19 European Convention on Human Rights, Article 5(5).
20 This is permitted in Scotland under the Public Health (Scotland) Act 2008.
21 European Convention on Human Rights, Article 5(1). Under the Public Health (Scotland) Act 2008.
22 See *A v The Scottish Ministers* 2001 SC 1 for a discussion on preventative detention and Article 5(1)(e).
23 *Aerts v Belgium* [1998] ECtHR 64.
24 (A/33) (1979–80) 2 EHRR 387
25 Hilary Patrick and Jill Stavert, *Mental Health, Incapacity and the Law in Scotland* (2nd edn, Bloomsbury Professional, 2016, new edn forthcoming 2025).

bedroom at night to prevent wandering or receiving medication to sedate them. In other cases, they might appear free to leave a particular living environment, but, in fact, compulsory measures would be used to detain them should they attempt to do so.[26] Further detailed guidance on whether particular circumstances amount to a deprivation of liberty can be found in Mental Welfare Commission Guidance published in 2021.[27]

In the *Bournewood* case,[28] (where a man with a learning disability which meant he was unable to consent to hospital admission, was admitted to a secure psychiatric hospital under the English law of 'necessity'), the court considered matters such as the patient's choice, the extent of free movement, his personal autonomy and contact with the outside world. It was held that he was, as a matter of fact, deprived of his liberty and was in no sense free to leave. A key factor in the decision was evidence that care professionals had 'complete and effective control over his care and movements' and that he was 'under continuous supervision and control' and 'not free to leave'.

In the subsequent case, *Cheshire West*, Lady Hale agreed with the view expressed in *Bournewood* that the key element of deprivation of liberty is 'whether a person is under the complete supervision and control of those caring for her and is not free to leave the place where she lives'.[29]

Where it appears a deprivation of liberty has taken place, it will be necessary to consider whether this is lawful, justified and proportionate.

Controls over person's life

14.9 The issue of deprivation of liberty occurs most commonly when there are significant changes in an adult's care or support, for example, when it is proposed that someone is moved from their home into residential care. However, issues can arise where incremental changes in an adult's care or treatment, perhaps as their condition deteriorates, will mean that arrangements which were not at the outset a deprivation of liberty, become one. If a person begins to be restrained on a regular

26 *Guzzardi v Italy* [1980] ECHR 5, p 92. Some studies show this is relatively common – see Professor Graham Thornicroft (Institute of Psychiatry), *Shunned: Discrimination against people with mental illness* (Oxford University Press, 2006).

27 For a full discussion on deprivation of liberty see the Mental Welfare Commission Guide: *Deprivation of Liberty* (2021) (www.mwcscot.org.uk).

28 *R v Bournewood Community and Mental Health Trust, ex parte L* [1998] 1 All ER 634, *HL v UK* (Application no. 45508/99) (2005) 40 EHRR 32.

29 *P v Cheshire West and Chester Council and another* and *P & Q v Surrey CC* [2014] UKSC 19 at para 49. This has been a consistent theme since *Stankov v Bulgaria* (Application 68490/01) (2009) 49 EHRR 7.

basis from leaving the place where they are living, it is difficult to suggest they are not being deprived of their liberty. Restraint might be by use of physical restraint, technology or medication.

Similarly, a person who lives in accommodation providing 24-hour care and supervision, who is not permitted to leave the accommodation without an escort, may be deprived of their liberty.[30]

In the *Cheshire West* case, the court took the view that deprivation of liberty can occur regardless of the living setting. Those placed in care settings that very much resemble ordinary domestic arrangements but who are under significant restrictions may well be considered to be deprived of their liberty.

Compliance or lack of objection to restrictions

14.10 In the *Bournewood* case it was emphasised that compliance or lack of resistance to restrictions is not a relevant factor to consider when deciding if someone has been deprived of their liberty, where they do not have capacity to consent to the restrictions (or where their compliance or consent has been obtained through use of medication). This was confirmed in *Cheshire West*, when it was stated that 'the person's compliance or lack of objection is not relevant; the relative normality of the placement…is not relevant; and the reason or purpose behind a particular placement is also not relevant'.[31]

It is now broadly accepted that compliance or lack of objection on the part of an incapacitated adult is irrelevant to the decision about whether or not a particular care regime amounts to a deprivation of liberty.

Moving to residential care – Social Work (Scotland) Act 1968, s 13ZA

14.11 The Adult Support and Protection (Scotland) Act 2007 amended the Social Work (Scotland) Act 1968 to include s 13ZA. This section explicitly states that local authorities have the power to move an adult into residential accommodation where necessary to provide them with appropriate community care services.[32] The Scottish Government has produced guidance to local authorities on how to interpret this provision.[33]

30 Mental Welfare Commission, *Justice Denied* (2008), paras 3.8ff.

31 *P v Cheshire West and Chester Council and Another*, Lady Hale at para 50.

32 Social Work (Scotland) Act 1968 (SW(S)A 1968), s 13ZA, as amended by the Adult Support and Protection (Scotland) Act 2007.

33 CCD5/2007, 'Guidance for local authorities: provision of community care services to adults with incapacity'.

The amendment followed concerns that local authorities were unsure about the extent of their statutory powers. Some local authorities routinely applied for guardianship or an intervention order in every situation where an individual lacked capacity and needed to move to residential accommodation. This caused delays, meaning that individuals remained in NHS hospitals for longer.

Before using this power, the local authority must take into account the general principles of the Adults with Incapacity (Scotland) Act 2000.[34] In addition, the power cannot be used where:

- a guardian or attorney with powers relating to the proposed steps has already been appointed;
- an intervention order relating to the proposed steps has been granted; or
- an application has been made (but not yet decided) for an intervention order or guardianship order with powers relating to the proposed steps.[35]

14.12 While s 13ZA was introduced to solve a practical problem, it has always been controversial and practice varies greatly in different local authority areas. The main issue is that a local authority must act in line with human rights. Section 13ZA contains no provision for review or appeal and so cannot authorise a move into care which amounts to a deprivation of liberty. Scottish Government guidance on hospital discharge confirms that 'using s13ZA to facilitate a discharge from hospital to a care home setting provides a level of legal authority for the move, but does not give authority for a person to remain/be held there'.[36] It may solve the immediate problem of discharging a patient to free up hospital beds but it creates a further problem of identifying what, if any, legal authority the care home has in relation to the individual. There has been much discussion over how to decide if particular living circumstances amount to a deprivation of liberty. However, the position is still very unclear, making it difficult for social workers and practitioners to be certain whether or not s 13ZA can be used in specific cases.

34 SW(S)A 1968, s 13ZA(3). See Chapter 5 for information about the general principles.

35 SW(S)A 1968, s 13ZA(4).

36 *Key actions managing the end to end discharge process of adults who lack capacity including legal measures* (Scottish Government, November 2020).

14.13 The need for formal authority to move an individual to a care home was considered by the sheriff court in Scotland in the cases of *Muldoon*[37] and *M, Applicant*.[38] The decisions in these cases caused some controversy and confusion, as the Sheriff did not specifically consider if the particular arrangements meant that the adult was detained within the meaning of Article 5. Instead, he concluded that if an adult is legally incapable of consenting to, or disagreeing with, a change in residence, the adult is deprived of their liberty and that this needs express statutory authority.

Some took the view that this meant additional authority was always necessary where an adult who lacked capacity was living in residential care and that s 13ZA could not be used. If correct, it would mean many people in Scotland were effectively deprived of their liberty and unlawfully detained. There were potentially huge resource implications for local authorities and the courts if guardianship was required in such a large number of cases.

The alternative view was that a distinction needed to be made between cases where there was, and was not, a deprivation of liberty. This should be decided on the basis of the facts in each individual case. Where an adult lacked capacity to make a decision on living arrangements the next step was to assess whether or not a particular placement amounted to a deprivation of liberty. If not, s 13ZA continued to provide valid authority for the move.

14.14 The extent to which s 13ZA can be relied on was placed in further doubt by the Supreme Court's broad approach to defining deprivation of liberty in the *Cheshire West* case. Particular reference is made to Lady Hale's comment at paragraph 46:

> '...what it means to be deprived of liberty must be the same for everyone, whether or not they have physical or mental disabilities. If it would be a deprivation of my liberty to be obliged to live in a particular place, subject to constant monitoring and control, only allowed out with close supervision, and unable to move away without permission even if such an opportunity became available then it must also be a deprivation of the liberty of a disabled person. The fact that my living arrangements are comfortable, and indeed

[37] 2005 SLT (Sh Ct) 52.
[38] 2009 SLT (Sh Ct) 185.

> make my life as enjoyable as it could possibly be, should make no difference. A gilded cage is still a cage'.

The current guidance on the use of s 13ZA is clear that this provision cannot be used where there is a deprivation of liberty.[39] In the light of the wide definition of deprivation of liberty set out above there are likely to be limited cases where s 13ZA can be used with certainty.[40]

14.15 The Scottish Law Commission looked at the issue of deprivation of liberty in detail in 2014[41] and the report produced provides a summary of the court decisions to date. Since then, there have been discussions and debates about how best to legislate to protect Article 5 rights. Suggestions include statutory guidelines, a separate system to authorise deprivation of liberty and introducing a stand-alone appeal.

14.16 In the current climate of uncertainty, it is preferable to seek court authorisation (by way of a guardianship order), for any placement where there is the likelihood of a deprivation of liberty. However, it is clearly undesirable that people remain in hospital or unsuitable placements while legal processes and procedures take place. In most of these cases there will be no legal authority to keep someone in hospital in any event, and it will be practical and sensible to move them to a more appropriate care setting while formal authority is put in place. In such cases, the general principles should be applied and consideration given to the use of s 13ZA. However, as soon as possible after the move the need for a guardianship order must be assessed to justify the placement continuing.[42]

[39] CCD5/2007, para 23.

[40] For detailed comments on the *Cheshire West* case see Alex Ruck Keene, '*Cheshire West*: the Supreme Court's right hook' and '*Cheshire West* – scoring criteria' (www.familylaw.co.uk).

[41] Scottish Law Commission, *Report on Adults with Incapacity* (Scot Law Com No 240, 2014). Available from www.scotlawcom.gov.uk

[42] The Mental Welfare Commission published an interesting report analysing the legal basis used in practice to move an individual to a care home from hospital: *Authority to discharge: Report into decision making for people in hospital* (Mental Welfare Commission, May 2021).

PRINCIPLES AND PRACTICE

When considering moving an adult without capacity into residential care the writers suggest local authorities should consider:

- Where should the adult live?
- What support does the adult need?
- Is the proposed support package suitable and of an acceptable quality?
- How do the principles apply to the situation?
- What, if anything, can be done to limit any restrictions on liberty?

Thereafter, the local authority should ask:

- Does the care regime amount to a deprivation or significant restriction of liberty? If so, an application for guardianship (or some other formal decision-making power) must be made.

The role of welfare attorneys

14.17 The extent to which a welfare attorney can authorise a deprivation of liberty remains uncertain. Most will have standard powers to decide where the granter lives and the care the granter receives. It is also true that many people signing powers of attorney have the possibility of moving into residential care in their minds. They will understand that their movements and freedoms will be restricted in a care setting and so could be said to have considered this when authorising their attorney to make the decision. However, given the fundamental importance of human rights, it is doubtful that these general powers can be implied to also authorise deprivation of liberty. For this reason, it has become more common for explicit wording to be included in powers of attorney. For example, a power might be included in the following terms:

> 'To decide what care, services and accommodation may be appropriate for me, including power to decide where I should reside at any time (whether permanently or otherwise). This includes the power to convey or have me conveyed there and to return me or authorise and/or arrange for others to return

> me to my place of residence should I leave without the consent of my Attorney.
>
> I acknowledge that I have been made aware that the exercise of such powers might, in certain circumstances, be considered to be a breach of my human rights under the European Convention on Human Rights and/or the Human Rights Act 1998 and I confirm that I have decided to consent at this time and in advance to the exercise by my Attorney of any of the powers detailed in this clause, having full faith and trust in my Attorney to exercise any of said powers in my interest and for my benefit.'

The legal effect of such a power has not been tested. Where included, it could be argued that the principles of autonomy and self-determination dictate that the powers the granter has specified should be exercisable. However, a deprivation of liberty can only be lawful if specific safeguards are in place. For example, there is a requirement for an independent periodic review of the need for the deprivation of liberty. It is likely further procedural safeguards would be needed before the exercise of such powers would be human rights-compliant.

The *Scottish Mental Health Law Review*[43] proposed the introduction of prescribed statutory wording. Where used, this wording would allow granters to provide advance consent to their attorney making decisions amounting to a deprivation of liberty. The Scottish Government agreed, in principle, and at the time of writing is consulting on this suggestion.[44] It is proposed that any power should reflect the following points:

- The granter has considered the circumstances in which it might be necessary to restrict their liberty or deprive them of their liberty, to safeguard their health or welfare, or that of others.
- The terms of Article 5 of the ECHR have been explained to the granter.
- Authority is given to the attorney/s alone.
- The attorney must be satisfied the action is necessary to safeguard the health or welfare of the granter.

[43] *Scottish Mental Health Law Review* (September 2022) (see archived report at https://webarchive.nrscotland.gov.uk/20230327160310/https:/cms.mentalhealthlawreview.scot/wp-content/uploads/2022/09/SMHLR-FINAL-Report-.pdf).

[44] Adults with Incapacity Amendment Act Consultation (July 2024), p 66.

- The attorney must act in accordance with the principles of the Adults with Incapacity (Scotland) Act 2000.
- The attorney will be subject to any directions of the court following any application under the Adults with Incapacity (Scotland) Act 2000, s 3(3). Where the adult objects at the time the power is exercised then there may be a requirement that a sheriff makes the final decision.[45]

There is also a suggestion that a stand-alone appeal will be introduced allowing the adult and other parties to appeal to the sheriff court for a decision on the lawfulness of a deprivation of liberty.[46]

14.18 When a power of attorney is being drafted, it is sensible for the granter to specifically consider and address how they want their attorney to make decisions about any move into residential care. It is also important for both the granter and the attorney to be clear on the extent and limitation of any powers granted. Until the law is clarified, it is likely to be safer to include an explicit power to restrict liberty.

The role of welfare guardians

14.19 In principle, a welfare guardian with specific powers can authorise a deprivation of liberty. This was considered by the Sheriff Appeal Court in *K v Argyll and Bute Council*.[47] In this case, the adult suffered from a serious delusional order which had a substantial detrimental impact on her life. She lacked capacity to make significant welfare decisions about her life. After hearing objections from the adult, the Sheriff initially granted powers '(a) to decide where the adult should live, to require her to live at that location, to convey her to that location and to return her to that location in the event of her absenting herself therefrom' and '(j) to decide where the adult is permitted to go and decide whether or not the adult should be accompanied by a person nominated by her guardian to assist with her personal safety and welfare'. On appeal, the adult argued that the Sheriff could not competently grant powers to a welfare guardian allowing them to deprive the person subject to the order of their liberty. The Appeal Court accepted that those powers were against the adult's express wishes. The court further agreed that the exercise of those powers would amount to a deprivation of liberty and frustrate her right to choose where she lived. However, in all the circumstances of the case these

45 Adults with Incapacity Amendment Act Consultation (July 2024), p 64.
46 Adults with Incapacity Amendment Act Consultation (July 2024), p 65.
47 [2021] SAC (Civ) 21.

powers were appropriate and should be granted in favour of the welfare guardian.

However, the powers must be reasonable in the circumstances of each individual case. Their validity may be questioned where appropriate procedures have not taken place. In the case of *Aberdeenshire Council v SF*[48], a guardianship order was not recognised in England due to the failure to allow the adult to express her views and the lack of provision for review. This case involved an adult living in supported accommodation in England, but habitually resident in Scotland, and under a Scottish guardianship order. The adult's living arrangements and the restrictions placed on her were considered to amount to a deprivation of liberty. The main factors in the decision not to recognise the order were firstly, the failure to provide the adult with an opportunity to be heard or represented and secondly the length of the order which was granted for seven years. Poole, J made the following comments in the judgment:

> 'Natural justice required that in a case where SF's liberty was being put into the hands of others for a period of seven years, she should have had an opportunity to be heard and/or an opportunity to be represented. SF's access to the court should not have been dependent on her taking the initiative. Effective access should have been secured for her. As it is, there were no measures taken to ensure that her Art 5(1) rights were upheld'.

It is essential that powers to deprive an adult of their liberty are appropriately drafted, time limited and regularly reviewed. The adult must have a real and meaningful opportunity to have their views heard.

In terms of reviews, local authorities were initially required to visit adults subject to welfare guardianship within three months of the order being granted and at least annually, thereafter. However, in 2014 changes were made allowing the local authority to set visits so the intervals between visits, after the second occasion, could exceed 12 months or even cease entirely.[49] This means some adults will only have two visits or reviews in the entire duration of their guardianship. This is not an appropriate safeguard for human rights purposes. It may be appropriate for local authorities to consider a mandatory six-month or annual visit where welfare guardianship powers are used to authorise a deprivation of liberty.

48 *Aberdeenshire Council v SF (No 2)* [2024] EWCOP 10.

49 The Adults with Incapacity (Supervision of Welfare Guardians etc. by Local Authorities) (Scotland) Regulations 2002 (SSI 2002/95) as amended.

In many cases, the chief social worker is appointed as the guardian and so monitoring by the local authority itself would not be considered a sufficient, independent safeguard. Guardianships of a shorter duration may be needed where authorisation of a deprivation of liberty is included among the powers granted, so that the court can review the need and use of those powers.

At the time of writing, the Scottish Government is proposing a stand-alone right of appeal to the sheriff court for a decision on the lawfulness of a deprivation of liberty.[50]

Assessment and removal orders

14.20 The Adult Support and Protection (Scotland) Act 2007 provides for formal court orders authorising the moving of an adult for the purposes of assessment or protection. These orders do not carry any right of detention and so, in some cases, they may have limited practical and legal use.

For example, a removal order allows the local authority to move an adult to a specified place. However, it is possible to envisage a situation where an adult attempts to get out of the vehicle transporting them. Locking the vehicle doors so that they are unable to leave appears to be authorised by the legislation, but there is an argument that such action would amount to an unlawful deprivation of liberty. This is because detaining an adult for their protection or to investigate harm against them is unlikely to fall within any of the categories that permit deprivation of liberty under Article 5 (unless the person has a mental disorder, in which case it may be possible to detain them under the Mental Health (Care and Treatment) (Scotland) Act 2003).

In practice, formal orders need careful consideration where an adult is likely to be non-cooperative. However, they may still be useful in some situations, such as where it is believed that the adult can be persuaded to cooperate if they are removed from a harmful situation.

Unlawful detention and compensation

14.21 Where an adult has been unlawfully detained or deprived of their liberty, a claim for damages may be made. In the 2015 case of *Essex CC v RF and Others,* the court agreed that a 91-year-old man who was moved into a care home had been detained without legal authorisation.[51]

50 Adults with Incapacity Amendment Act Consultation (July 2024).

51 [2015] EWCOP 1.

A compromise agreement for damages was agreed between the parties as a result of the breaches of Article 5 (right to liberty) and Article 8 (right to respect for private and family life). The court was required to approve this, given the adult lacked capacity. Damages of £60,000 were agreed. The local authority also agreed to waive £25,000 in outstanding care fees and to exclude the compensation from future financial assessments calculating contributions towards care. This was based on previous cases awarding between £3,000 and £4,600 a month for unlawful detention in similar circumstances.[52]

This can be contrasted with the case of *Bostridge v Oxleas NHS Foundation Trust*[53] where the Court of Appeal held that where there was no loss, a claim for damages for unlawful detention would attract only nominal damages. This case involved detention under the Mental Health Act 1983 and the court was satisfied that the claimant's treatment and discharge arrangements would have been precisely the same had the detention been lawful from the outset.

The case of *Esegbona v King's College Hospital NHS Foundation Trust*[54] involved a claim for failure to follow the deprivation of liberty requirements in England. The adult was admitted to hospital in October 2010 following a diagnosis of pulmonary oedema. Her condition deteriorated and she developed a cognitive impairment, though there was no evidence of a meaningful assessment of capacity. She repeatedly asked to go home to her family and a move to care was against her and her families wishes. She was discharged to a care home on 14 June and died 19 days later. The court determined that she had been unlawfully detained for 119 days. The Court distinguished the case from *Bostridge* on the basis that had Mrs Esegbona not been detained the outcome may have been different and she could have been discharged home as she had requested. The unlawful detention element of her claim attracted an award in damages of £15,470.[55]

Respect for private and family life

14.22 Under Article 8 of the Convention, individuals have the right to conduct their life privately and, importantly, without interference from

[52] See *London Borough of Hillingdon v Neary* [2011] EWHC 3522 (Fam) and *Local Authority v Mrs D* [2013] EWCOP B34.

[53] [2015] EWCA Civ 79.

[54] [2019] EWHC 77 (QB).

[55] For further discussion see: *London Borough of Haringey v Emile* [2020] MHLO 70 (CC).

the state, provided the rights of other people are also respected. Article 8 states that:

- everyone has the right to respect for his private and family life, home and correspondence; and
- there shall be no interference by a public authority with the exercise of this right except such as is in accordance with the law and is necessary in a democratic society in the interests of national security, public safety or the economic well-being of the country, for the prevention of disorder or crime, for the protection of health or morals, or for the protection of the rights and freedoms of others.

The terms 'family life' and 'private life' are not defined in the Convention but have been given wide meanings.[56] They include lifestyle choices, as well as the right to develop personal relationships. The right also means information about an individual should only be shared without consent, in limited circumstances.[57]

14.23 Article 8 means an individual should be able to enter or leave their home as they wish and have control over who else is allowed into their home. Public authorities can only interfere with the rights protected by Article 8 where they can show that their action is lawful, necessary and proportionate to protect national security, public safety, the economy, health or morals, disorder or crime or the rights and freedoms of other people. For example, the police may enter premises where they have a warrant authorising entry, or where this is justified in all the circumstances to prevent a crime, notwithstanding the intrusion this causes to a person's home.[58]

14.24 The case of *London Borough of Hillingdon v Steven Neary* considered circumstances where a young man with autism and a severe learning disability was moved to a residential institution for a year without his family's agreement. The case found that Hillingdon Council had breached the adult's human rights by failing to consider the implications of

[56] For example, 'Respect for family life must also comprise to a certain degree the right to establish and develop relationships with other human beings' *Niemietz v Germany* (1993) 16 EHRR 97.

[57] *MS v Sweden* (1999) 45 BMLR 133. See Chapter 13 for further discussion on confidentiality.

[58] For example, see *Moffat v McFadyen* 1999 GWD 22-1038.

removing him from his family home for a considerable period of time.[59] However, it should also be noted that in *M, Applicant* the argument that there should be a presumption that incapacitated adults stay at home with their family was rejected. The court stated that the right to family life and private life were distinct considerations and that '...elements of private life, such as the right to personal development and the right to establish relationships with other human beings and the outside world, may not always be entirely compatible with existing family life...'.[60]

14.25 Many of the possible interventions by public authorities in adult protection cases could involve interfering with the rights safeguarded by Article 8. This means a public authority should be mindful of Article 8 and be able to justify its actions as lawful, necessary and proportionate. This will particularly be the case where formal action is taken without the adult's consent.

Undue pressure and human rights

14.26 Under the Adult Support and Protection (Scotland) Act 2007, it is possible for an order to be granted, or action to be taken, without the adult's consent where they have been unduly pressured. This concept of undue pressure raises interesting issues in the context of human rights.

Existing legal concepts allow an individual's actions to be set aside if they have been unduly influenced or pressured. For example, disappointed beneficiaries sometimes challenge wills where they believe a relative was pressured unfairly to leave money or property to a particular individual. As the deceased is clearly unable to give evidence about their wishes, undue influence must be established by looking at other circumstances.

In addition, contracts can sometimes be declared invalid where one party has been threatened or deliberately misled.[61] Such a claim is normally made when the individual is incapable of understanding the contract or can provide other evidence that they were pressured to sign.

However, the concept of undue pressure under the Adult Support and Protection (Scotland) Act 2007 goes further, in that it allows an order to be granted on the application of a third party, even where an adult is capable of making their own decisions and does not agree they have been unduly pressured.

59 [2011] EWHC 1377 (COP).

60 *M, Applicant* 2009 SLT (Sh Ct) 185.

61 For example see *Bank of Scotland v Bennett* [1997] 3 FCR 193.

While it is understandable that the state may wish, and indeed have a duty under human rights law,[62] to protect someone who it feels is being unduly pressured to resist help, such decisions raise serious human rights issues. It is suggested that if an order was granted in such circumstances, the adult might be able to argue that overriding their wishes would infringe their rights to respect for private life, as well as (depending on how the order is exercised) potentially constituting an unlawful deprivation of liberty under Article 5. If the local authority wishes to take action in such a situation, legal advice may be necessary.

THE UN CONVENTION ON THE RIGHTS OF PERSONS WITH DISABILITIES

14.27 Although the rights contained in the original UN Declaration of Human Rights apply to everyone, the reality is that some groups remain likely to encounter physical, social and economic barriers. This has meant it is still difficult for everyone to enjoy their rights and fully participate in society. As a result, there has been a move towards additional conventions designed to bring benefits to specific groups.

As part of this effort, on 30 March 2007, the UK was among 82 countries to sign a UN Convention on the Rights of Persons with Disabilities[63] ('the UN CRPD'). Although the UK Parliament subsequently ratified the UN CRPD on 8 June 2009, international treaties can only be relied on in the UK if made effective by an Act of Parliament.[64] This means that while the UN CRPD can be referred to in cases (and this increasingly happens) it will not, in itself, dictate the decisions of the courts. However, the UK is bound, under international law, to comply with its obligations under the UN CRPD and so the standards can be considered influential, if not legally enforceable at national level.

The European Court of Human Rights will also interpret the European Convention on Human Rights in the light of the UN CRPD.[65] Public bodies must act in a way that respects, and does not unjustifiably infringe, the rights contained in the UN CRPD.

62 See UN Convention on Rights of People with Disabilities, Article 12(4).

63 See www.un.org for the full text of the UN CRPD.

64 The ECHR was ratified in 1951. It was not incorporated into UK law until the Human Rights Act 1998.

65 *Glor v Switzerland* (Application no. 13444/04) [2009] ECHR 2181.

14.28 The purpose of the UN CRPD was to provide an international standard for the human rights of people with disabilities. This was in recognition of the fact that people with disabilities still face additional barriers and are less likely to get jobs, be able to access services and benefit fully from education and health services.

Article 1 defines people with disabilities as those who have long-term physical, mental, intellectual or sensory impairments which, in interaction with various barriers, may hinder their full and effective participation in society on an equal basis with others. This covers a range of people, including those with learning disabilities, mental health difficulties and degenerative conditions such as dementia. The UN CRPD also recognises that disability is an evolving concept.[66]

14.29 The UN CRPD does not create any new rights or additional entitlements, but rather expresses existing rights in a way considered relevant to people with disabilities. For example, Article 12 expands on the support people with disabilities need to have access to justice and Article 14 emphasises that any deprivation of liberty should be on an equal basis with the general population. There are also provisions designed to develop the right to live independently and expanding the definition of respect for privacy, home and family life.[67]

Under Article 12, persons with disabilities have the right to equal recognition before the law and access to justice. This requires appropriate measures to be put in place to allow an individual to use their legal rights. This could include the provision of advocacy, information and use of the Vulnerable Witnesses (Scotland) Act 2004.[68]

The right to live independently and be included in the community is provided for by Article 19.

14.30 A controversial General Comment on Article 12 (Equal Recognition before the Law) of the UN CRPD was adopted by the UN Committee in 2013.[69] The comment reaffirms the right to equality and reinforces the presumption that all those with disabilities have full legal capacity and that any 'perceived or actual deficits in mental capacity' should not be used to justify restrictions on legal rights. However, it goes on to say that status

66 UN Convention on the Rights of Persons with Disabilities, Preamble (e).

67 UN Convention on the Rights of Persons with Disabilities, Articles 19, 22 and 23.

68 See Chapter 12.

69 CRPD/C/11/4.

-based systems, including guardianship regimes, should be abolished and there should be a move to supported decision making models.

This General Comment has been heavily criticised as being based on older guardianship laws, which stripped people of all legal capacity, rather than the more flexible and proportionate modern regimes. There was also a lack of consultation before the comment was adopted. If the guardianship and mental health legislative regimes were to be abolished, this would actually infringe human rights rather than protect them. For example, it is surely essential that there is a mechanism whereby those who lack capacity to exercise their legal rights can have those rights protected by others. In addition, repealing mental health legislation would deprive seriously ill individuals of the care and treatment that they need.

It seems unlikely that guardianships will be abolished in Scotland in the light of this General Comment; and there is no such proposal contained in the Scottish Government's current (at time of writing) consultation on reform of this area.

CONCLUSION

14.31 Human rights have already had a significant impact in Scotland. The Adults with Incapacity (Scotland) Act 2000 and Adult Support and Protection (Scotland) Act 2007 are largely based on making sure that those with reduced capacity have their rights both respected and exercised on their behalf. The principles of the legislation are designed to make sure that adults are involved in decisions about their lives and that any restrictions are necessary and proportionate. They attempt to strike a balance between creating duties to investigate and protect adults at risk with the need to respect the autonomy of every individual.

In any circumstance where an intervention will interfere with a human right, the public authority must make sure that this is lawful, necessary, justified and proportionate. Even where a public authority has been given a legislative power to take action, it must still respect human rights when deciding whether and how to exercise these powers.

INDEX

[All references are to paragraph numbers]

Abuse and harm *see* **Harm and abuse**
Access to funds
financial support and advice, and, 10.15–10.17
Access to records
local authorities, and
ASP(S)A 2007, under, 8.13
MH(CT)(S)A 2003, under, 8.22–8.23
Accommodated children
public bodies' duties and powers, and, 11.12–11.15
Additional support
education authority duties, and, 11.22–11.23
Adult
information requirements, and
ASP(S)A 2007, under, 2.12
AWI(S)A 2000, under, 2.33
MH(CT)(S)A 2003, under, 2.22
transition to adult protection, and, 11.1
Adult at risk
definition, 2.3
financial harm and abuse, and, 7.2
'Adult carer support plan'
public bodies' duties and powers, and, 11.11
Adult protection
human rights, and *see* **Human rights**
meaning, 1.2
relevance
AWI()SA 2000, and, 2.32
MH(CT)(S)A 2003, and, 2.21
risk, and, 1.4
Adult protection committees
accountability, 3.10
Adult protection committees – *contd*
ASP(S)A 2007, and, 2.10
conclusion, 3.12
convenors, 3.6
functions, 3.2
generally, 3.1
governance, 3.10
large scale investigations (LSIs), 3.11
learning reviews, 3.11
membership
convenors, 3.6
further member/attendees, 3.8
generally, 3.5
statutory members/attendees, 3.7
organisations and agencies, and, 3.4
procedures, 3.9
role, 3.3–3.4
status, 3.2
statutory basis, 2.10
Adult protection law
balancing risk and protection, 1.4
development, 1.1–1.6
framework *see* **Legal framework**
principles
ASP(S)A 2007, in, 5.5
AWI(S)A 2000, in, 5.3
background, 5.2
conclusion, 5.12
human rights, and, 5.8
indemnity, 5.10
introduction, 5.1
legal impact, 5.9
MH(CT)(S)A 2003, in, 5.4
promotion, 5.11
SC(SDS)(S)A 2013, in, 5.6–5.7
scope of legislation, 1.3
wider context, 1.5

Adult Support and Protection (Scotland) Act 2007
access to records, 8.13
adult protection committees, 2.10
'adults at risk', 2.3
assessment orders
appeals, 8.12
applications, 8.9
consent of adult, 12.18–12.19
grounds, 8.8
impact, 8.11
incapacity, 12.19
introduction, 8.7; 12.17
limits to powers, 8.10
serious harm, 12.22
undue pressure, 12.20–12.21
banning orders
appeals, 12.46
applications, 12.41–12.45
breach, 12.37–12.39
consent of adult, 12.18–12.19
emergency applications, 9.5; 12.42
expiry, 12.40
financial harm and abuse, and, 7.24–7.25
generally, 12.31
grounds, 12.32
impact, 12.34
incapacity, 12.19
introduction, 12.17
perpetrator aged under 16, 12.33
power of arrest attached, 12.38
protecting adult, 12.44
protecting adult's interests, 12.43
recall, 12.36
returning banned person to court, 12.38
serious harm, 12.22
service, 12.45
temporary measures, 12.35
undue pressure, 12.20–12.21
variation, 12.36
codes of practice, 2.34
concept of 'capacity', 2.4
cooperation
examination of records, 13.8–13.9

Adult Support and Protection (Scotland) Act 2007 – *contd*
cooperation – *contd*
general duty, 13.2
general practitioners (GPs), 13.4–13.7
generally, 13.1
provision of medical records, 13.7
reporting harm, 13.4–13.6
scope of provisions, 2.8
sharing of information, 13.3
court orders, 2.9
emergencies
applications to JP, 9.3
generally, 9.2
involvement of adult, 9.4
temporary banning orders, 9.5
use of measures, 9.6
general practitioners (GPs)
provision of medical records, 13.7
reporting harm, 13.4–13.6
generally, 2.2
harm and abuse, 6.6
information requirements of adults, relatives and carers, 2.12
inquiries and investigatory powers, 2.7
interviews, 8.5
local authorities' duty to investigate harm
access to records, 8.13
assessment orders, 8.7–8.12
banning orders, 12.31–12.46
duty, 8.2
interviews, 8.5
medical examinations, 8.6
outcome of inquiries, 8.14
removal orders, 12.16–12.30
visits, 8.3
warrants for entry, 8.4
medical examinations, 8.6
outcome of inquiries, 8.14
people covered, 2.3
principles, 5.5
provision of medical records, 13.7

Adult Support and Protection (Scotland) Act 2007 – *contd*
removal orders
consent of adult, 12.18–12.19
contact conditions, 12.27
duration, 12.30
emergencies, and, 9.2–9.6
expiry, 12.30
generally, 12.23
grounds, 12.24
impact, 12.25
incapacity, 12.19
introduction, 12.17
no detention, 12.26
protection of property, 12.29
recall, 12.28
serious harm, 12.22
undue pressure, 12.20–12.21
variation, 12.28
reporting harm, 13.4–13.6
scope
adult protection committees, 2.10
cooperation, 2.8
court orders, 2.9
generally, 2.6
inquiries and investigatory powers, 2.7
'unwilling or unable', 2.5
use, 2.11
visits, 8.3
warrants for entry, 8.4
Adults
information requirements, and
ASP(S)A 2007, under, 2.12
AWI(S)A 2000, under, 2.33
MH(CT)(S)A 2003, under, 2.22
transition to adult protection, and, 11.1
Adults at risk
definition, 2.3
financial harm and abuse, and, 7.2
Adults with Incapacity (Scotland) Act 2000
attorneys, 2.27
bank accounts, 2.28
codes of practice, 2.34
Adults with Incapacity (Scotland) Act 2000 – *contd*
cooperation, and, 13.12
emergencies
generally 9.7
interim guardianship, 9.8
generally, 2.23
guardianship orders
appeals, 12.14
applications, 12.10
complaints about guardian, 12.8
generally, 12.7
human rights issues, 12.15
introduction, 12.5
non-compliance with decisions of welfare guardian, 12.16
notice to adult and other parties, 12.11
overview, 2.31
procedure, 12.9–12.16
protecting adult's interests, 12.13
harm and abuse, 6.5
'incapacity', 2.24
information requirements of adults, relatives and carers, 2.33
interim guardianship, 9.8
intervention orders
appeals, 12.14
applications, 12.10
complaints about intervener, 12.8
generally, 12.6
hearing, 12.12
human rights issues, 12.15
introduction, 12.5
non-compliance with decisions of welfare guardian, 12.16
notice to adult and other parties, 12.11
overview, 2.31
procedure, 12.9–12.16
protecting adult's interests, 12.13
local authorities' duty to investigate harm
duty, 8.16
generally, 2.26; 8.15
making medical decisions, 2.30

Adults with Incapacity (Scotland) Act 2000 – *contd*
managing bank accounts, 2.28
managing residents' finances, 2.29
medical decisions, 2.30
people covered, 2.24
principles, 5.3
relevance to adult protection, 2.32
residents' finances, 2.29
scope
attorneys, 2.27
generally, 2.25
guardianship orders, 2.31
intervention orders, 2.31
investigation of harm, 2.26
making medical decisions, 2.30
managing bank accounts, 2.28
managing residents' finances, 2.29
Advance directives
support for adults, and, 10.22
Advance statements
scope of MH(CT)(S)A 2003, and, 2.20
support for adults, and, 10.23
After-care
public bodies' duties and powers, and, 11.16–11.18
Alcohol abuse
harm and abuse, and, 6.19
Ante-natal depression
public bodies' duties and powers, and, 11.9
Antisocial behaviour orders
generally, 12.47
Appeals
banning orders, 12.46
guardianship orders, 12.14
intervention orders, 12.14
removal orders, 9.13
Appointees
financial harm and abuse, and, 7.19–7.20
Appointment of attorney
financial harm and abuse, and, 7.9–7.13
support for adults, and, 10.25–10.26
Appointment of named person
support for adults, and, 10.27
Assessment orders
appeals, 8.12
applications, 8.9
consent of adult, 12.18–12.19
generally, 12.17
grounds, 8.8
human rights, and, 14.20
impact, 8.11
incapacity, 12.19
introduction, 8.7
limits to powers, 8.10
right to liberty and security, and, 14.20
serious harm, 12.22
undue pressure, 12.20–12.21
Attorneys *see also* **Welfare attorneys**
appointment
financial harm and abuse, 7.9–7.13
support for adults, 10.25–10.26
persons involved in adult protection cases, 4.34
scope of AWI(S)A 2000, 2.27
Bank accounts
scope of AWI(S)A 2000, and, 2.28
Banning orders
appeals, 12.46
applications, 12.41–12.45
breach, 12.37–12.39
consent of adult, 12.18–12.19
emergency applications, 9.5; 12.42
expiry, 12.40
financial harm and abuse, and, 7.24–7.25
generally, 12.31
grounds, 12.32
impact, 12.34
incapacity, 12.19
introduction, 12.17
perpetrator aged under 16, 12.33
power of arrest attached, 12.38
protecting adult, 12.44
protecting adult's interests, 12.43
recall, 12.36

Banning orders – *contd*
returning banned person to court, 12.38
serious harm, 12.22
service, 12.45
temporary measures, 12.35
undue pressure, 12.20–12.21
variation, 12.36
Behaviour changes
harm and abuse, and, 6.27
Capacity
concept and ASP(S)A 2007, 2.4
Care Commission *see* **Healthcare Improvement Scotland**
Care home residents' finances
financial harm and abuse, and, 7.26–7.27
Care Inspectorate
adult protection committees, and, 3.4
complaints, 4.9–4.10
enforcement, 4.11–4.12
functions, 4.5
generally, 4.5–4.6
inspections, 4.7–4.8
principles, 4.6
Care providers
generally, 4.29
Carers
information requirements, and
ASP(S)A 2007, under, 2.12
AWI(S)A 2000, under, 2.33
MH(CT)(S)A 2003, under, 2.22
public bodies' duties and powers, and
'adult carer support plan', 11.11
'young carer statement', 11.11
Carers (Scotland) Act 2016
'adult carer support plan', 11.11
community care services, and, 10.8
'young carer statement', 11.11
'Children in need'
public bodies' duties and powers, and, 11.12–11.15
Chronically Sick and Disabled Persons Act 1970
community care services, and, 10.9
generally, 2.37
Codes of practice
generally, 2.34
'Coercive control'
harm and abuse, and, 6.20
Community based treatment orders
generally, 12.3
Community care assessments
community care services, and, 10.7
public bodies' duties and powers, and, 11.8
Community care services
Carers (Scotland) Act 2016, under, 10.8
community care assessments, 10.7
free personal and nursing care, 10.11
generally, 10.6
MH(CT)(S)A 2003, under, 10.10
provision of suitable housing, 10.12
services under Chronically Sick and Disabled Persons Act 1970, 10.9
Compensation
right to liberty and security, and, 14.21
Compulsory detention in hospital
generally, 12.3
Compulsory supervision orders
public bodies' duties and powers, and, 11.8
Confidentiality
data protection, 13.15
disclosure of information
generally, 13.11
legal basis for disclosure, 13.16
freedom of information, 13.17
Continuing care
public bodies' duties and powers, and, 11.16–11.18
Convenors
adult protection committees, and, 3.6

Cooperation
ASP(S)A 2007, and
examination of records, 13.8–13.9
general duty, 13.2
general practitioners (GPs), 13.4–13.7
provision of medical records, 13.7
reporting harm, 13.4–13.6
scope of provisions, 2.8
sharing of information, 13.3
AWI(S)A 2000, and, 13.12
conclusion, 13.18
data protection, 13.15
disclosure of information
generally, 13.11
legal basis for disclosure, 13.16
examination of records, 13.8–13.9
family and friends, 13.14
freedom of information, 13.17
general practitioners (GPs), and
provision of medical records, 13.7
reporting harm, 13.4–13.6
generally, 13.1
independent sector, 13.13
informal carers, 13.14
inquiries by local authorities, 13.10
legal basis for disclosure, 13.16
MH(CT)(S)A 2003, and
disclosure of information, 13.11
inquiries by local authorities, 13.10
scope of provisions, 2.17
parents, 13.14
provision of medical records, 13.7
reporting harm, 13.4–13.6
sharing of information, 13.3
voluntary sector, 13.13
Coordinated support plans (CSPs)
education authority duties, and, 11.24–11.26
Council officers
generally, 4.3
Counselling
support for adults, and, 10.28
Court measures of protection
abusers, against
family orders, 12.51
Court measures of protection – *contd*
abusers, against – *contd*
generally, 12.49
interdicts, 12.50
non-harassment orders, 12.52
antisocial behaviour orders, 12.47
ASP(S)A 2007, under
assessment orders, 12.17
banning orders, 12.31–12.46
guardianship orders, 12.5–12.16
intervention orders, 12.5–12.16
protection orders, 12.17–12.46
removal orders, 12.23–12.30
assessment orders
consent of adult, 12.18–12.19
incapacity, 12.19
introduction, 12.17
serious harm, 12.22
undue pressure, 12.20–12.21
banning orders
appeals, 12.46
applications, 12.41–12.45
breach, 12.37–12.39
consent of adult, 12.18–12.19
emergency applications, 9.5; 12.42
expiry, 12.40
generally, 12.31
grounds, 12.32
impact, 12.34
incapacity, 12.19
introduction, 12.17
perpetrator aged under 16, 12.33
power of arrest attached, 12.38
protecting adult, 12.44
protecting adult's interests, 12.43
recall, 12.36
returning banned person to court, 12.38
serious harm, 12.22
service, 12.45
temporary measures, 12.35
undue pressure, 12.20–12.21
variation, 12.36
community based treatment orders, 12.3

Court measures of protection – *contd*
compulsory detention in hospital, 12.3
conclusion, 12.54
family orders, 12.51
forced marriage protection orders, 12.48
generally, 12.1
guardianship orders
appeals, 12.14
applications, 12.10
complaints about guardian, 12.8
generally, 12.7
human rights issues, 12.15
introduction, 12.5
non-compliance with decisions of welfare guardian, 12.16
notice to adult and other parties, 12.11
procedure, 12.9–12.16
protecting adult's interests, 12.13
interdicts, 12.50
intervention orders
appeals, 12.14
applications, 12.10
complaints about intervener, 12.8
generally, 12.6
hearing, 12.12
human rights issues, 12.15
introduction, 12.5
non-compliance with decisions of welfare guardian, 12.16
notice to adult and other parties, 12.11
procedure, 12.9–12.16
protecting adult's interests, 12.13
mental health tribunals, 12.2
MH(CT)(S)A 2003, under, 12.3
non-harassment orders, 12.52
protection orders
banning orders, 12.31–12.46
consent of adult, 12.18–12.19
incapacity, 12.19
introduction, 12.17
removal orders, 12.23–12.30
serious harm, 12.22

Court measures of protection – *contd*
protection orders – *contd*
undue pressure, 12.20–12.21
removal orders
consent of adult, 12.18–12.19
contact conditions, 12.27
duration, 12.30
expiry, 12.30
generally, 12.23
grounds, 12.24
impact, 12.25
incapacity, 12.19
introduction, 12.17
no detention, 12.26
protection of property, 12.29
recall, 12.28
serious harm, 12.22
undue pressure, 12.20–12.21
variation, 12.28
sheriff court, 12.4
vulnerable witnesses, 12.53
Court orders
scope of ASP(S)A 2007, and, 2.9
Criminal injuries compensation
support for adults, and, 10.29
Criminal justice system
Crown Office Procurator Fiscal Service, 4.40–4.41
organisations, and
Crown Office Procurator Fiscal Service, 4.40–4.41
introduction, 4.37
police, 4.38–4.39
Procurator Fiscal, 4.40–4.41
Criminal offences
financial harm and abuse, and, 7.23
Crown Office Procurator Fiscal Service
generally, 4.40–4.41
Data protection
confidentiality, and, 13.15
Deprivation of liberty
authorisation
welfare attorneys, 14.17–14.18
welfare guardians, 14.19

Deprivation of liberty – *contd*
right to liberty and security, and, 14.7
Detention
police power to remove and detain, and
emergency, in, 9.17
generally, 9.16
right to liberty and security, and
assessment orders, 14.20
compensation for unlawful detention, 14.21
compliance with restrictions, 14.10
conditions for detention, 14.7
controls over person's life, 14.9
deprivation of liberty, 14.7
generally, 14.7–14.8
lack of objection to restrictions, 14.10
moving to residential care, 14.11–14.16
removal orders, 14.20
welfare attorneys, 14.17–14.18
welfare guardians, 14.19
scope of MH(CT)(S)A 2003, and, 2.18
Detention and treatment orders
public bodies' duties and powers, and, 11.9
Direct payments
financial harm and abuse, and, 7.28–7.30
generally, 2.38–2.40
principles, 5.6–5.7
Disclosure of information
generally, 13.11
legal basis for disclosure, 13.16
Disclosure Scotland
Protection of Vulnerable Groups Scheme, 2.41–2.43
Domestic abuse
harm and abuse, and, 6.20
Drug abuse
harm and abuse, and, 6.19
Eating disorders
harm and abuse, and, 6.18
Education authority duties
additional support, 11.22–11.23
coordinated support plans, 11.24–11.26
generally, 11.19
school age, 11.20–11.21
Emergencies
ASP(S)A 2007, under
applications to JP, 9.3
generally, 9.2
involvement of adult, 9.4
temporary banning orders, 9.5
use of measures, 9.6
AWI(S)A 2000, under
generally, 9.7
interim guardianship, 9.8
banning orders, 9.5
conclusion, 9.19
generally, 9.1
interim guardianship, 9.8
medical treatment, 9.18
MH(CT)(S)A 2003, under
generally, 9.9
police power to remove and detain, 9.16–9.17
removal orders, 9.10–9.15
police power to remove and detain
emergency detention, 9.17
generally, 9.16
removal orders under ASP(S)A 2007
applications to JP, 9.3
generally, 9.2
involvement of adult, 9.4
temporary banning orders, 9.5
use of measures, 9.6
removal orders under MH(CT)(S) A 2003
appeals, 9.13
applications, 9.11
cancellation, 9.15
effect, 9.12
generally, 9.10
introduction, 9.9
place of safety, 9.14
variation, 9.15
temporary banning orders, 9.5

Emergencies – *contd*
urgent medical treatment, 9.18
warrants for entry
applications to JP, 9.3
generally, 9.2
involvement of adult, 9.4
use of measures, 9.6
Emergency detention certificates
generally, 12.3
Enforcement
Care Inspectorate, 4.11–4.12
Examination of records
cooperation, and, 13.8–13.9
Family orders
generally, 12.51
Financial attorneys
financial harm and abuse, and, 7.9–7.13
Financial guardians or interveners
financial harm and abuse, and, 7.14–7.17
Financial harm and abuse
'adult at risk', 7.2
appointees, 7.19–7.20
appointments
appointee, 7.19–7.20
financial attorney, 7.9–7.13
financial guardian or intervener, 7.14–7.17
withdrawer, 7.21–7.22
attorneys, 7.9–7.13
banning orders, 7.24–7.25
care home residents' finances, 7.26–7.27
categories
harm by companies or strangers, 7.7–7.8
harm by individual with no formal role, 7.6
introduction, 7.4
misuse of formal authority, 7.5
companies, by, 7.7–7.8
conclusion, 7.32
criminal offences, 7.23
definitions, 7.2–7.3
direct payments, 7.28–7.30
Financial harm and abuse – *contd*
financial attorneys, 7.9–7.13
financial guardians or interveners, 7.14–7.17
generally, 7.1
individual with no formal role, by, 7.6
Mental Welfare Commission, and, 7.3
misuse of direct payments, 7.28–7.30
misuse of formal authority, 7.5–7.6
overview, 6.23
Public Guardian, and, 7.3
recovery of funds, 7.31
remedies
appointee, 7.19–7.20
banning orders, 7.24–7.25
care home residents' finances, 7.26–7.27
criminal offences, 7.23
direct payments, 7.28–7.30
financial attorney, 7.9–7.13
financial guardian or intervener, 7.14–7.17
recovery of funds, 7.31
withdrawer, 7.21–7.22
removal
appointee, 7.19–7.20
financial attorney, 7.9–7.13
financial guardian or intervener, 7.14–7.17
withdrawer, 7.21–7.22
residents' finances in care homes, 7.26–7.27
strangers, by, 7.7–7.8
withdrawers, 7.21–7.22
Financial interveners *see* **Financial guardians or interveners**
Financial support and advice
access to funds, 10.15–10.17
appointees, 10.14
generally, 10.13
management of funds in residential homes/hospitals, 10.18–10.20
Forced marriage
generally, 6.21
protection orders, 12.48

Formal inquiries
Mental Welfare Commission, and, 4.25
Free personal and nursing care
community care services, and, 10.11
Freedom of information
generally, 13.17
General practitioners (GPs)
co-operation duties, and
provision of medical records, 13.7
reporting harm, 13.4–13.6
Guardians *see also* **Welfare guardians**
generally, 4.34
Guardianship orders
appeals, 12.14
applications, 12.10
complaints about guardian, 12.8
emergencies, and, 9.8
generally, 12.7
human rights issues, 12.15
introduction, 12.5
non-compliance with decisions of welfare guardian, 12.16
notice to adult and other parties, 12.11
overview, 2.31
procedure, 12.9–12.16
protecting adult's interests, 12.13
public bodies' duties and powers, and, 11.10
Harm and abuse
alcohol abuse, 6.19
categories
alcohol abuse, 6.19
domestic abuse and 'coercive control', 6.20
drug abuse, 6.19
eating disorders, 6.18
financial abuse, 6.23
forced marriage, 6.21
human trafficking, 6.22
introduction, 6.7
neglect by third party, 6.14–6.15
physical abuse, 6.8–6.9
psychological abuse, 6.10–6.11
self-harm, 6.17
Harm and abuse – *contd*
categories – *contd*
self-neglect, 6.16
sexual abuse, 6.12–6.13
'coercive control', 6.20
conclusion, 6.29
definitions
ASP(S)A 2007, in, 6.6
AWI(S)A 2000, in, 6.5
generally, 6.2
MH(CT)(S)A 2003, in, 6.3–6.4
domestic abuse, 6.20
drug abuse, 6.19
eating disorders, 6.18
financial *see* **Financial abuse and harm**
forced marriage, 6.21
generally, 6.1
human trafficking, 6.22
neglect by third party, 6.14–6.15
physical abuse, 6.8–6.9
psychological abuse, 6.10–6.11
recognition of
concerns raised following behaviour changes, 6.27
disclosure by adult, 6.25
disclosure by third party, 6.26
generally, 6.24
medical care and treatment, 6.28
self-harm, 6.17
self-neglect, 6.16
sexual abuse, 6.12–6.13
Health boards
adult protection committees, and, 3.4
Health care providers
generally, 4.4
Healthcare Improvement Scotland (HIS)
adult protection committees, and, 3.4
enforcement, 4.16
functions, 4.14
generally, 4.13–4.14
inspections, 4.15
Home support
public bodies' duties and powers, and, 11.8

Housing (Scotland) Act 1987
generally, 2.44
Human rights
adult protection, in
protection of those at risk, 14.6
right to liberty, 14.7–14.21
right to respect for private and family life, 14.22–14.25
undue pressure, and, 14.26
conclusion, 14.31
generally, 14.1
guardianship and intervention orders, and, 12.15
Human Rights Act 1998, 14.3
principles, and, 5.8
private and family life, 14.22–14.25
protection of those at risk, 14.6
public authorities, 14.5
right to liberty and security of person
assessment orders, 14.20
compensation for unlawful detention, 14.21
compliance with restrictions, 14.10
conditions for detention, 14.7
controls over person's life, 14.9
deprivation of liberty, 14.7
detention, 14.7
generally, 14.7–14.8
lack of objection to restrictions, 14.10
moving to residential care, 14.11–14.16
removal orders, 14.20
welfare attorneys, 14.17–14.18
welfare guardians, 14.19
right to respect for private and family life, 14.22–14.25
Scotland, in
generally, 14.2
Human Rights Act 1998, 14.3
public authorities, 14.5
Scotland Act 1998, 14.4
UN Convention on the Rights of Disabled People, 14.27–14.30
undue pressure, and, 14.26
Human trafficking
harm and abuse, and, 6.22
'Incapacity'
scope of AWI(S)A 2000, and, 2.24
Indemnity
principles, and, 5.10
Independent advocates
ASP(S)A 2007, under 10.4
generally, 10.2
legal right to advocacy, 10.3
MH(CT)(S)A 2003, under, 10.3
principles, and, 10.5
Informal carers
cooperation, and, 13.14
Information requirements
adults, relatives and carers, of
ASP(S)A 2007, and, 2.12
AWI(S)A 2000, and, 2.33
MH(CT)(S)A 2003, and, 2.22
Inquiries
local authorities
cooperation, and, 13.10
scope of ASP(S)A 2007, and, 2.7
Mental Welfare Commission, 4.25
Interdicts
generally, 12.50
Interim guardianship
emergencies, and, 9.8
Interveners *see* **Financial guardians or interveners**
Intervention orders
appeals, 12.14
applications, 12.10
complaints about intervener, 12.8
generally, 12.6
hearing, 12.12
human rights issues, 12.15
introduction, 12.5
non-compliance with decisions of welfare guardian, 12.16
notice to adult and other parties, 12.11
persons involved in adult protection cases, and, 4.34
procedure, 12.9–12.16
protecting adult's interests, 12.13
scope of AWI(S)A 2000, and, 2.31

Investigation of harm
access to records
ASP(S)A 2007, under, 8.13
MH(CT)(S)A 2003, under, 8.22–8.23
ASP(S)A 2007, under
access to records, 8.13
assessment orders, 8.7–8.12; 12.17
banning orders, 12.17, 12.31–12.46
duty, 8.2
interviews, 8.5
medical examinations, 8.6
outcome of inquiries, 8.14
removal orders, 12.17–12.30
visits, 8.3
warrant for entry, 8.4
assessment orders
appeals, 8.12
applications, 8.9
generally, 8.7
grounds, 8.8
impact, 8.11
limits to powers, 8.10
AWI(S)A 2000, under
duty, 8.16
generally, 2.26; 8.15
choice of procedures, 8.24
conclusion, 8.25
generally, 8.1
medical examinations
ASP(S)A 2007, under, 8.6
AWI(S)A 2000, under, 8.15
MH(CT)(S)A 2003, under, 8.21
MH(CT)(S)A 2003, under
access to records, 8.22–8.23
co-operation with local authority, 8.19
duty, 8.18
generally, 2.16; 8.17
medical examinations, 8.21
removal orders, 9.9–9.15
warrants for entry, 8.20
visits
generally, 8.3
interviews, 8.5
warrants, 8.4

Investigation of harm – *contd*
warrants for entry
ASP(S)A 2007, under, 8.4
MH(CT)(S)A 2003, under, 8.20
Investigations *see also* **Large scale investigations (LSIs)**
local authorities' duty to investigate harm *see* **Investigation of harm**
Mental Welfare Commission, and, 4.22–4.24
MH(CT)(S)A 2003, under, 2.16; 8.18
Public Guardians, 4.18–4.19
Large scale investigations (LSIs)
adult protection committees, and, 3.11
Learning reviews
adult protection committees, and, 3.11
Leaving care
public bodies' duties and powers, and, 11.16–11.18
Legal framework
Adult Support and Protection (Scotland) Act 2007
adult protection committees, 2.10
'adults at risk', 2.3
concept of 'capacity', 2.4
cooperation, 2.8
court orders, 2.9
generally, 2.2
information requirements, 2.12
inquiries and investigatory powers, 2.7
people covered, 2.3
scope, 2.6–2.10
'unwilling or unable', 2.5
use, 2.11
Adults with Incapacity (Scotland) Act 2000
attorneys, 2.27
generally, 2.23
guardianship orders, 2.31
information requirements, 2.33
intervention orders, 2.31
investigation of harm, 2.26
making medical decisions, 2.30

Legal framework – *contd*
Adults with Incapacity (Scotland) Act 2000 – *contd*
managing bank accounts, 2.28
managing residents' finances, 2.29
people covered, 2.24
relevance to adult protection, 2.32
scope, 2.25–2.31
Chronically Sick and Disabled Persons Act 1970, 2.37
codes of practice, 2.34
conclusion, 2.45
Housing (Scotland) Act 1987, 2.44
Mental Health (Care and Treatment) (Scotland) Act 2003
advance statements, 2.20
cooperation, 2.17
detention, 2.18
information requirements, 2.22
introduction, 2.13
investigation of harm, 2.16
mental health tribunals, 2.19
people covered, 2.14
relevance to adult protection, 2.21
scope, 2.15–2.20
Protection of Vulnerable Groups (Scotland) Act 2007, 2.41–2.43
Social Care (Self-directed Support) (Scotland) Act 2013, 2.38–2.40
Social Work (Scotland) 1968, 2.36
Vulnerable Witnesses (Scotland) Act 2004, 2.35
Local authorities
adult protection committees, and, 3.4
banning orders
appeals, 12.46
applications, 12.41–12.45
breach, 12.37–12.39
consent of adult, 12.18–12.19
emergency applications, 9.5; 12.42
expiry, 12.40
financial harm and abuse, and, 7.24–7.25
generally, 12.31
grounds, 12.32
Local authorities – *contd*
banning orders – *contd*
impact, 12.34
incapacity, 12.19
introduction, 12.17
perpetrator aged under 16, 12.33
power of arrest attached, 12.38
protecting adult, 12.44
protecting adult's interests, 12.43
recall, 12.36
returning banned person to court, 12.38
serious harm, 12.22
service, 12.45
temporary measures, 12.35
undue pressure, 12.20–12.21
variation, 12.36
duty as education authority
additional support, 11.22–11.23
coordinated support plans, 11.24–11.26
generally, 11.19
school age, 11.20–11.21
duty to investigate harm *see* **Investigation of harm**
parties involved in protection cases, and
council officers, 4.3
generally, 4.2
removal orders under ASP(S)A 2007
consent of adult, 12.18–12.19
contact conditions, 12.27
duration, 12.30
emergencies, and, 9.2–9.6
expiry, 12.30
generally, 12.23
grounds, 12.24
impact, 12.25
incapacity, 12.19
introduction, 12.17
no detention, 12.26
protection of property, 12.29
recall, 12.28
serious harm, 12.22
undue pressure, 12.20–12.21
variation, 12.28

Local authorities – *contd*
removal orders under MH(CT)(S) A 2003
appeals, 9.13
applications, 9.11
cancellation, 9.15
court measures of protection, and, 12.3
effect, 9.12
generally, 9.10
introduction, 9.9
place of safety, 9.14
public bodies' duties and powers, and, 11.10
right to liberty and security, and, 14.20
variation, 9.15
Looked after children
public bodies' duties and powers, and, 11.12–11.15
Managing bank accounts
scope of AWI(S)A 2000, and, 2.28
Managing residents' finances
financial support and advice, and, 10.18–10.20
scope of AWI(S)A 2000, and, 2.29
Mediation
support for adults, and, 10.28
Medical care and treatment
harm and abuse, and, 6.28
Medical decisions
scope of AWI(S)A 2000, and, 2.30
Medical examinations
ASP(S)A 2007, under, 8.6
AWI(S)A 2000, under, 8.15
MH(CT)(S)A 2003, under, 8.21
Medical treatment
emergencies, and, 9.18
harm and abuse, and, 6.28
Mental Health (Care and Treatment) (Scotland) Act 2003
access to records, 8.22–8.23
advance statements, 2.20
codes of practice, 2.34
community care services, and, 10.10
Mental Health (Care and Treatment) (Scotland) Act 2003 – *contd*
cooperation, and
disclosure of information, 13.11
inquiries by local authorities, 13.10
local authority, with, 8.19
scope of provisions, 2.17
court measures of protection, and, 12.3
detention, 2.18
emergencies
generally, 9.9
police power to remove and detain, 9.16–9.17
removal orders, 9.10–9.15
harm and abuse, 6.3–6.4
independent advocates, and, 10.3
information requirements of adults, relatives and carers, 2.22
introduction, 2.13
local authorities' duty to investigate harm
access to records, 8.22–8.23
co-operation with local authority, 8.19
duty, 8.18
generally, 2.16; 8.17
medical examinations, 8.21
removal orders, 9.9–9.15
warrants for entry, 8.20
medical examinations, 8.21
mental health tribunals, 2.19
people covered, 2.14
police power to remove and detain
emergency detention, 9.17
generally, 9.16
principles, 5.4
relevance to adult protection, 2.21
removal orders
appeals, 9.13
applications, 9.11
cancellation, 9.15
effect, 9.12
generally, 9.10
introduction, 9.9

Mental Health (Care and Treatment) (Scotland) Act 2003 – *contd*
removal orders – *contd*
place of safety, 9.14
variation, 9.15
scope
advance statements, 2.20
cooperation, 2.17
detention, 2.18
generally, 2.15
investigation of harm, 2.16
mental health tribunals, 2.19
warrants for entry, 8.20
Mental health tribunals
scope of MH(CT)(S)A 2003, and, 2.19
Mental Welfare Commission
financial harm and abuse, and, and, 7.3
formal inquiries, 4.25
generally, 4.21
inquiries, 4.25
investigations, 4.22–4.24
overlap of role with other bodies, 4.28
role, 4.21
visits, 4.26–4.27
Misuse of direct payments
financial harm and abuse, and, 7.28–7.30
Misuse of formal authority
financial harm and abuse, and, 7.5–7.6
Named person
generally, 4.35
planning for the future, and, 10.27
Nearest relative
generally, 4.35
Neglect by third party
harm and abuse, and, 6.14–6.15
Non-harassment orders
generally, 12.52
Nursing home provision
public bodies' duties and powers, and, 11.8
Organisations and individuals
adult protection committees
accountability, 3.10
Organisations and individuals – *contd*
adult protection committees – *contd*
conclusion, 3.12
functions, 3.2
generally, 3.1
governance, 3.10
membership, 3.5–3.8
procedures, 3.9
role, 3.3–3.4
status, 3.2
statutory basis, 2.10
attorneys, 4.34
Care Commission, 4.13
Care Inspectorate
adult protection committees, and, 3.4
complaints, 4.9–4.10
enforcement, 4.11–4.12
functions, 4.5
generally, 4.5–4.6
inspections, 4.7–4.8
principles, 4.6
care providers, 4.29
conclusion, 4.42
council officers, 4.3
criminal justice system
Crown Office Procurator Fiscal Service, 4.40–4.41
introduction, 4.37
police, 4.38–4.39
Crown Office Procurator Fiscal Service, 4.40–4.41
friends and neighbours, 4.33
generally, 4.1
guardians, 4.34
health care providers, 4.4
Healthcare Improvement Scotland (HIS)
enforcement, 4.16
functions, 4.14
generally, 4.13–4.14
inspections, 4.15
independent advocates, 4.36
individuals, 4.33
intervention orders, and, 4.34

Organisations and individuals – *contd*
local authorities
council officers, 4.3
generally, 4.2
Mental Welfare Commission
formal inquiries, 4.25
generally, 4.21
inquiries, 4.25
investigations, 4.22–4.24
overlap of role with other bodies, 4.28
role, 4.21
visits, 4.26–4.27
named person, 4.35
nearest relative, 4.35
persons supporting an adult
attorneys, 4.34
guardians, 4.34
independent advocates, 4.36
intervention orders, and, 4.34
named person, 4.35
police, 4.38–4.39
Procurator Fiscal Service, 4.40–4.41
professional regulators, 4.30–4.32
Public Guardian
generally, 4.17
investigations, 4.18–4.19
overlap of role with other bodies, 4.20
role, 4.17
regulators, 4.30–4.32
relatives, 4.33
Social Care and Social Work Improvement Scotland
adult protection committees, and, 3.4
complaints, 4.9–4.10
enforcement, 4.11–4.12
functions, 4.5
generally, 4.5–4.6
inspections, 4.7–4.8
principles, 4.6
Parental responsibility
transition to adult protection, and, 11.3–11.5
Parents
cooperation, and, 13.14
Persons supporting an adult
attorneys, 4.34
guardians, 4.34
independent advocates, 4.36
intervention orders, and, 4.34
named person, 4.35
nearest relative, 4.35
Physical abuse
harm and abuse, and, 6.8–6.9
Place of safety
removal orders, and, 9.14
Police
adult protection committees, and, 3.4
generally, 4.38–4.39
Principles
ASP(S)A 2007, in, 5.5
AWI(S)A 2000, in, 5.3
background, 5.2
generally, 5.1
human rights, and, 5.8
indemnity, 5.10
legal impact, 5.9
MH(CT)(S)A 2003, in, 5.4
promotion, 5.11
SC(SDS)(S)A 2013, in, 5.6–5.7
Private and family life
human rights, and, 14.22–14.25
Procurator Fiscal Service
generally, 4.40–4.41
Professional regulators
generally, 4.30–4.32
Promotion of wellbeing and social development
public bodies' duties and powers, and, 11.9
Protection of Vulnerable Groups Scheme
generally, 2.41–2.43
Protection orders
assessment orders
consent of adult, 12.18–12.19
incapacity, 12.19
introduction, 12.17
undue pressure, 12.20–12.21

Protection orders – *contd*
banning orders
appeals, 12.46
applications, 12.41–12.45
breach, 12.37–12.39
consent of adult, 12.18–12.19
emergency applications, 9.5; 12.42
expiry, 12.40
generally, 12.31
grounds, 12.32
impact, 12.34
incapacity, 12.19
introduction, 12.17
perpetrator aged under 16, 12.33
power of arrest attached, 12.38
protecting adult, 12.44
protecting adult's interests, 12.43
recall, 12.36
returning banned person to court, 12.38
serious harm, 12.22
service, 12.45
temporary measures, 12.35
undue pressure, 12.20–12.21
variation, 12.36
consent of adult, 12.18–12.19
incapacity, 12.19
introduction, 12.17
removal orders
consent of adult, 12.18–12.19
contact conditions, 12.27
duration, 12.30
expiry, 12.30
generally, 12.23
grounds, 12.24
impact, 12.25
incapacity, 12.19
introduction, 12.17
no detention, 12.26
protection of property, 12.29
recall, 12.28
serious harm, 12.22
undue pressure, 12.20–12.21
variation, 12.28
serious harm, 12.22
undue pressure, 12.20–12.21

Provision of suitable housing
community care services, and, 10.12
Psychological abuse
harm and abuse, and, 6.10–6.11
Public authorities
human rights, and, 14.5
Public bodies' duties and powers
accommodated children, 11.12–11.15
'adult carer support plan', 11.11
after-care, 11.16–11.18
ante-natal depression, 11.9
application to children and duties, 11.7–11.9
application to those aged over 16, 11.10
'children in need', 11.12–11.15
community care assessment, 11.8
compulsory supervision orders, 11.8
continuing care, 11.16–11.18
detention and treatment orders, 11.9
generally, 11.6
guardianship orders, 11.10
home support, 11.8
leaving care, 11.16–11.18
looked after children, 11.12–11.15
nursing home provision, 11.8
promotion of wellbeing and social development, 11.9
removal orders, 11.10
'young carer statement', 11.11
Public Guardian
financial harm and abuse, and, 7.3
generally, 4.17
investigations, 4.18–4.19
overlap of role with other bodies, 4.20
role, 4.17
Recovery of funds
financial harm and abuse, and, 7.31
Regulators
generally, 4.30–4.32
Relatives
generally, 4.33
information requirements, and
ASP(S)A 2007, under, 2.12
AWI(S)A 2000, under, 2.33
MH(CT)(S)A 2003, under, 2.22

Removal orders (ASP(S)A 2007)
consent of adult, 12.18–12.19
contact conditions, 12.27
duration, 12.30
emergencies, and
applications to JP, 9.3
generally, 9.2
involvement of adult, 9.4
temporary banning orders, 9.5
use of measures, 9.6
expiry, 12.30
generally, 12.23
grounds, 12.24
impact, 12.25
incapacity, 12.19
introduction, 12.17
no detention, 12.26
protection of property, 12.29
recall, 12.28
serious harm, 12.22
undue pressure, 12.20–12.21
variation, 12.28
Removal orders (MH(CT)(S)A 2003)
appeals, 9.13
applications, 9.11
cancellation, 9.15
court measures of protection, and, 12.3
effect, 9.12
generally, 9.10
introduction, 9.9
place of safety, 9.14
public bodies' duties and powers, and, 11.10
right to liberty and security, and, 14.20
variation, 9.15
Residents' finances
financial harm and abuse, and, 7.26–7.27
scope of AWI(S)A 2000, and, 2.29
Right to liberty and security of person
assessment orders, 14.20
compensation for unlawful detention, 14.21
Right to liberty and security of person – *contd*
compliance with restrictions, 14.10
conditions for detention, 14.7
controls over person's life, 14.9
deprivation of liberty, 14.7
detention, 14.7
generally, 14.7–14.8
lack of objection to restrictions, 14.10
moving to residential care, 14.11–14.16
removal orders, 14.20
welfare attorneys, 14.17–14.18
welfare guardians, 14.19
Right to respect for private and family life
human rights, and, 14.22–14.25
School age
education authority duties, and, 11.20–11.21
Scotland Act 1998
human rights, and, 14.4
Self directed support
generally, 2.38–2.40
principles, 5.6–5.7
Self-harm
harm and abuse, and, 6.17
Self-neglect
harm and abuse, and, 6.16
'Serious harm'
protection order under ASP(S) A 2007, and,12.22
Services under Chronically Sick and Disabled Persons Act 1970
community care services, and, 10.9
Sexual abuse
harm and abuse, and, 6.12–6.13
Sharing of information
cooperation, and, 13.3
generally, 12.4
Social Care and Social Work Improvement Scotland
adult protection committees, and, 3.4
complaints, 4.9–4.10
enforcement, 4.11–4.12

Social Care and Social Work Improvement Scotland – *contd*
functions, 4.5
generally, 4.5–4.6
inspections, 4.7–4.8
principles, 4.6
Social Care (Self-directed Support) (Scotland) Act 2013
generally, 2.38–2.40
principles, 5.6–5.7
Social development
public bodies' duties and powers, and, 11.9
Social Work (Scotland) 1968
generally, 2.36
Statement of wishes and feelings
support for adults, and, 10.24
Support for the adult
access to funds, 10.15–10.17
advance directives, 10.22
advance statements, 10.23
appointment of attorney, 10.25–10.26
appointment of named person, 10.27
Carers (Scotland) Act 2016, under, 10.8
community care assessments, 10.7
community care services
Carers (Scotland) Act 2016, under, 10.8
community care assessments, 10.7
free personal and nursing care, 10.11
generally, 10.6
MH(CT)(S)A 2003, under, 10.10
provision of suitable housing, 10.12
services under Chronically Sick and Disabled Persons Act 1970, 10.9
conclusion, 10.30
counselling and mediation, 10.28
criminal injuries compensation, 10.29
financial support and advice
access to funds, 10.15–10.17
appointees, 10.14
Support for the adult – *contd*
financial support and advice – *contd*
generally, 10.13
management of funds in residential homes/hospitals, 10.18–10.20
free personal and nursing care, 10.11
future planning
advance directives, 10.22
advance statements, 10.23
appointment of attorney, 10.25–10.26
appointment of named person, 10.27
generally, 10.21
statement of wishes and feelings, 10.24
generally, 10.1
independent advocates
ASP(S)A 2007, under 10.4
generally, 10.2
legal right to advocacy, 10.3
MH(CT)(S)A 2003, under, 10.3
principles, and, 10.5
management of funds in residential homes/hospitals, 10.18–10.20
mediation, 10.28
provision of suitable housing, 10.12
services under Chronically Sick and Disabled Persons Act 1970, 10.9
statement of wishes and feelings, 10.24
Temporary banning orders
generally, 9.5
Third party disclosure
harm and abuse, and, 6.26
Transition to adult protection
'adult', 11.1
conclusion, 11.28
duties and powers of public bodies
accommodated children, 11.12–11.15
'adult carer support plan', 11.11
after-care, 11.16–11.18
ante-natal depression, 11.9

Transition to adult protection – *contd*
duties and powers of public bodies – *contd*
application to children and duties, 11.7–11.9
application to those aged over 16, 11.10
'children in need', 11.12–11.15
community care assessment, 11.8
compulsory supervision orders, 11.8
continuing care, 11.16–11.18
detention and treatment orders, 11.9
generally, 11.6
guardianship orders, 11.10
home support, 11.8
leaving care, 11.16–11.18
looked after children, 11.12–11.15
nursing home provision, 11.8
promotion of wellbeing and social development, 11.9
removal orders, 11.10
'young carer statement', 11.11
duties of local authority as education authority
additional support, 11.22–11.23
coordinated support plans, 11.24–11.26
generally, 11.19
school age, 11.20–11.21
generally, 11.1–11.2
incorporation of the UN Convention on the Rights of the Child, 11.27
parental responsibility, 11.3–11.5
UN Convention on the Rights of Disabled People
generally, 14.27–14.30
UN Convention on the Rights of the Child
incorporation, 11.27
Undue pressure
human rights, and, 14.26
Undue pressure – *contd*
removal orders under ASP(S)A 2007, 12.20–12.21
Urgent medical treatment
emergencies, and, 9.18
Visits
local authorities, and
generally, 8.3
interviews, 8.5
warrant of entry, 8.4
Mental Welfare Commission, and, 4.26–4.27
Voluntary sector
cooperation, and, 13.13
Vulnerable witnesses
generally, 12.53
Vulnerable Witnesses (Scotland) Act 2004
generally, 2.35
special measures, under, 12.53
Warrants for entry
ASP(S)A 2007, under, 8.4
emergencies, and
applications to JP, 9.3
generally, 9.2
involvement of adult, 9.4
use of measures, 9.6
MH(CT)(S)A 2003, under, 8.20
Welfare attorneys
deprivation of liberty authorisation, 14.17–14.18
Welfare guardians
deprivation of liberty authorisation, 14.19
Wellbeing and social development
public bodies' duties and powers, and, 11.9
Withdrawers
financial harm and abuse, and, 7.21–7.22
'Young carer statement'
public bodies' duties and powers, and, 11.11